W9-AXF-372

Carol Channing

Just Lucky I Guess

I Guess

A Memoir of Sorts

Simon & Schuster   New York London Toronto Sydney Singapore

SIMON & SCHUSTER
Rockefeller Center
1230 Avenue of the Americas
New York, NY 10020

SIMON & SCHUSTER and colophon are registered trademarks
of Simon & Schuster, Inc.

For information regarding special discounts for bulk purchases,
please contact Simon & Schuster Special Sales at
1-800-456-6798 or business@simonandschuster.com

Designed by Karolina Harris

Manufactured in the United States of America
10   9   8   7   6   5   4   3   2   1

Library of Congress Cataloging-in-Publication Data
Channing, Carol.
  Just lucky I guess : a memoir of sorts / [Carol Channing].
    p.   cm.
  1. Channing, Carol.   2. Actors—United States—Biography.
3. Singers—United States—Biography.   I.   Title.
PN2287.C494 A3   2002
792.6'028'092—dc21   2002026994

ISBN 0-7432-1606-7

Acknowledgment

o Michael Korda who is giving me a chance to start my life over again. Did you ever hear of that before? My fitness trainer says, "Grandma Moses?" But she was only seventy.

This book is dedicated to Roger Denny.

Just
Lucky
I Guess

*T*he name of my book is *Just Lucky I Guess,* referring to the old joke

Client to prostitute: What's a nice girl like you doing in a place like this?

Prostitute: Just lucky I guess.

I have a right to repeat this old joke because I have been prostituting myself all of my life. I've been making love to an audience since the fourth grade. It's interesting to me that what I do onstage is legal, whereas what's done in bed is not. That's odd, don't you think? I would suppose that the sweetest part of a girl's body is where she wants sex, wouldn't you? I don't know if it's the same with a man. I have to ask, since I'm not one. Well, it seems sweet to a girl, provided somebody thinks all the rest of her is sweet, too. According to my generation, you don't get to find that out until you're married.

My parents told me I came home from kindergarten and said to them, "All the little girls hit the little boys."

Parents: Do you?

Me: Oh no, I pet them.

I don't remember this, but my petting them was far from illegal, because we were all in kindergarten and unaware of sex as yet. I simply shifted all my sweetest feelings to the school auditorium stage and imitated only people with whom I was entranced.

By the fourth grade I knew I was suddenly attractive provided I could turn into people who seemed to me to be attractive to the boys . . . like Margery Gould or Barbara Sperb, who I thought were the two cutest girls in the school. These girls wiggled their little buns and acted the way I felt like acting toward the boys, so I did it onstage, in my campaign speech for student body secretary—"This is Margery Gould," "This is Barbara Sperb."—and won the election.

I also did the principal of the school, Miss Berard, who was apparently the forerunner of Julia Child . . . fascinating! I had her say, "When you fill out your ballots, vote for Carol." I won again. I used to find any excuse to go in her office, she was so fascinating, and found out later what she had was called adenoids. Unlike Danny Kaye's teachers who, he told me, locked him up in the dean of boys' office for being obstreperous, my teachers loved being imitated. They must have sensed one cannot imitate somebody one doesn't hold dearly.

When I get philosophical like this, people usually cut me off, but not this time. This is *my book*! I can dwell on any subject as long as I want. This is not a conventional autobiography and was never meant to be one. It is only what I remember of my life, and it is selective. I find I cannot relate anything at all if the memory is negative or critical of the places I have been, the people I've met, what I've learned and, most importantly, what I've eaten.

It's a joy to write your own book with no help, and since it's a free country, you also can skip reading anything you want. That way, we're all happy. I do hope you proceed, but at your own risk of boredom or your own impatience with unraveling disorganization.

Whenever I've read a book, organization in itself has never interested me. I just want to know what makes life worth living to the author. Well, I've tried to tell you eventually what makes life worth living to me. Don't think I'm not aware that at times it's a little circuitous or off the point I was starting to make, but I do hope I did finally make it. My point, that is.

y mother thought it would be nice to name me Suzanne. My father, who was city editor of the *Seattle Star* at the time, objected and said, "Peggy, no newspaperman can name his child anything that doesn't fit in the thirteen Linotype headline." My father also wanted a first name he felt was euphonious with Channing. I forget the word for it, but it's like Walter Kerr, the great *New York Times* theatre critic. He was indeed great. Well, he gave *me* lovely reviews, didn't he? He named his offspring Christopher Kerr, Kitty Kerr, Colin Kerr, et cetera.

So my father came up with Carol. In those days there had to be a lot of juggling to make people's names fit into the headline and still get the rest of the story in. This is how Elizabeth Taylor got to be Liz, which she hates. It isn't exactly easier than Elizabeth, but it's only two and a half spaces.

So it goes . . . five for Carol, half for the space between Carol and Channing, and, with half for the *i*, seven and a half in Channing. That makes the ideal thirteen Linotype. See?

I was explaining all this to Carol Burnett and Carole Bayer Sager—that as far as my parents knew, I was the first Carol. Before me, female people named Caroline, Carolina, Carolyn, et cetera, had parents who didn't think of just plain Carol. I go so much further back than Burnett and Bayer Sager, they hadn't realized any of this.

To make my point, I've often seen in headlines "Burnett's Ratings Highest" or "Bayer Sager Still in Top 10," but mine reads full name, "Carol Channing Still Touring," and I say to myself, "Thank you, Daddy."

Also, the word *carol* means a song or a dance . . . like "singing a Christmas carol" or "the villagers were caroling on the green." So our three sets of parents must have wished upon us what happened to us.

Alcohol has plagued the news world. Murphy Brown taught us that. I checked this statement with Tom Johnson, editor in chief of CNN, and he said, "Yes, it's true. Alcohol has plagued the news world." Well, on graduating from Brown University, my father, George Channing, got a job first on *The Providence Journal*, then on the *Detroit Free Press*, where he met my mother, who was the secretary for Detroit Mayor Johnny Smith. This was just before World War I. So I surmise the mayor must have been stuck on her. My father thought the mayor was too. When I asked my mother, she said, "Oh, Carol, a secretary's job is the hardest. They casually ask for the Ford papers. Now, how is a poor secretary to know where she put those?" My father enlisted in the army. He went over to Ypres, France, pronounced "Wipers" by our American soldiers on the *Leviathan*. On Armistice Day, he returned to my mother and the *Free Press* and apparently celebrated the armistice with his newspaper cronies in the nearest bar to the *Free Press* for several years.

My parents got involved in a downtown Detroit traffic jam, threw their hands up, and left for Seattle to raise chickens on an Alderwood, Washington, farm. My cousin Richard Long came to live with them because my aunt Elsa, his mother, my mother's only sister, read a book on free love, decided she liked it, but apparently didn't think it was the right atmosphere for a child.

Dickie loved my parents, and when the girl down the road asked my mother if she was expecting a child, my mother said, "Yes." Dickie couldn't wait until I got here. Therefore, my first word was "Dickie," and I have adored him ever since. He was seven years old when I was born. He's eighty-eight now and the most attractive, gorgeous-looking human being since my father, maybe. My mother lived to be a hundred, but she was gorgeous before that.

Dickie tells me my mother had a talk with him. She said, "George and I are trying to build a life together, so Carol will have to be your ward. You must help and look after her." Now, Dickie is a born daredevil. He never could stop taking chances. To this day his hobby is getting into a glider, to the consternation of the inhabitants of Southern California. He steers just clear of jagged California mountains. He's always lived in the fast lane.

Well, since I was his ward, he said he hitched my baby carriage onto the back of his tricycle and we went careening around the streets of

Seattle on "terror rides." He tells me now I'm lucky to be alive. I don't know who to thank, certainly not Dickie, but it *is* part of his devastating charm.

Anyway, my father gave up alcohol, cold turkey. Mother pointed out that Christian Science might help him. (There was no AA at that time.) He embraced Christian Science. So did my mother. I was born in a Christian Science home. It was a hospital without medicine, Mrs. Whittamore's Home, it was called. There are many people who tell me they were born in the same bed at the same time, but it doesn't seem likely, because where would our mothers all have fit?

The first time I played Seattle (in my first starring part, *Gentlemen Prefer Blondes*) I was standing in a reception line to benefit some disease, shaking hands with hundreds of people. One of them was a cuddly little old lady. She said, "I was there when you were born. Right after Mrs. Whittamore and I delivered you, I said, 'She's going to be tall,' " and she promptly walked on. I tried to call her back as she left me, but she just kept walking, wearing a satisfied, superior smile. There I stood, over six feet tall in my high heels, wanting to find out more. Still, it gave me satisfaction, knowing I had proven her right.

Here it is the beginning of my book, and I'm already off the track. My point was my cousin Dickie was there when I was born and told me it was true what my father said, that he sent a wire to his newspaper cronies in Detroit: "Carol came singing into the world." My father told me I sang "La, la, la" when born, not the more traditional "Waaaa," but apparently that singing voice only lasted until I had to do eight shows a week. Pity, isn't it?

After years of those weekly eight shows, my voice just struggles and sometimes croaks because I'm always trying to sound like the character I'm playing. But my father and I spent my growing up years singing together. He harmonized gorgeously, and I had a singing voice that seemed to make him laugh and cry. My mother told me her happiest times were sitting in the car's backseat watching our heads rocking in unison, pouring our souls out into music, driving and singing all day long.

Sometimes we'd start with:

Roll, Jordan, roll,
Roll, Jordan, roll.

> I want to go to heaven when I die
> for to hear sweet Jordan roll.

Daddy's counterpart would get more and more complicated; we'd modulate up every new verse, and it got wilder and funkier till we decided we had wrung that one dry. Next might be, "Do You Call That Religion?"

Maybe the next song was a hymn. No, it wasn't a hymn, I recently learned it is gospel, which few of our current generations are heir to. Such as

> Good Lord, I don't feel no wise tired
> I am bound to shout to glory when this world is on fire
> Children, o-oh Glory Hallelu-oo-*oo*-oo-jah.

The one we laughed at most was

> Ezekiel saw the wheel
> Way up in the middle of the air

Me (an octave higher):

> The little wheel run by faith

Daddy (an octave or two lower):

> And the big wheel run by the grace o' Gawd

Both (Daddy in glorious harmony):

> It's a wheel in a wheel
> Way in the middle of the air. (pronounced almost eye-uh)

The deepest beat was:

> Oh, Mary, don't you weep, don't you moan
> 'Cause Pharaoh's army got drownded
> Oh, Mary, don't you weep

Well, I am having such a good time remembering this, I'm just sorry you can't hear what I hear—my father's voice harmonizing. These and more are, of course, still my favorite songs, so I sing them to myself and hear his voice every time, as strong as it ever was. Whenever I walk I sing, so he sings with me, in my mind. Or when the subway treads to a beat, I hear him handing the rhythm of it to me.

Most of these were Southern Baptist hymns. That is, I always thought they were Southern Baptist hymns and wondered why Baptists didn't know them. But Liz Carpenter (Lyndon and Lady Bird Johnson's right arm) told me, when I asked her to join me singing hymns and she couldn't, "Those are not hymns, Carol. You are singing gospel. How do you know these songs?"

I couldn't assimilate fast enough what she had just asked me, so I couldn't answer her, but slowly I came to know my father's roots were deeper into gospel lore than I ever realized. Growing up, I never asked him how he learned these songs in his "birthplace," Providence. I never even wondered.

Daddy had two distinctly opposite accents around the house, each used equally. One was grand New England stentorian sounds, like when he spouted Keats, Shelley, and Mccaulay's essays in the alleys of Providence after school and work and beans and bread. With resounding Shakespearean tones he would swing into Elizabeth Barrett Browning's

Sweet, sweet, sweet, O Pan!
Piercing sweet by the river!
Blinding sweet, O great god Pan!
'Till the sun on the hill forgot to die,
And the lilies revived, and the dragonfly
Came back to dream by the river.

The first words I'd hear in the mornings as Daddy spread his arms wide looking out the window were "And Aurora, the rosy fingered goddess of the dawn, rolled back the crimson clouds and everything was ready for the coming of the sun." Then sure enough he'd haul that sun up single-handedly for all the rest of us to see. His "Aurora" greeting told me he was awake, so I could come running to him.

Daddy: Who am dat in de Emperor's Palace?

His rich, full bass resonated his imitation of the Emperor Jones. I thought every father had two accents. I was surprised to find out how one-cylindered other people's fathers were.

Well, I didn't think it was coming this soon, but now I can't continue this part of the saga of my childhood unless I tell you that when I was sixteen years old, packing for leaving home alone for the first time to go to Bennington College, my mother announced to me I was part Negro. "I'm only telling you this," she said, "because the Darwinian law shows that you could easily have a black baby." In those days, 1937, this was unique. Now, thank God, Americans are truly mongrel pups, which is what gives us our strength. No hemophilia here, especially nowadays. Anyway, she went on to say that that was why my eyes were bigger than hers (I wasn't aware of this) and why I danced with such elasticity and why I had so many of the qualities that made me me.

She said when my father was born his birth certificate had a small *c*, which stood for "colored," after his name, but that fortunately the city hall of Augusta, Georgia, burned down, leaving no evidence of this. "Augusta, Georgia? I thought he was born in Providence, Rhode Island." "No," she said, "he was as white as he is now [which was white], but his mother took him and his sister Alice [after their Nordic German-American father died and she could save enough money] to Providence, where they would never recognize Daddy's full features, his shining, evenly shaped teeth, or his magnificent, wide-ranged voice." She said my paternal grandfather left my grandmother all his earnings, but my grandfather's brother, being a lawyer, had it all taken away from her easily because she was "colored" and in the South. She got the two children to Providence, enrolled them in public school, opened a little grocery store, and later became a domestic in a family home.

My mother said she didn't know how old Daddy and Aunt Alice were when their mother died, but my father finished growing up in Classical High School without his mother. My mother's surmise was Daddy's mother didn't want anyone to see her around her children. Daddy had a job sewing buttonholes in a tailor's shop, which afforded him a can of beans and a loaf of bread daily. He won a scholarship to Brown University and graduated summa cum laude. My mother added that the reason Daddy was so fastidious and bathed so often and adored 4711 perfume was because "all Negroes smell, you know." My father never, ever smelled. I ought to know, I hugged him a lot. No African-American that I danced with ever smelled.

For the sake of the truth, I had to tell you that the spice of my life was singing with Daddy. That is, once my cousin Dickie had to be returned to his mother, Aunt Elsa, in Los Angeles when he was twelve years old. I was, of course, devastated when he left. No Dickie to love.

Aunt Elsa, after years of practicing her book on free love, finally married Uncle Wally Pritchard, a distinguished, kind gentleman who took his obligation to Dickie and me seriously. He taught Dickie to brush his teeth, clean the sink and mirror, and use a clean mop before leaving the bathroom. We liked him a lot. Dickie tells me now that his mother, Elsa, ruined Uncle Wally's life. I was raised by both parents with the daily reminder "Don't be like your Aunt Elsa," meaning she was the darling of anyone's living room—singing, dancing, and keeping her family entertained with stories—but undisciplined enough to remain totally unfocused and unconscientious.

I was bedazzled by Aunt Elsa. Children, I've noticed, love anyone with sex appeal. I didn't know it was sex appeal yet. I just couldn't resist her glamour. She had the narrowest and fullest lipsticked Cupid's bow mouth of the flapper era, clothes with belts around her hips, tumbling black, naturally curly hair, and she wore it all with joy and freedom. How could any child not want to be like her aunt Elsa? But I kept it my secret.

My mother was beautiful and, like most siblings who go the opposite of one another, she had a lovely puritanical quality. Does everyone feel his mother is beautiful and smells beautifully? It was Harriet Hubbard Ayer powder, she told me. I repeated to her often how I loved to breathe the scent of her. I understand Chan, my son, when he was first brought in to me in the hospital after he was born, sniffing all around me, and finally his mouth landing on my nose because he thought it was my breast. He was pure contentment. Mothers do smell like the perfumes of Arabia, don't they?

oth sisters were raised in a convent in Quincy, Illinois. On leaving the convent they . . . We must stop here for the sake of clarity, which I needn't tell you is not my forte. I just found out when it comes to sequence my mind works something like Henny Youngman's. It would be nice to be as funny as Henny Youngman was, but who is? This was Henny's sense of sequence: Henny gave me a diamond pin. It turned out to be a dime glued to a safety pin (dime and pin). He pinned it on me and then said, "And speaking of China" (no one had mentioned it), "I took my mother-in-law to Mexico for the Kaopectate Festival. Bought her a gorilla coat. Beauty-full . . . sleeves too long."

One night recently, Loretta Young, yes, the great movie star and my dear friend, introduced me to her priest, Father Benedict Groeschel, in case he might help me through the trauma of my marriage with Charles. He certainly did. I told him, "One person thinks my deified love for my father is unnatural. I know it never was. Sometimes I pray straight to him, looking at his picture."

Father Groeschel: Your father loved you unconditionally like a good parent. Remember, God *is* love.

Thank you, Father Benedict.

Loretta knew I'd cotton to him because he arrived at her house looking like something left over from the bubonic plague. By that I mean he wore his everyday garb, a gray wool robe with a hood and a rope belt like the monks who salvaged the little that was left of civilization after practically everybody died. I had to tell him how admirable I think people are who dress uniquely to suit themselves.

He said: It also saves a lot of money on clothes.

If Loretta picked him to proselytize for her, she certainly picked the right one. Loretta's main concern in life was to convert only those she cared for and worried about to Catholicism. The only reason it didn't work out with me is because I do not know which part of me is me and which is Christian Science. I guess I never will know and none of us does. Are we each a pillar of influences or would we have been the way we are anyway?

efore I ever attended any live theatre or concert or opera, my mother asked me if I'd like to volunteer to deliver *Christian Science Monitor*s on Saturdays to the back stages of all the then legitimate theatres in San Francisco, where we lived. I was told I was a cooperative and tractable child, so I agreed in order to live up to being cooperative and tractable.

We went first to the Curran Theatre, but not to the lobby or the box office, no. We walked down that long, dark alley leading to the Curran's huge stage door, which is still there. I must have been small, because the iron bolt that's so easy for me to slide open today when we play San Francisco was nearly impossible for me to budge at that time. The door was a clean, newly painted gray. I remember I decided the paint must be sticking it closed, so I put down my *Monitor*s to tackle it. My mother opened the heavy door quite easily. I stepped inside and stood still. I was overcome with the feeling that here was hallowed ground. I couldn't move. I could see the stage even in the dark, through what I now know to be "3." (Stages are usually divided into five sections.) It came over me that I was looking at the stage and backstage of a cathedral, a temple, a mosque, a mother church. I know I'm using adult words to describe a child's feelings, but I don't know how else to tell you this simple reaction of a child to a holy place. Children know it. They sense it's holy.

I put the publications in the rack by the door and have no idea how long I stood there. I remember my mother seemed to have someplace else to go, because I was alone and still in awe and unrushed. Beyond that stage door, when we finally got it open, lay the *real* life . . . the only real life there is, not just the mundane facts of life, the mathematical statistics, but a world created by human beings who have caught a glimpse of creation and then re-created their glimpse to put it inside that door and onto the stage. I didn't want to leave.

When Mother returned to me she said, "Now we'll go next door to the Geary Theatre and then to the old Tivoli Opera House," where I later saw Leo Carrillo in some play about a pushcart vendor selling garlic and onions, played to an audience howling with laughter. And then on to the President Theatre, where Charlotte Greenwood played with Joe E. Brown in *Elmer the Great* . . . hilarious . . . and Henry Duffy and Dale Winter presented *Sally, Irene, and Mary* . . . beautiful! Of course, at that moment I hadn't seen *any* live shows yet. At that time, I wanted only to kiss the floorboards of these religious monuments. But how did I know then they were really churches? Children sense things, don't they?

M y first taste of life in front of a live audience came when I was in the fourth grade, while I was sitting in the audience of the auditorium of the Commodore Sloat grammar school (first to sixth grades) in St. Francis Wood (one of the residential sections of San Francisco). The occasion was the school assembly meeting, which took place on Fridays. This meeting was for the purpose of nominating the next term's school officers. An electric shock went through me when Bobbie Schmaltz nominated me for secretary of the student body. If you were nominated, the procedure was to walk forward to the stage, go up the six steps to center stage, and tell your fellow students why they should vote for you. I was ossified with fright on the walk up because naturally I couldn't think of one reason why they should vote for me. I got as far as when I was supposed to speak.

I was an only child, and like so many only children I had nightly imaginary visits with anyone I met that I thought was eccentric or funny or adorable or had an accent different from mine. During these "visits," I spread out teacups over the assembled chairs and carried on conversations with all of these fascinating people. Guests would often ask my parents, "Who are all of those people upstairs with Carol?" My mother would reply, "No, that's only Carol. She's playing by herself." "No," the skeptical guests would say, "who are all of those voices?"

So, in the morning assembly, in the school auditorium, with my knees shaking, I did the thing I did best . . . turned into somebody else. I did an imitation of the principal of the school, Miss Berard, saying, "When you fill out your ballots, vote for Carol." I told you about her in my introduction. . . . My classmates yelled their recognition of Miss Berard, applauded, and everyone laughed, including Miss Berard. Even she enjoyed it! My knees were steadier now.

In the middle of the stage, suddenly I was no longer an only child. What I laughed at alone in my room, everyone else laughed at. I suddenly realized we're all alike. What I was excited with, everyone else seemed to be excited with. We all go toward the same things or away from them. We laugh or cry at the same things. We're safe and close together under one roof, experiencing reactions simultaneously. Nothing else in the world matters. Only this delicious moment. We don't care what's wrong with any of us, we're free! We were soaring above all the faults we are supposed to have. And at that moment, *all* of our happiness quotients were soaring, including mine. To the sound of applause, I ran off the stage, into the cloakroom, hid behind the coats, and cried, "Oh, God, I'll do anything to get back on that stage again. I'll go without food, water, sleep, or anything."

That night I told my parents, "Something happened to me today. I can't stop thinking of it." They listened. I told them all about it. My father, after focusing intently on what I said, announced, "There's an adage that says, 'Be careful what you set your heart upon for you shall surely get it.'"

Me: You mean I can lay down my life right now?

Daddy: You can lay down your life at seven or at seventy-seven or whenever. The happier people are not the ones who get *out* of work. The happier people are the ones who are lucky enough to *find* their work. I noticed he said happi*er*. None of us is completely happy, because challenges seem to be a constant in our lives. Maybe sometime we'll find out why.

At school we were given until the next Friday to get our campaign speeches together. First I rehearsed mine on my mother, who was always there when I got home from school. Then I tried it on my father an hour before dinner, when he got home from the office, and then on any of their dinner guests, who were not the best comedy audience in the world since they usually had an incurable problem or two or they wouldn't have been Christian Scientists. But I soon found out, after I won the election (naturally I won, because my campaign speech created holy chaos). I found out that the fewer rehearsal laughs there were from my parents' friends, the better the final performance for my fellow students went.

The best part of running for secretary was that the auditorium held only one-third of the student body, so we had to do three assembly meetings. On the first one I wasn't so good. The second I was better. By the third I was swinging, and that's when I learned to like long runs.

*M*y adolescent years were spent in Aptos Junior High (now called Middle School). Joy! I had an entire new battery of faculty members and students to take home with me in my imagination. However, in this school, parliamentary procedure took place only in each *individual* class of about thirty. The president and vice president functioned with, and were elected by, the entire school. So, naturally, I ran this time for vice president of the entire student body. I gravitated to the school band because I needed them for my campaign song.

The leader of the school band was Harry Kullijian. I was so in love with Harry I couldn't stop hugging him. In hindsight, I realize how disciplined he was and what a sense of responsibility he had.

Remember, these were times way before the Pill. Now condoms are necessary, we hear, but the Pill, I'm sure we all agree, caused the sexual revolution. It wasn't so bad using discipline instead. I was free to adore Harry, to sink into his protection and dearness. It was thrilling and sweet to have his arms around me. Anyway, I was eleven and Harry was fifteen, a little older than most in our class because his Armenian family didn't believe in starting children in school until later. I know how right they were, because I started kindergarten early for those days, four and a half years old, and skipped second grade, so I was younger than everybody all our growing up years. I still feel most of the world is smarter than I am. It may be, but it leaves one with a weird lack of conviction in comparison with the positive statements other people seem to make. My son, Channing, also graduated high school at sixteen. He seems to be all right, though.

Harry confided to my mother how affectionate I was to him. By this time we were twelve and sixteen. He had a serious talk with both my parents (without me), assuring them, "I will never get your Carol into any kind of trouble." They told me about the talk.

My father said, "I like that boy."

Harry was the most exotic, beautiful thing I had seen since Uday Shan Kar, India's greatest concert dancer, who appeared at the Curran Theatre. Harry had silken, bronze skin; long, almond-shaped eyes that stretched almost to his ears; and that sweet, contented smile with which camels in the Holy Land are born. His profile had the graceful line of that on an Egyptian coin. Standing in the sun he was an antique bronze god, so you can imagine why I could not stop hugging and kissing him. His father looked like a throwback to the Ottoman Turk Army . . . the one that fought the Crusaders in the medieval days, at least according to the drawings in our school history texts. Gorgeous! None of the family was tall, but neither was the Ottoman Turk Army. Years later, on a press junket to Istanbul with Hedda Hopper, I was surprised to find this out. The Turks are built with wide shoulders and great strength. I was taller than Harry, but we never noticed it. I simply felt extremely girly-girl standing next to a boy-boy, and he treated me as such.

Now the campaign song! I didn't tell you what it was. At the time, Eddie Cantor came bouncing out of our Majestic radios every Sunday night, followed by Jack Benny, Walter Winchell, Gladys Swarthout, Louella Parsons, et cetera. Those programs were a family ritual that took place in most homes, so everyone knew the melody of the Eddie Cantor theme song. We borrowed that melody, and the band and I wrote lyrics. It started with the band singing:

Band:

We want Carol, we want Carol

Me:

When *I'm* vice president
When *I'm* vice president
We'll all leave school at one o'clock
When *I'm* vice president

Band:

We want Carol, we want Carol

There were several verses. We kept it up till most of the students joined in.

My father used to come home with vice presidential campaign slogans for me. One I remember was "If Carol's your Vice it's a virtue." Isn't that clever? He made these up during his lunch hour at the office. Today, his function would perhaps have been called the Christian Science public relations office. There he would stay in touch with newspapers, radio, and all the media for Christian Science. He also spoke in the legislature in Sacramento to protect the church's democratic rights. But busy though he was, many campaign slogans for me were made up in that office and during legislative meetings.

Naturally, it was the most difficult thing in the world not to make love to Harry, not that I knew anything about *how* to make love, or what it was leading to. I just wanted to be close to him and hug him from head to toe. But he would distract me, and we'd rush to the beach to see (for twenty-five cents, through a periscope pointing downward) how the man buried alive was doing or run to Golden Gate Park, where Joe DiMaggio was training every Saturday and Sunday.

How did we know that Joe was great even then? I told about growing up at the same time as Joe on a TV interview in New York. We all worshiped Joe. Decades later, I was one of hundreds on a big TV special called *Night of 100 Stars*. The entire cast was assembled for a picture. A voice called from behind me, "We miss you out at the ballpark, Carol."

I turned around and, yes . . . you knew: It was Joe! With that smile you could only describe as sunny Italy. You died only a few years ago, Joe, but I wish I could correct you. It wasn't the *ballpark*. It was where Eighth Avenue enters Golden Gate Park in San Francisco. There was a big clearing there with nothing but grass. You had only one or two other players to throw you your ball. I always wanted to straighten you out about that, but I never had the nerve to go and talk with you, even though, at the time, I was starring in *Gentlemen Prefer Blondes*. You didn't *have* a ballpark to practice in then. You never stopped concentrating long enough to look up and see the same group of school-children watching you every Saturday and Sunday with no one else there. I think nobody knew you were *you* then, except us, and we surely knew . . . years ahead of time.

It was USSR Armenia all during my Armenian Period. My mother told me the strangest thing was happening to my face during that three-year time. Instead of my father's round, open eyes, mine were becoming more almond-shaped or doe-eyed and elongated, stretching almost to my ears.

"You're looking Armenian!" she said. See? My father's quotation of the adage "Be careful what you set your heart upon for you shall surely get it" was turning out to be true in my case.

Anyway, back to my campaign for vice president. George Fenneman was running for president. Years later, as an adult, he became very popular on television on the Groucho Marx show and on many others.

Girls weren't allowed to run for president then (maybe they still aren't), but once George and I won—yes, we won by a landslide—George made an excellent president. We got along fine, except that I wanted to raise the flag once a week. I suggested he could do it every day except my day. Whoever I asked thought I was crazy. Miss Cole, the vice principal, almost got angry with me. George was irritated. Even I wondered what was the matter with me. Why couldn't I sit quietly and behave myself like that pretty little ingenue Barbara Currier that George was stuck on? So I wondered if I had some kind of metabolic imbalance that didn't show on the surface. Why did I feel it was only fair if I led the entire school in the pledge of allegiance to the flag every, for instance, Friday? And I would have done it so well, I thought.

Well, I never got to. I still wonder why not. I stuck to getting them all to clean up the girls' yard dressed as Harpo Marx and to promoting all the girls to wearing a uniform of navy pleated skirt with a middy or boys' shirt. Miss Cole asked me to help her with this last item. She asked the right person, because that was *my* most becoming outfit, so I promoted it heavily. We all looked pretty spiffy, though, as a result.

*A*t the school dances I taught all the little boys how to dance and then found them partners once they learned. It wasn't magnanimous of me, I had a motive—nobody asked *me* to dance. I was too tall (for that generation), so I put myself to work. Harry was busy conducting the band, so I couldn't dance with him. Besides, he danced like the excellent soccer player he was. Outside of school, he booked his band most every Friday and Saturday night for weddings, anniversaries, and receptions. My parents asked him what I did when I tagged along with him, and he said I was the mascot. But he had me sing "When Irish Eyes Are Smiling" and "Loch Lomond" and "Danny Boy." (As I say, this was before I lived through eight shows a week on Broadway, so I sang clear and sweet like a girl-girl.) I don't remember ever being happier than during the three laugh-filled years with Harry on clarinet, Sammy Parotta on drums, Alex Merrick on piano, and Jimmy Furée on violin or bass.

Again in hindsight, Harry must have been smart at making money, because we never had a dearth of it. We always had gas for the car. We'd run out of school at 3:10 P.M. and jump into the car. I got delivered to flamenco dance class with Rita Hayworth's brother José Cansino or to ballet or modern dance class, while Harry went to his violin teacher. The band played soccer or rehearsed for the next booking.

My ballet mistresses were Madame Hirsch and Mademoiselle Arnold. I was thirteen years old when they submitted my name to Adolph Bolm, the choreographer and master of the San Francisco Opera Ballet. He accepted me! My first appearance was in the ballet *Petrouchka*—on pointe. The second was with Elizabeth Rethberg singing something by Wagner. Third, the Russian Ballet. All bit parts. I dressed with all of the Russian ballerinas, but time stood still when

Tatiana Riabouchinska asked me, in Russian, to hook her tutu up the back. I knew what she was asking me to do because it wasn't hooked. I had watched her dance for years, every time she came to San Francisco, and never thought I'd meet her.

As I say, San Francisco is a deliriously enchanting city! Where else could this happen? I took lessons from Yeichi Nimura, Japan's greatest dancer, and learned his "Saw Dahce" (Sword Dance). Then I studied with La Argentina, Spain's world-renowned flamenco dancer. I saved my allowance for fifty-cent seats in the top balcony of the Curran or Geary Theatre and saw Kreutzberg and Giorgi, Mary Wigman, Trudi Schoop (dance pantomimist) from Berlin, Angna Enters from Paris, and Uday Shan Kar from India. I can still do his neck wiggle, but you had to have started doing it when you were little.

Now is my time to tell you that San Francisco is an inspiring city in which to raise children. It's really a metropolitan art colony because of its dramatic beauty. Therefore, Sol Hurok found a guaranteed audience for his booking of world-renowned dance concert artists. It was also the most thriving theatre town west of the Mississippi.

The Palace of the Legion of Honor offered Impressionist painters who were considered "modern." When I was little, Renoir, Monet, Picasso, Seurat, Gauguin, van Gogh . . . a big Rodin exhibit arrived. Could you find that in Wichita? My mother exposed me to all that, and I'm still grateful. I wish I could have done the same for Chan, but he found his own way to museums and galleries, thank goodness. He took an art course at Smith College while still attending Williams that I'm sure led to his immediately recognizable hilarious drawings of faces in the news.

His position now is editorial cartoonist on . . . the Fort Lauderdale *Sun-Sentinel*. Several years ago he was a Pulitzer Prize finalist. He has many awards, and he won the award voted on by his peers in the United States. So he really is just as brilliant as most every mother thinks her son is, I'm sure. Charles, my husband, and I thought he was excruciatingly funny, and I know he is, but also Chan agreed with us politically. Some people write to his paper and syndication, "Chan Lowe: why don't you send him back to communist China where he came from?" I guess they think his name is Chan Lo. Chan says it's important for a political cartoonist that he be controversial.

Yul Brynner

*I*t seems to me now that I began getting ready for my first meeting with Yul Brynner when I was eleven or twelve years old. I met him when I was about twenty-six, and it took me all that time to prepare.

At the Curran Theatre in San Francisco there arrived a revue called *Chauve Souris*, French for "Smiling Cat," I think. Why it was called that, I don't know. It had nothing to do with a cat. And it wasn't at all in French. It was completely in Russian. Maybe that's why I didn't hear anything about a cat. The creator of it was a man named Nikita Balieff, it said on the posters. I had already saved my allowance in case something earth-shattering like this came along. I saw it for a $2.50 orchestra seat. Pow! It inspired me into my entire Russian period.

Student tickets in those days were fifty cents in the uppermost balcony. I saw it from then on every Saturday matinee for weeks. In the first row I saw the red circles on their cheeks, the eyelashes painted in black on their eyelids, the bright red cupid's bow mouths. In the top balcony I could make out the body movements and hear those wild Slavic shrieks. There was one song sung by three people called "Katzeenika." Pronounced "*Kah*tzinka." Little Katja stood center of her two parents, Mominka on her right and Popinka on her left. I wanted to perform that song with my whole soul, but naturally I wanted to do all three parts.

There was a vermilion wool dress in the window of the Czechoslovakian Import Shop on Sutter Street, between Powell and Mason. It had peasant embroidery on the neck and sleeves. I looked at it after ballet class every weekday. Finally my mother said she'd help me to buy it. Anything you love like that turns out to be the most becoming thing you've ever owned. I wore it all my growing-up years and through Bennington College and after. As I grew, it became a tunic, then a blouse, and finally I had the wardrobe woman for Ted Shawn and Ruth St. Denis add wide strips of black on the bottom . . . first one, then two, then three, till I became the height I am now. I parted my hair in the middle, pulled it straight back to a black bow at the nape of the neck, like the Ballets Russes, and went to school, Sunday school, and dinner with my parents' friends that way. I never took it off except when my mother brought it to the cleaners. I appeared in this ensemble at the stage door of the Curran Theatre to ask for Mr. Nikita Balieff. Oh, I forgot the black, knee-high boots. Very authentic.

So after a matinee I knocked on that stage door and asked for Mr. Balieff. He came . . . a darling, jolly yet sophisticated, Russian-accented man dressed in a regular business suit. Why did I think he'd be wearing a tunic? Anyway, *I* was. The hairdo, the whole shmeer. He was dressed like the European entrepreneur he was.

Mr. B: Come in, little girl. Are you Russian?

Me: No sir, I'm going through my Russian period, which began the first time I saw your show.

Mr. B: You must have enjoyed it.

Me: Oh I do! But I wanted to ask you if you could please teach me those Russian sounds in your song "Katzeenika."

Mr. B (immediately): Come with me.

We walked together through the hall. On the left was a door. He opened it, and there was an old, brown wood, beaten-up upright piano. We sat on the bench together. I had my school notebook and a pencil. As he sang the song, I asked him to stop while I wrote it down phonetically . . . that is, phonetic to *me*. I wrote:

Yah nee biz mahny*air*off
Pliny*a*yoo oftz*air*off
B*oo*doo yaha s*nee*mee
Das po*l*iakoo tantza*watz*.

I sang it back to him.

Mr. B: That *boodoo* is "bwoodoo," with the first *oo* pronounced like *good* or *wood*. The second is *oo* as in *who*.

Me: Aha! Yes!

On we went, yet the next *oo* was "doohoochk*oo*v," as in *root*. I learned right then that if you want something badly enough, you can grab it the first time. I sang the whole song back to him, enjoying the intricacies he had just taught me . . . the little differences. He gave me the sheet music, which I told him I would treasure for the rest of my life. But the lyrics were written in triangles, *E*'s turned sideways, and pyramids, so I was totally dependent on the huge kindness of Mr. Balieff and the memory of his pronunciation. It never left me. I did treasure it. I kept the music in an envelope file until, years later, after attending college, Mark Blitzstein asked me to do a benefit. I rehearsed the song with the pianist and did it. It went like knishes at Coney Island, except that we were near Coney Island and the audience was probably full of knishes. They seemed to understand Russian. I don't know how it would go elsewhere. I tried it once on the Grand Ballroom circuit. It didn't go there.

After we opened in *Lend an Ear* on Broadway in 1947, Yul Brynner asked me to join him for one of his TV shows. He wanted me to do a duet with him. I asked him if he knew "Tziganka."

"Oh, everybody in Eastern Europe and all of Russia knows 'Tziganka.' "

There was only one TV channel then in New York, and we had to wear brown lipstick because the red went white on the receiver. I wore the bright red Czechoslovakian tunic, which also went white, I heard. Only the embroidery stood out. We looked like we were just off the boat. We went to an apartment building way up on the West Side. We broadcast out of a small room that was about ten stories up. I remember because it had a view here and there between other buildings of the Hudson River.

Yul grabbed his guitar for "Tziganka," and we shrieked up a storm. We were wild. But only a few people had TV sets in 1947, so we never knew if it appealed to anyone. The chorus of "Tziganka" demanded screaming "Gar*i*, gar*i*," which means "Burn, burn." It's a Cossack song about coming up over mountains in Russia on horseback, riding faster and faster down into the villages, whipping the horses to the beat of the music, raping the women, including the grandmothers, burning the thatched roofs—oh, it's cruel! We wallowed in it while discovering each other.

I was always, along with many other women, crazy about Yul. He was married at the time to Virginia Gilmore, a movie star, and I was married to a pro football player on the Ottawa Rough Riders, but I don't think either of those people crossed our minds while we were televising this song. I had already heard Nastia Poliakova, the Queen of the Gypsies of the entire world, down at the Russian Kretchma on East Fourteenth Street, sing "Tziganka," while she threw knives at a Cossack-uniformed man. Oh, God, she was great! But she wasn't any louder or shriller than Yul and I were. We sat back and laughed our heads off when we finished that song because we so loved the song and we loved the way we did it. Nothing ever came of it, with only about seven TV viewers, but this is what cemented our friendship, so it's important to me.

Everybody recognized Yul in show business as his peers' friend. At least I did. He had a strange habit of looking out for all his fellow actors while fighting constantly with the management. Not too smart, I always thought, for a man as knowledgeable businesswise as Yul. He even included me among his responsibilities. At the second opening of *Hello, Dolly!* on Broadway, Pia Lindstrom's TV review said something to the effect of "I'd like to tell you what I thought of *Hello, Dolly!* but I was sitting right behind Yul Brynner and he gave Ms. Channing so many standing ovations I missed too much of it."

That was our Yul. We were together in London for two command performances. I gave two more without him, but by that time he had taught me good. He whispered the rules every step of the way: "Get your gloves on quickly before the Queen arrives and shakes hands with you. Never start a new subject with her. Let her do it. Bow to the floor when I nudge you. I'll remain next to you, don't worry."

Maria Riva (Dietrich's daughter, you know) adored him, and she tells in her book *Marlene* that in her growing-up years he slept with her mother constantly and Maria knew it. She continued to adore him. Wouldn't we all have loved to sleep with him?

One time I said: Now, Yul, I read in an interview with you that you were born in Shanghai and raised in Indonesia. The last time I saw you, you told me your mother was a Bessarabian Gypsy and your father was from Outer Mongolia.

Yul: Whatever I last said, that's what I am!

He also told me his mother taught him the Gypsy signal used, for instance, in the grand ballroom of the Russian Imperial Embassy. When the signal is given, all the lights go off for one half-second. When they flash on again, the jewels on all the women are gone.

Me: Oh, Yul, tell me the signal.

Yul: You think I would tell you? On my mother's grave I'd never tell anyone. Not even you!

I know this sounds as if there were a romance between Yul and me. There wasn't. We were just crazy about each other, that's all.

But Charles dictated a letter to me to send Yul that Charles told me was wise business, something I wouldn't understand. Charles cut things like that off at the most excruciating time. He enjoyed that. But he didn't need to. My roots are from that generation that has to marry anyone she talks to alone after 10:00 P.M. Isn't that frustrating? The poor audience gets all my frustrations smack in the face. I wonder if I make love to them in my own way instead. My own way being love-making that's totally unrecognizable as such, I've been told. Maybe that's why I'm cured of anything or feeling better by the end of each show, though. Who knows?

Another time I had a pain in my shoulder from a sudden stop in a taxi. Lying down made it even worse, so I had to sit up or walk. I couldn't sleep a wink for three nights, which is dangerous when you must not ever miss a show, so Charles told me to call Yul. He knew he was the king of pain. As I say, Charles enjoyed controlling Yul's and my friendship. We each had matinees that day, so Yul made an 11:00 A.M. doctor's appointment.

Yul ushered me through a tall double door, stood in front of it facing a patient-filled waiting room, held on to my arm, and announced, "No autographs please. She never signs autographs." Nobody had asked me. The patients slowly put their papers and magazines down to lackadaisically observe what the noise was all about. Yul charged on through the next set of double doors, right into the doctor's office. He talked to the doctor while he told me to sit down and cry it out, that it would ease the pain and nervous sleeplessness. He kept handing me Kleenexes. He asked the doctor what to do with me.

The doctor put a wire up each nostril with cotton on the end of it dipped in something. He told me to inhale through my nose. In about half an hour he took out the wires. I cried all the way to the theatre; Yul kept handing me Kleenexes. He delivered me to Tiv, my dresser, and by the time Tiv got me microphoned, made up, wigged, and dressed, I walked out onstage and did a matinee that was so terrific I was never so terrific before or since. Tiv said I was chewing up the scenery, and he thought I was going to hold on to the curtain and go up and down with it for the final bows like the Duncan Sisters did for that historic tour in *Topsy and Eva*. You don't know about it? The Duncan Sisters, that is? Well, it was spectacular.

No one came backstage after that matinee, so it's possible it wasn't as spectacular as I thought it was. By the way, the pain didn't diminish that much. When the doctor arrived in my dressing room after that matinee, Tiv took me into his room, where my usual fish dinner was being heated up in the wig oven along with that evening's show's red Dolly wig. *That* room, Tiv's room, always in every theatre was connected to mine. Tiv told me he didn't think I should take any more of the doctor's painkillers and went on to say, "I think you should tell the doctor, 'Thank you very much, you cured me.' " Now if you've ever had a dresser, you know he or she is your everything, not just your dresser. You'd better do whatever he or she wants, or this theatre marriage isn't going to work. So I did what he said, as always. Tiv was never wrong about anything anyway, so why shouldn't I?

In London, for Yul's and my second command performance, he was doing "A Puzzlement" and "Shall We Dance?" I did "Diamonds Are a Girl's Best Friend" again and "Hello, Dolly!" with a full British cast of waiters, cooks, busboys, et cetera.

Yul had to rehearse a full hour entering and going down six steps. You see, Yul was sixteen years old when the acrobats miscalculated and he fell from the high wire in the Europe-Asia circus. There was no net. He was still three or four inches short of his full growth, so he grew only on the side of him that was not all banged up. He had a four-inch lift always under his right heel. "Oh, my darling, I am a cripple, you should know," he would say, and that's why he most always took his famous stance with feet wide apart and fists on hipbones in order to maintain his balance. Descending those six steps took up the hour.

I stayed with him during that hour, downstage of him and out on the runway, because I had to go over the *Hello, Dolly!* number and re-measure my steps for this stage, since I seem to have this proclivity for disappearing from the audience into the orchestra pit if something keeps me from counting out the number of steps to the pit. When I disappear, the cast and musicians seem disconcerted for a moment, but they get over it right away and just keep going. Because of being near-sighted, I keep my glasses on for rehearsals and memorize the number of steps for each new theatre. So far, I've broken the left knee joint; right wrist and thumb (in a cast for a year); both arms, the right one had a cast and sling for six months, the left for eight—wasn't I lucky it wasn't the other way around as I'm right-handed; and a fractured bottom vertebra so I sat on an inflated inner tube for the run of *Jerry's Girls*. On travel days, Charles used to give orders, "Get the madam seated in the plane onto the picture frame."

For years Yul went through a brown era, during which everything had to be brown, including his two soft-boiled eggs for breakfast in their brown shells.

The King and I, Lena Horne, and *Dolly* were all touring simultaneously, so we ran into one another in airports (Yul in a wheelchair with his brown fedora down to his eyebrows). We followed one another in the same theatres across the country, so Lena and I often landed in dressing rooms with newly painted brown walls, brown furniture and vanities, brown sinks, johns, showers, shower curtains, and towels. It did hurt me that when Elizabeth Taylor was touring just before us with Richard Burton in *Private Lives*, Yul had the lavender and crystal dressing room they prepared for her at the Sanger Theatre in New Orleans covered with brown paint, so I missed its splendor. Anyway, in Memphis, the resident stage manager told me he had a hard time finding Miss Horne in her dressing room as she was also brown. He said he called, "Half hour, Miss Horne. Miss Horne?" She said, "I'm heah."

In her show she mentioned the movies decided "light Egyptian" was the correct Pan-Cake for her, but I think she looks even more beautiful brown, don't you? Well, I suppose Yul would have thought so, anyway.

When Yul opened *The King and I* at the Uris in New York, the audience section walls were all white and gold Rococo with gold leaf angels flying around the proscenium arch and a turning mirrored chandelier in the center of the house. I needn't tell you what he did to all of that. He was so right. And he reopened as a smash hit! We know one reason why, don't we? The show was the center of focus. Oh, he was so knowledgeable.

*T*o the Curran Theatre in San Francisco came Katherine Cornell and Brian Aherne in *The Barretts of Wimpole Street* and *Romeo and Juliet*, the Lunts in *The Guardsman*, *Amphitryon*, and Robert Sherwood's play *Idiot's Delight*. Also Otis Skinner, and then his daughter Cornelia, who captured me only with her playwriting, not her acting. Children know, don't they? She didn't wear her clothes well. No style. No sex appeal. That's the first telltale sign that a performance is not going to stay with you forever. Alla Nazimova was magnetic as Mrs. Alving in Ibsen's *Ghosts*. Watching her I learned that there is no reason why an actress playing a woman with a grown son can't be a svelte fashion plate and have her own clothing, makeup, and extreme coiffure. She certainly kept a female child in her audience riveted on her. It even enhanced her last scene. This extremely attractive creature was holding her adult son in her arms while he died of syphilis. She poured her heart out to him with very few lines. I thought at the time that these emotions I'm experiencing with her are far deeper than a dear little old lady's. Her womanly feelings were strong, and they showed she was in the prime of life.

I didn't get to know the theatre critic Walter Kerr until after he retired. He and Jean Kerr invited us often to their home *after* he retired. There he told me he found out watching Nazimova onstage in Chicago that it is very possible to be hypnotized by an actress just from sitting in her audience. He said she held him in her spell for four whole days after he'd seen her. On the fourth day he was waiting for a bus in Evanston, Illinois, where he lived. At that point she released him so that he was able to count the change for his bus fare. Yes! She held me, too. When I had that reaction to Lynn Fontanne, Ethel Waters, or Fanny Brice, for instance, I was unable to stop walking and talking like them. Finally I'd completely turned *into* them for several days . . . to the annoyance of everyone around me. My suspicion is Walter simply *wrote* about them instead. Each of us has his own way of reacting to hypnosis, and that kind of hypnosis never seems to be a bad influence on a victim.

My parents took me to the first musical I ever saw. It was Marc Connelly's *The Green Pastures*, with Rex Ingram playing the Lord and with the Hall Johnson Choir, each member of it singing his heart out. There were also three sunflowers in the Garden of Eden. I wanted to play one of those sunflowers so badly (and still do). I was about six years old then. The Lord walked by the sunflowers and asked (two octaves lower than anyone), "How you, sunflowers?" Their brown faces were the centers of the sunflowers. "We's fine, Lord," they answered, with bored-with-paradise but contented smiles. They were the funniest people in the show, I felt.

Later, I saw Helen Hayes in *Ladies and Gentlemen* and *Twelfth Night*, Francis Lederer and Julie Haydon in *Autumn Crocus*, Willie and Eugene Howard in (I longed to be Louella Geer, who stood between them) *George White's Scandals*. It was good for me that I had to save my allowance to go alone to a matinee. I think I appreciated it more.

Then it happened! From a third-row orchestra seat I saw *As Thousands Cheer* with Ethel Waters. It was the first musical that was as well thought out as a play—by Moss Hart and Irving Berlin, no less. But at one point the curtains opened all the way back to the brick wall of the Curran Theatre. As I mentioned to you before, most stages at that time were divided into five sections, with a curtain that could be closed on each section. Well, there against the back brick wall stood this monumental figure of a woman with a bandanna tied around her head, leaving her eyes and lips in bold relief to tell this next story. The beat began with a mighty *auschpannen*, as Mary Wigman, the world's first modern dancer, from Berlin, referred to it. Mary Wigman was prior to Martha Graham, and even looked a lot like her, long, swinging hair and all. This *auschpannen* amounts to a big, silent, slow inhale from the orchestra and then swings up and around into the first downbeat, which lands with a crash. Later, when I worked often with Huddie Ledbetter (billed Leadbelly) for Max Gordon at the Village Vanguard in New York, it was called "funk," but this performance by Ethel Waters was the first time I heard it in a live theatre.

Waters stepped forward from "5" *on* the downbeat—5's curtains closed behind her. *Auschpannen* again . . . her second step simultaneous with the following crash. Now she was in "4" (curtains close), "3" (curtains), "2" (curtains), now she was in "1," right on the footlights, towering over us, her voice rising to "Supper Time" as the last curtain closed behind her. On it was the silhouette created with lights of a man hanging from the bough of a tree, neck and head bent toward one shoulder, legs dangling but held still.

This is what my Georgia-born father used to tell Mother and me about. He told us that as newspapermen they were never allowed to mention lynchings in their stories (even up North), and this was the first time anyone had depicted such a thing. It took Moss Hart and Irving Berlin to defy the rule, allowing this woman's enormous artistry to reach out and sing it to us. I forgot to tell you she was a Negro, which is important because it made her thoughts stand out like neon against her brown skin, and therefore there was no getting away from her emotions. Her singing voice was bottomless and topless, seemingly created just to tell this story. There was another number, then the lights went on for intermission. I was embarrassed that my heart was still pounding till I shook because of Ethel Waters and the subject matter of a lynching. I was surprised to see the audience was thumbing through programs, talking, stretching, et cetera. I think they didn't realize what a lynching was.

After intermission came "Easter Parade." Then Waters sang "Heat Wave" while Grace and Kurt Graff's dancers did the sexiest choreography I ever thought possible. It was thrilling! This was show business. You could do things onstage that the movies never allowed, at least at that time.

Years later, after Ethel Waters appointed herself my son Chan's official grandmother, which she took very seriously from the time he was three. I asked her who thought of that theatrical beginning to "Supper Time."

Ethel Waters: They *had* to do that, Carol. They had to set the stage for the next scene, so they stuck me down in "1" until the next set got onstage.

Me: Who did the orchestration?

Waters: Oh, Irving Berlin planned it himself. He timed the music to the set change.

Can you imagine, after all these years, that I remember every note and almost every move she made? It was the high spot of the show.

I grew up with my father saying things like "There is no power on earth as strong as the individual." To me, it's true. No onstage helicopter landing and taking off, no swimming pool, no crashing chandelier has the profound emotional impact of the individual person. The feelings of those actors stay with you whenever you think of them, for the rest of your life.

Ethel was the first Afro-American to come downtown to Broadway. She was a huge hit at the Cotton Club in Harlem with Cab Calloway and his orchestra with her tag "Sweet Mama Stringbean." She was asked to appear in the chic revue *The Little Show* with Marilyn Miller and Clifton Webb, and plays like *Mamba's Daughters* and Carson McCullers's *Member of the Wedding.* Musicals like, as I told you, *As Thousands Cheer* and *Cabin in the Sky.* I was able to see her in everything. Some people that I trust tell me she could be murderous when frightened, but Julie Harris and I never saw a glint of that side of her. She and Chan used to come and sit in the stage left box of the Biltmore Theatre in L.A. for many matinees of my one woman show, Chan's platinum blond head shining under her chin as he sat safely and happily on her lap. I forgot to tell her of my heritage because I forgot all about it, but now I realize how grateful I am for it, so I'm telling you of it. All Ethel needed from me was that Chan and I adored her.

et me tell you how to pass an IQ test so that you will have one of the best ratings in the country and therefore be accepted by any college or university that you have your heart set on. If I can do it, anyone can do it. These SAT tests have absolutely nothing to do with how smart we really are.

I wanted to go to Bennington and nowhere else. I wanted it all the time I attended Lowell High School, but I worried about my chances because Bennington was famous for all its students possessing the highest IQs in the country. Still, I simply had to go there because at that time it was the only college at which you could major in the arts. (Well, actually, at Reed College in Oregon you could, but they didn't have either the endowments or the faculty.)

Our drama teacher at Lowell, Mr. Polland, had us write compositions on articles or pictures that appeared in *Theatre Arts Monthly*, the only magazine of its kind at the time. It was full of stories on the pioneers of modern dance, of drama, of music, and on playwrights and set designers, many of whom were on the Bennington faculty. So! I went to Heald's Engineering College in San Francisco and took a summer course in aptitude tests. The favorite questions were:

If a train is going 65 miles an hour and an oncoming train is going 100 miles an hour and they both start at 6:14 A.M., from 78 miles apart, at what time will they cross?

And:

If two trains are going in the same direction and they both start at 6:14 A.M. and one train arrives at its destination at 12:22 P.M., the other at 2:14 P.M., how many miles an hour faster was the first train going than the second?

Yes. I know you don't care any more than I did. However, this is how our intelligence is judged. Can you believe it? Have you noticed what kinds of letters people with high IQs write?

Dear Sir: With regards to your overcharging me $50.00.

Now, I'm not going to send my regards to someone who overcharged me fifty dollars. Are you? And no matter how many times you explain to them that you don't send regards to someone who overcharged you, they go right on doing it.

I've also noticed that brilliant brains like that often don't do much of anything in life except pass high on IQ tests. Oh, I know, I'm just jealous, that's all. I'm on the defensive. I should respect them, and I do, actually. Their brains just are different from the rest of ours, that's all.

After I took that course, getting the answer became a routine procedure. I naturally can't remember it now, but getting the answer became unbelievably simple. For no reason at all you take the speed of the first train, divide it by the second train's, add what time they started, multiply it by God knows what, and there's your answer. Just memorize the order of the adding and subtracting like a piece of choreography. Like the children of this current generation with computers, at age five I was phenomenal with choreography. The ballet master "talked" sixteen steps to the dancers, we memorized them on the spot in our heads and then did them. He'd say, "Glissade tour jeté plié relevé into second arabesque, batma, and pas de bourrée, four déboulés to right, four to left . . ." Oh well, I'm simply showing off because I'm so mad at myself for not being able to work computers like my four-year-old friend, Seth, who declared me "hopeless."

My point is, relate the entire IQ test to something you care about, like choreography or whatever it is you're at home with. There is no reason under the sun why you find the answer to *any*thing by following what the engineering teacher taught me, you just memorize the procedure; then *why* it gives you the answer is someone else's problem, not yours, but you pass the test with flying colors.

There was only one hitch. After one year at Bennington, they give you the same type of IQ test. I didn't expect *that*! I was off into Strindberg, Ibsen, Chekhov, and all that crowd. My counselors, Martha Hill and Mary Jo Shelley (great names in the New York dance world), said, "What happened? You had one of the highest IQs when we accepted you here." So my warning to you is, Find out if they're going to give you another one of those inconsequential tests that relates to nothing concerning anyone's life, and go over your notes carefully before taking it. My brain simply sank right back to where it had been comfortable and happy.

By the end of the second year, I got better grades in sociology, human biology, and literature than I did in drama or dance, and drama/dance was my major. I got bad grades in my major.

But my lit teacher was no less than Henry Simon, the older brother of Richard Simon, cofounder of Simon & Schuster or maybe now he's some Simon's grandfather or great grandfather. Like most of us, I forget how old I am, which is probably just as well. He gave me an A for a thesis on Gustave Flaubert, author of *Madame Bovary*. Naturally, I had great affection for him for that, and he opened literary portals for me I didn't know existed. He had a wife who wrote a book that was a bestseller at the time. I think. At least it was a huge success with me. I remember her writing of "Henry's sartorial driftwood," and sure enough, he came to class every weekday wearing three pieces of sartorial driftwood, his jacket, his trousers, and his shirt. He looked pretty cute in his driftwood, too, but then he did give me an A, so I viewed him especially positively.

I only took lit because of Marion Hepburn, one of Katharine's younger sisters. She was my friend and a lit major. She was a senior when she came to welcome us freshmen. I was so entranced with her because she had Katharine's vocal cords, teeth, and family accent, but all of that came out of a huggable Dolly Dimple plumpness. Actually, she was fat. Well, fat is what it was that she was, but very pretty. There was no other family in any country that had any accent remotely like that of this Hepburn family, especially in Hartford, where they lived. Wouldn't you think they would have been influenced by everyone else around them? Not at all. Marion was friendly to me because she wanted to know how once onstage I could turn into all those students around campus. Years later, Marion told me she wanted to know the process so she could do it too. It never entered her mind, she said, that it was a gift, and she laughed at herself embarrassedly. She said she was only engulfed in "lit-raht-yewah" (literature) and was conscious of little else.

Peggy Hepburn, the third sister, was a tearing beauty but not exaggerated like Kate. She looked, as Noël Coward said, as if God shot for Peggy, missed, and first got Katharine instead. Later, He created the perfect Peggy. I know Peggy's looks were perfect, but is that the goal? *Time* magazine called Kate "muscle-faced." I think that's far more valuable, don't you? Especially since no one else in the world has ever been muscle-faced? Or can you tell that Peggy never gave me the time of day, and Marion was around me a lot, much to my enjoyment and pride?

Bennington lived up to its reputation. It was a marvelous school, mostly because the classes were limited to twelve students, so that if Martha Hill chose to ignore you or lose her temper at you, it was very noticeable. See, I had already been teaching dance at Mills College, across the bay from San Francisco, as a member of the Allied Dance Group. The San Francisco Opera Ballet master, Adolph Bolm, recommended me. They tried me out three times, and allowed me to be a member. They were all teachers, including Tina Flade (pronounced "Flahduh," isn't that interesting?), head of the dance department of Mills. I was still a student at Lowell High School when we were all working out new forms of choreography. As Nanette Fabray once said to me when I asked her how she went over in her show, "With all due humility, I was fantastic." What else do you say when someone asks if you were good at something? Thank you, Nanny. I was, too . . . fantastic . . . and humble, okay? We're all good at something.

We have a great president of Bennington, we all agree . . . Liz Coleman. She told me, "I'm sorry you were given Martha Hill, Carol, not only as your dance teacher but as your personal counselor." I told her, "Liz, if one can live through Martha Hill, one can live through *any*thing." And that statement proved to be true. Apparently Martha's venom came through to Liz when she looked up my grades and comments by Martha. Lovely, brilliant Katherine Drexel Henry told me before she died of cancer in her thirties in New York, "Oh, I wasn't good enough for Bennington, Carol." Antoinette Larrabee said the same about herself. Many art majors said that to me, but never the science majors or human biology or sociology, et cetera. I'm convinced art in any form cannot be taught and should not be. The student should only be exposed to it and then exercise it at first without influence.

I left Bennington after two years, even though I was accepted into the senior division. I refused it. I felt that Martha's goal was the annihilation of my entire being; I also felt that I deserved it. At sixteen and seventeen, one believed her. I believed Martha, that I was not good enough for Bennington either. I believed Martha Hill right up until a few years ago, when Liz Coleman straightened me out. Liz is brilliant at straightening people out. I've got to get Dustin Hoffman to Liz Coleman. Once when he was asked, "How do you feel if you read a bad review of yourself?" he answered, "I feel they've caught up with me. They're on to me." Of course, one bad review and I'm right back with Martha Hill, just like Dustin is with one isolated criticism. It's our job to reach the guy that wrote that bad review. If that man can write such a thing, then we've failed. I didn't learn anything at all from Martha Hill. I learned things I'm still drawing on from the faculty members Arch Lauterer and José Limón . . . mostly kindness and understanding of and care for one another's work.

José Limón (pronounced "Lee-*mone*") had an old automobile. He used to fit five of us students in it if we split the gas expenses. He drove. On one of the rides to New York City I was going to split a hotel room with one of the drama boys in the car. Mr. Limón looked at me pleadingly and said, "Don't do this, Carol." I got his message clearly, as if to say, It's not for you. It won't make you happy. So I didn't. I was so deeply touched by the way he cared about his students and that I was one of them worth his bother. I was a virgin. How did he know? Does that sort of thing show with all of us, do you suppose? I mean, to someone who cares about us? No! Of course not. Mr. Limón was a most unusual man. He was born in a tepee in Mexico and became one of the world's greatest artists. He was a dance pioneer with his well-trained and -disciplined group. And he was very gentle. His choreography was so durable that to this day younger dancers receive his training and tour with it all over the country and perhaps the world.

I used to hear often of another drama teacher at Northwestern University. She never worked professionally in the theatre, by the way, which I think is revealing. Under her tutelage, seven students walked into Lake Michigan and drowned themselves. We all know it may be our most vulnerable age, all of us, but the faculty who has been forced to *teach* instead of *doing* what they wanted should be carefully watched. I'm the only one of her students who did the work I wanted Martha to teach me. These are her words: "You, Miss Channing, must have been a big frog in a very small pond in San Francisco and you kid yourself that you're important. I thought you were Bennington standards when I came to San Francisco to interview you. Now that you're here I realize you are nothing like I thought you were. And I recommended you. I get the blame for misjudging." I slowly got so sick I landed in the infirmary for weeks. I couldn't stand up or stop throwing up or face anyone. As I say, I believed Martha, of course. Actually, at any age you do. I was pleasantly surprised when Bennington asked me to deliver the baccalaureate address at graduation several years later.

What kept me going till I left was I did jazzy musical shows up in the college auditorium at night. I wrote lyrics for me to sing while impersonating my favorite fellow students. I put the lyrics to then-current Broadway tunes. The girls all packed the place and laughed up a storm. Many of the girls I did were extreme individuals and fascinating. I had excellent material. As I told you, in my mind it was devoid of disapproval. I wasn't aware of why they as an audience thought it was so bitingly satiric. I just thought the girls I chose as characters to play were eccentrically, darlingly funny.

One day at Drama Seminar, when I finished doing scenes from Shaw's *St. Joan*, Arch Lauterer made his theatre commentary after other faculty members finished theirs. Mr. Lauterer was always busy doing the sets for Martha Graham's concerts in New York. He pointed to where I was dangling my feet over the end of the stage in what was supposed to be the Loire River. "There has always been a question as to which is more important to the theatre . . . the playwright with his ensemble piece, or star quality in a star vehicle." He said to the entire auditorium of students and faculty very matter-of-factly, "Now here we have this example. This play is a starring vehicle requiring whoever plays the title character to bring herself up to it. Since Carol achieved that, Shaw's goal for his play is achieved. In the scenes before this (of *Juno and the Paycock*) it is a well-written ensemble piece. Which is more important is only to be judged by the audience and the box office." He said this so factually that nobody (including me) thought it was any particular compliment to me. However, his almost exact words have stayed with me all these years, and I honestly wonder again what he saw that made him make such an encouraging (for me) statement.

Someone on the faculty, I don't know who, switched me to Hope Miller, the opera singing teacher, for my final six months. I learned all I know about singing from her. I liked her. She was a mine of just what I wanted to know. But I'm sure my voice isn't the best advertisement for an opera coach. I found out from Hope, singing correctly is a cinch. But musical comedy people want to sing like the character, at least I do. Also Ezio Pinza missed more shows in *South Pacific* than any

of the rest of us ever heard of. Opera singers cancel out constantly. I'm
on the defensive again.

Can you imagine how happy I was to see Henry Simon? Approval!
Also, he had no snobbery concerning the arts. Intellectual snobbery
seems to be the key to recognizing lousy teachers. I've already said it,
but especially during the first year of college, all students' lifelines are
hanging by a thread. But the standard of teachers at Bennington was
known as not only fine but current. We learned from Leon Hender-
son, who was economic adviser for the Roosevelt administration.
When we got him, he headed the Securities and Exchange Commis-
sion, so I didn't understand him, but he was unusually left-wing for an
eastern college to beckon him. We also heard lectures from prominent
conservatives.

I studied singing also in New York with Hope Miller during our
winter fieldwork period, and the result is there in my seven-inch rib
expansion while dancing and singing simultaneously. I'm proud of the
breath endurance she taught me. Mr. and Mrs. Ferguson were fine
teachers of Method acting, which has stayed with me all my working
life. I'm telling you all this because I just wanted you to know Bennington was and is a marvelous school. Walter Kerr, who was an incomparable writer himself, said in one of his reviews, "It is the
teacher's fate never to be incomparable himself; he frees ability to go
where he cannot go." That was the caliber of the Bennington faculty I
worked with. In retrospect, I am grateful to Martha Hill. We all eventually do live through a few vital threats like that, I'm sure, before we
can learn to survive. Right?

When I talked to the Theatre Guild about doing a George Bernard
Shaw play, Bennington had already taken the fear away from attacking
such projects. What a gift Bennington bestowed on its students!

any people ask me, "Carol, how did you get into the theatre?" I never mind being asked that question because I do so dearly love to hear my own answer. So, during my winter period from Bennington I went first to the William Morris Agency. I was warming the bench outside Mr. Lastfogel's (the president's) office waiting to go in. On my right were Betty Comden and Adolph Green, two members of the Revuers who had appeared at the Village Vanguard just once, and I saw them. They were an innovation! Judy Holliday was one of their group. No one had heard of the Revuers yet or any of their names.

On my left was Alfred Drake, who wasn't the great Alfred Drake at all yet. Mr. Lastfogel's door finally opened. His secretary pointed at us and said, "You! Come in." Betty said to me, "She pointed at you, Carol." I said, "I could swear she pointed at you and Adolph." "No! Go in. Go!" Betty said.

I picked up my little Haitian drum, went through the door, and began my first audition. Years later I opened my *Carol Channing and Her Ten Stout-Hearted Men* show at the Drury Lane Theatre in London with that story.

Mr. Lastfogel was a man who was known as having a touch of genius, and so of course as a result he never saw anyone, excepting occasionally Katharine Hepburn, or John Wayne, or Mrs. Lastfogel—he saw *a lot* of her. But now, there I was face to face with the great man himself. He was a rugged tycoon who could make or break anyone's career with a single bite on his cigar. I swung right into my first number—something I was sure of because it was a big hit with the girls at Bennington—a simple ancient Gallic dirge, in obsolete Vercingetorix French. Vercingetorix was a conqueror before all Gaul was hauled together. This dirge was adapted from the original Greek tragedy,

Orestes, and this was the most thrilling part of the whole thing, the Orestes Funeral Chant.

I remember how Mr. Lastfogel's eyes filled with wonderment as I showed him how the women of the Greek chorus lamented the ravages of war and the shortage of men. As I say, I had my little drum, this was in 9/5 time, very difficult. I chanted in obsolete French. Then, while beating my breasts, I swung into the rousing finale, "Oo—oo—oo."

Well, Mr. Lastfogel thought I should do someone better known than Orestes, like Sophie Tucker. I sensed I was losing the great man's attention, so I said, "Wait, Mr. Lastfogel, please. I have another song here that the girls at Bennington just love. It's a Haitian corn-grinding song rendered by the natives as they stomp out the kernels with their feet. They sing of their lost youth and pray for rain." The lyrics were in patois, a Haitian bastard form of French.

Mr. Lastfogel thought he could see some signs of improvement but that perhaps it would be wiser for me to get out of ethnic music and into the straight classics, like Ethel Merman. As he was ushering me to the door and telling me not to phone him that he would phone me, I said, "Wait, Mr. Lastfogel, please. I have one more song here that I ran across in my studies on Mittel European cultures." And before he could close the door in my face I sang it. I sang from the middle to the end of "Roumania" here in Galitzianer Yiddish.

"Wait," Mr. Lastfogel said, "I think I see a glimmer of talent in this girl." He said his grandmother used to sing songs like this to him when he was a little boy. And, do you know, Abe Lastfogel and I sang this song together. He was my agent all my working life.

From there he sent me over to Marc Blitzstein, who was writing modern American operas: *The Cradle Will Rock* and this new *No for an Answer*. I got the job, my first job on Broadway, and then I thought I was on my way. Well that's what lots of people think, but I learned. After Blitzstein, I used to do free benefits for the Knights of Columbus, the Shakespeare Club, the Elks, the Shriners, the Hadassah, and bingo games for the Catholics. But that's how I got into the theatre.

Now once Mr. Lastfogel arranged a meeting for me with Marc Blitzstein, Marc treated me as if I were dear and tender. I was so grateful I talked, sang, and danced for him everybody that I had seen on Broadway, mostly because he seemed delighted with my renditions and I enjoyed making him happy. He was trying to find a girl to do his one comedy song in *No for an Answer*. The song he handed me was to be sung by a young girl at a roadside bar, who didn't know who she was yet. Perfect! Well, I still don't know, but I was nineteen then so I had a good excuse. The name of the song was "I'm Simply Fraught About You"—very subtle and sophisticated lyrics, but I threw everything but the kitchen sink into it, which Marc said was just the right thing to do.

I asked him if I could make parts of it Merman, parts Gertrude Lawrence, others Bea Lillie or Sophie Tucker. He said, "Absolutely! That's why I want you to do this song." He was right. We did the show in a huge theatre that was then called Mecca Temple or the Shrine Auditorium. Now it's the City Center Theatre on Fifty-sixth Street west of Avenue of the Americas, but they've cut it up or done something to it. It's not as big. However, the distinguished classical music critic Virgil Thomson on *The New Yorker* magazine gave me one encouraging sentence in his good review of Marc's work. "You will surely hear more about a satirical chanteuse named Carol Channing." I'll never forget that sentence. Of course he was "distinguished." He was to me, anyway.

But let me back up. During rehearsals the company constantly told me to write to my congressman and complain about something. I could never remember what. I'd get to Mecca Temple the next day and they'd say, "Well? Did you write to your congressman?" I finally said, "Look. I was nailing my lyrics and rehearsing them all last evening. I can't do two things at once. Let me get this song right first." I never got off the song. I don't when I have a performance to do. Who does? Sometime later, the McCarthy era began. I used to read some of their names in the daily papers.

Why didn't the hearings ever call on me? How did those unconstitutional, undemocratic McCarthyites know I was always busy with my fabulously funny lyrics? I was in the same show as these accused people. *No for an Answer* was about the formation of a labor union. Apparently being any part of singing the story of building the labor unions automatically labeled you a Communist. But then, why did *I* come out smelling like a rose? Almost all the actors I knew lived in terror they'd be called in and suddenly labeled Communists, which as we know ended their careers. I was even worried for myself. There must have been a spy or spies in that company who knew I was too obsessed with my own performance to think of anything else.

I just looked it up on the Internet. Marc Blitzstein openly declared himself a card-holding member of the Communist party at the Mc-Carthy hearings in 1958. I never knew that! No wonder everyone wanted me to write my congressman and complain. They took it for granted I shared their political views if I was in the show. Most of the company seemed to be Russian Jews whose parents were still celebrating having a congressman to write to and not being executed for it. They couldn't stop writing to him they were so happy to be Americans. It never occurred to me there was anything un-American about forming a labor union. I still don't see that there is. Do you? Equity, SAG, and AGVA are surely sustaining me now, and they were never Communists. Ronald Reagan was president of SAG for years, and you know to him Russia was the Evil Empire, so he wasn't either a Communist . . . or a card holder . . . or anything . . . and we love him.

After *No for an Answer* a group of very good young male country singers and songwriters asked me to be their only girl and vocalist. I was happy to be working some more. I sang:

> Franklin Roosevelt
> Told the people how he felt
> We damn near believed
> What he said
> He said "I hate war
> And so does Eleanor
> But we won't be safe
> Till everbody's dead"

We sang a lot more, for benefits and group meetings all over Manhattan. Then Mildred Weber, the great organizer of the New and Unknown Talent Department of William Morris, put me on the Borscht Circuit for one summer at Camp Tamiment in the Catskills, pronounced by the clientele "Cahmb Dowmnt" in the "Kedzgls." Betty Garrett and I were assigned as roommates, only tentmates is what we were. We lived in a tent with a wooden roof over it and Betty's twelve cats and a drawing of Ethel Waters that Betty did for me. I framed it and hung it above my cot.

Most of the cats were housebroken, but we got used to the cat litter within twenty-four hours and it never bothered me, mostly because

Betty was the best roommate and friend anyone could have. She was so in love with Larry Parks, later her husband and father of her two sons. He was just great starring in the movie *The Jolson Story*. Then the House Un-American Activities Committee axed his career, and no movie people dared touch him again. He died young. Who could live through that? If he wanted to overthrow democracy, Betty would have known it, I swear. I mean, even I wrote a paper at Bennington called "The Difference Between Communism, Socialism, and Democracy," figuring I would therefore know all this for the rest of my life. All I can remember now is communism and socialism didn't work and democracy did; I could tell that just from researching the facts.

I was fired shortly before the end of the season for having no talent and after much degrading name-calling from Max Liebman, our director, always in front of the entire company. I don't remember doing a bad show there. Actually, I was in my element . . . revues.

Anyway, Jerome Robbins was our choreographer. The steps he gave me I wallowed in, so he'd give me more. They required a body elasticity that I knew I could give them as soon as he demonstrated them to me. I was crazy about those steps! I can't say I was crazy about Jerry because I never got to even talk with him, just to say "uh huh" and "I see what you want." I knew him only through the dances he gave me. He paid no attention to me as I remember. He was hell-bent on trying out the extent of his own choreography. I certainly don't blame him. He was on a divine mission. He was also living with a girl who was one of his dancers, and that took up the rest of each day. He rehearsed all day Saturdays and Sundays, though. Her husband and little boy arrived every weekend.

We did three shows a week, all different and never repeated. Betty and I did one sketch I remember. We played switchboard operators for a legal firm. We'd answer, "Beaton Barton Batten and Button, good morning." It got more and more complicated. We adored the way we did it. So did the cats and the audience.

Some of the musicians said, "Why don't you yell back at Max Liebman? He has to have a 'patsy.' He dishes it out to anyone who'll take it." Finally, Max screamed at me rehearsing onstage, "You're nothing but a dirty chozzer [pig]. You're fired!" Betty and one of the musicians took me for a walk along the lake until I could breathe again. They must have had humanitarian natures. I asked them what I had done wrong. "Nothing!" Betty kept saying. It's one thing to be fired from the Bake Shop at Macy's, which I had been because I ate the blueberries that had fallen out of the blueberry muffins into the pan. Then there were the blueberries that almost fell out, and the next one that could have fallen out. And finally I was fired because there were holes in the blueberry muffins, though I was their fastest helper because I made the work into a piece of choreography, so the hours flew by. To be fired from the Bake Shop at Macy's is bad enough, but to be fired for the one excuse for your existence is numbing.

The reason Max had such an indentation on me was because he was the producer and director of the biggest TV musical and sketch show for years, *Your Show of Shows*, starring Sid Caesar, Imogene Coca, and Marguerite Piazza. So I felt he had to be a man to be respected. He wasn't. Well, he hated me, didn't he?

When the dinner gong rang and everyone went to the dining room, I began walking down the road to Unity House, the summer camp place for the ILGWU—the International Ladies' Garment Workers' Union.

There was a big wave coming up over the lake. I thought, How convenient. I could accidentally drown. But, better yet, a truck was coming toward me down the road. That would really look like an accident. I tried to get in its way, because this pain would all be over if I could get in front of it. But as in the nightmare of not having a voice to yell back at Max, my legs wouldn't take me to the front of the truck. Of course I wouldn't have done it, but it was slightly comforting to realize there is another way out.

Mr. and Mrs. Dubinsky were sitting in rocking chairs on the wooden front porch at Unity House (Dave Dubinsky was the president and organizer of the ILGWU). As they rocked Mrs. Dubinsky said, "You look like death, Carol. What is it?" I told them I just got fired. Dave said, "Your only cure is to get right up on our stage here and do the best performance you can. Someone, get Perry Bruskin to come and rehearse the piano with her." Perry rehearsed a samba for my Carmen Miranda with me and "Happy Birthday" for my Tallulah. He knew "Mama Goes Where Papa Goes" for my Sophie Tucker and got the drummer for Ethel Waters's *auschpannens*. We did a show that went over like knishes at Coney Island. I always liked Perry Bruskin (you don't know him, I'm sure), but that night I was devoted to him. I decided Dave Dubinsky had a touch of greatness. What a remarkable man to take such an attitude toward someone who wasn't even a member of his union (me). His nature was simply like that, and so was his wife's. I wish I had told him what he had done for me. He was right. When one is thrown from a horse, get right back on it and keep riding. Don't wait, or you'll never get back on.

It was necessary for me to tell you my Max Liebman experience because only a few years later, just as *Gentlemen Prefer Blondes* opened on Broadway, *Time* magazine put me on their cover. They had to interview Max for the story. He came into my dressing room at the Ziegfeld raging angry. "*Why* did you tell them I fired you? I *discovered* you! How dare you say that?" I answered him, "Because, Max, it proves something important in the arts. The reaction to an artist's work is all in the eye of the beholder. It's only a matter of opinion. People who fail at any time could remember that." And that *is* true, isn't it?

Speaking of that *Time* cover, there used to be a newsstand on the corner of Commonwealth and Mass Avenues in Boston. The man who owned the stand told me many years ago, but after my father was gone, that he'd see my father walking home from his office. Even after new issues of *Time* came out, the newsstand man kept the old one with me up for weeks. He said, "It made my day just to see your father's face as he looked at it."

Most of us would like to have somewhat repaid our parents by letting them know they helped us achieve some of our goals. Wasn't I lucky? I got to before it was too late.

I auditioned for everything and everybody on or off Broadway while living alone in New York after being fired from the Borscht Circuit by Leibman. I talked alone with Lee Shubert in his office. He asked, "Well, what do you want to be in the theatre? Do you want to be like Eve Arden or Margaret Dumont or Charlotte Greenwood or who? You're very tall." I tried to explain that I wanted to be in a revue and play all different characters when, all of a sudden, I started to cry out of frustration because I couldn't succinctly tell him. He handed me a box of Kleenex and kept smiling at me. I was now nineteen years old, which is always an interesting age to older people. Finally, he sent me to the director and playwright of a play called *So Proudly We Hail*. I got the job! We closed within a few months.

More auditions for the Rainbow Room, the Village Vanguard (where I got the job), little clubs like Spivey's Roof, and more shows like

Nancy Hamilton's *2 for the Show* (a revue). This one was at her home. They were welcoming to me, but they already had an understudy.

Finally, I saw in *Variety* that Vinton Freedley was producing a musical that had just opened at the Colonial Theatre in Boston. It was Danny Kaye's first starring part, costarring Eve Arden. I got myself to Boston, where my parents were living in Mary Baker Eddy's home on Commonwealth and Mass Avenues because that's where the first reader of the Mother Church and his family live during the reader's tenure.

I went straight to the Colonial. Mr. Freedley was an aristocratic, lovely gentleman. I asked if I could audition for him as Eve Arden's understudy. He said, "Certainly. Go onstage right now and I'll sit in the audience." Danny Kaye remembered me from the Borscht Circuit. He decided to sit next to Mr. Freedley for this. Again, I was doing everybody I had ever seen on Broadway. Vinton was laughing, and both of them seemed to be enjoying my program. Finally, Danny said, "Oh, Vinton, give her the job. It'll save you money. She'll fit into Eve's costumes."

I got the job and went right to work. Danny was always my dear friend after that, inviting me into his dressing room to talk while he made up.

I must tell you that decades later, when I had to leave *Hello, Dolly!* in Chicago to film *Thoroughly Modern Millie*, Mr. Merrick replaced me for four months with Eve Arden. I had just told the company that I had understudied her once. So Eve got up and told them the reason Mr. Merrick wanted her for this *Dolly* job was because she fit into my costumes! The cast embraced her immediately.

I wound up understudying everybody in *Let's Face It*, that is most of the women, because Vinton saw how eager I was to do it. I talked him into my standing by for Edith Meiser, Vivian Vance, and the entire chorus. I never went on for Vivian or Edith, which was a blessing because they were playing elderly society matrons. You know how it is when you're nineteen—you don't realize you're young. But filling in for the chorus gave me an excellent opportunity to try out different makeups.

One time I tried an interesting Uday Shan Kar effect, whitening my cheekbones so they appeared high and wide and putting brown shadow below them, which made my cheeks look sunken, I thought. The eyes were elongated to much wider than my own in a Cleopatra influence. I was able to get into one of the chorus girls' short costumes but was a head taller than all the rest of them.

Danny and Benny Baker were singing their duet in front of the chorus when Danny happened to look back, double-took on me, and couldn't remember his next lyric. So Benny looked to see what was throwing Danny and couldn't remember *his* next lyric. Myself, I felt I had looked pretty exotic in the mirror, but the entire number fell apart because of Danny's and Benny's reaction. It was the last time they let me fill in for anyone but Eve, and I was told to report to the stage manager so he could check me before going on for that.

any people have to have gone through the same experiences I have . . . trying for jobs, being rejected, walking home to a single room past buildings lit up with people moving around inside, families having dinner, sometimes in the winter Christmas trees—all that. Again, "Be careful what you set your heart upon for you shall surely get it." I dreamed of being allowed into a family like one of those, and that is how I found myself married to Ted Naidish, the son of an emigrated Russian Jewish family.

Ted was a waiter for the summer on the Borscht Circuit in order to support himself while writing a novel that was contracted with Charles Scribner's Sons publishers. He was one of Maxwell Evarts Perkins's protégés. It was stimulating for me to learn from him about those who were considered current novelists, like Scott Fitzgerald, Ernest Hemingway, John O'Hara, Thomas Wolfe, William Faulkner, and to read their books.

There is nothing so safe and secure and warm as an immigrant, for-eign-language-speaking family all around you. It was a dream come true for me. They look after you, you look after them. They make chick'n in the pot if you're sick. You learn new marvelous-sounding words every minute. When Eve Arden had a cold and let me go on one Wednesday matinee (in her costumes), the whole family had to hear all about it. Eve gave me a huge bottle of perfume after doing it, saying, "For an understudy that really studies." It and the note had to be passed to every member of the family for examination. They were happy for me.

All the family boys were in uniform, in training to go overseas. They were so beautiful—all in full bloom. You know that unbelievable blossoming that comes over crepuscular skin types at sixteen and stays until about twenty-five? The girls have it, too. I never went through it. They hoped I'd make it someday on Broadway. We were all about the same age.

This kind of celebration was totally new to an only child (me). I thought I'd finally done something right and died and gone to heaven.

On Sundays Dad Naidish (Abe) would take us to Café Royal on St. Mark's Place and Third, or Ratner's for Milchecheh (dairy), or Suss-man Volks, with dozens of sausages hanging in the window, but often and most happily of all to a restaurant on Third Avenue in the heart of the Lower East Side called Moskowitz and Lupowitz's.

Walter Matthau said to me years later, "You know how you got a reservation there? You call Gramowitz 4-55 et cetera." But the impor-tant part about what Walter said was that it was truly just as exciting there as I thought it was. I didn't simply get carried away with my own feelings about that place, as I often do. It was just that thrilling to him, so I'm accurate. The loongen goulash (lung stew) was just that nour-ishingly soul satisfying, he said. But then Walter and I had very much the same talent. He could play anybody he really liked, so it may be something to do with our emotional structure. I should ask a certified public accountant or some such, if I run into one that's still alive since Moskowitz and Lupowitz.

The family and I really went there to hear Paysach Bourschstein (probably spelled Pesach Burstein) sing "Brazil" in Yiddish. I couldn't get enough of him. He began every song over the wild Mittel Euro-

pean violins with one note: "Mmmmmmm Brahzil." I didn't know
whether I was laughing or being titillated. It was somehow hair-
raisingly funny to hear the often first-on-the-hit-parade "Brazil" done
in Yiddish. Of course he sang "Roumania," too. That's where I first
heard it, and it's stayed with me ever since. His vocal cords turned into
a crying violin joining the fast-vibrating fiddles, and there was a wail in
there of sunken homesickness.

Years later, Barbara Walters took me to a Los Angeles benefit.
Somehow I wound up in the middle of the stage singing "Roumania."
I remember it clearly because it was the most overwhelming experience for me until the effect of Gower Champion's original *Hello, Dolly!*
on an audience. The main thrill about the performance of "Roumania" was that the orchestra played it just like the one at Moskowitz and
Lupowitz. Singing it with them, I was able to turn into a veritable Pesach Bourschstein.

"Ech Rou-mania, Roumania" (faster) "Roumania" (even faster)
"Rou-mania" (high note) "Roumania mmmmmmm Roumania, Roumania" (all one note, but Pesach made it vibrate, so I did, like little violins only vocally). Then a big sting from the first violin; he held the
note and I continue on the same note with caressing, complicated Yiddish. I realized at that moment, from experience, that if the orchestra
is full of goyem, it's impossible to do it properly, but I did it properly
that night because they weren't goyem and they all seemed to be
homesick for sweet Romania and they were all divine reflections of
Ziggy Elman and Benny Goodman. They went all the way with me as
we accumulated the rhythm, never any faster, never any slower than I
went. They played with respect for me. They must have felt my respect for them.

The audience stood here and there, dancing to it with snapping fingers over their heads. More and more joined in clapping. The orchestra and the audience loved that song as much as I did. At the end, we all
cheered together for the longest time. I kissed the conductor and ho-
raed back to Barbara and her table. Barbara was proud of me. That was
show business! Barbara surely forgets this. It couldn't have meant as
much to her as it does to me because she is not in musical work, but I
felt my friendship with Barbara was closer at that moment than it ever
was. I learned then that I can do that song and probably other Yiddish

songs I've learned from Sophie Tucker and Molly Picon provided the musicians feel the same way I do about the songs. When I was alone I sang them for myself "acapulco" (as Jimmy Durante called it) because one cannot carry an orchestra around with one. I had to sing them at unexpected times to make myself happy. I had to sing them as often as I sang my father's childhood songs.

Stephen Birmingham's first book, *Our Crowd*, was about the German Jews (the Litvaks). He had to write a second book, *The Rest of Us*, because the Galitziane (Russian Jews) complained, "What about the rest of us?" so he called it just that. In it he told how Yiddish Art Theatre was illegal in Russia, so the Jewish theatre lovers (that's redundant, isn't it?)—I mean, *Jewish* and *theatre lover* are two terms of the same meaning so that one of them is unnecessary, well then, let's say the rabid theatre lovers—huddled together in one another's basements, covered up any little windows, lit candles for footlights, and put on their own shows. They took the chance of being jailed or even executed, but they couldn't do without theatre.

After schlepping across Siberia to Shanghai or Hong Kong, they waited years sometimes to get on a boat to New York, which accounts for why, at around eighty years old, my mother looked more and more like the fishing ladies on the Kowloon side of Hong Kong. You know, the ones with the bamboo bars across their shoulders with nets or tackle hanging on each end? I was struck dumb over one lady I was standing next to in Hong Kong. I leaned over to look into her face and almost said, "Mother?" She wasn't unfriendly. She just kept looking at me exactly the way my mother did. This lady was old, too. I wonder if she was as beautiful as my mother was when she was younger.

The Russian and German Jews arrived at Ellis Island, near the Lower East Side, settled there, and all that pent-up theatre exploded into Broadway musicals. George Burns, his nephew Lou Weiss, and all the old gang at the Morris office know this history well. All their grandparents schlepped across Siberia, they tell me. Naturally I asked, "What about Cole Porter?" "Oh, he's one of us. We've decided he just doesn't know it." You don't suppose they knew more than Cole, do you? I used to hear them talking at William Morris about Goldie Hahn. The original Salvation Army girl in *Guys and Dolls*, Isabel Bigley, was Isabel Bagel, and you've surely heard of Ed Solomon's TV show. It was all true. They weren't joking. But then, those were the days when their biggest hero besides President Roosevelt was Vinsdn Tzutsle (Winston Churchill). It certainly used to be fun to go to the Morris office.

While Ted was writing his novel, we moved near his grandparents, who lived in Brighton Beach. Grandpa told me his name in Russia was Chaim Dubekolieff. When he finally came through Ellis Island, the immigration officer told him his name was now Sam Cohen—simply because the dummkopf officer couldn't pronounce his given name. Grandpa said he was so pleased. He thought, Aha, I have a good American name and I'm proud to have it. He went on to say, "Little did I know upstairs is Rosie Cohen, downstairs is Yenta Cohen, everywhere de memmis Cohens."

I used to watch old Jews in Brighton Beach on the boardwalk, then step behind them to be sure I got the walk accurately. Grandpa Cohen introduced me to some of them. They were delighted that I almost ate them up alive because they were so funny, especially since such appreciation was coming from what we all thought then was a shiksa (me). I never heard Yiddish or Hebrew before coming to New York, but I understood these boardwalk conversations because every night Grandpa would read us the geshichtas from the *Yiddisheh Daily Forvitz* (*The Forward*) and the *Tug* (*The Day*). The stories were mostly about the Vibileh (wife) and the Buminka (other woman). The Vibeleh always won, and the Buminka got thrown out once the gontsa meshpucha caught on to what a threat she was to the family, and Papa was glad to see the light before she got all his gelt. These were running stories, like soap operas today. I couldn't wait to find out what happened the next night until I found out they were pretty much all the same.

The first sentence I learned was *Meineh grampeleh ist ein alta gonif*, "My grandpa is an old crook," taught to me by all the relatives to tease Grandpa. I soon spoke really rapid-fire Yiddish because it sounded so complicated and required a facile tongue that longed for that kind of exercise. It eventually came in very handy with the William Morris office of Abe Lastfogel's, Nat Lefkowitz's, and Lou Weiss's generation. Now William Morris is all flattened out into assembly-line American businessmen with no knowledge whatsoever of their rich heredity or jargon. They even had in this last generation one token Italian, who was Pearl Bailey's and my agent, and another one in the New York office, Kenny DiCamillo, both brilliant. The one on the West Coast was Tony Fantozzi.

I must disgress again to tell you we took Tony and his father to the immigration office to be tested for his American citizenship papers. When they asked his father who the first president of the United States was, he said, "Giorgio Washingmachine."

Brighton Beach relatives are not that colorful either anymore. Nobody's relatives are that colorful anymore. We're all getting homogenized. Surely some good will come out of this that I don't yet see. Well, probably the elimination of racial prejudice, but then we'll all think of something else to get fatootsed about.

My five-year marriage to Ted ended in a disoriented daze. While he wrote his novel, *Watch Out for Willie Carter*, our life had disintegrated into poverty. There was no money for food, clothing, or housing, so I simply wasted away. I cut myself off from my own family and put all of my trust in Ted.

Like Jack Matsumoto. Jack was fourteen years old when he arrived in San Francisco from Japan. I was seven. He always had that "ill wind that blows out of the East" expression on his face. But I was fascinated by his face because it was carved like a fine Japanese antique. My desk adjoining his was just on his left for three years. I admired him. He was so silent. I walked home with him from school (if he said I could).

Jack, none of us knows how to reach you, but if you're still alive, I hope you're still painting your watercolors of cypress trees around your Japan . . . each branch growing horizontally, reaching toward the ocean. You must have been homesick. I remember seeing you create your watercolors during lunch hour. I paid you a quarter from my allowance to do one for me. They were so gently gorgeous, they would heal anything.

Well, I just found out from a close friend in our class that Jack turned out to be the Admiral Matsumoto who sank our United States fleet at Pearl Harbor. I checked, and it's the same Jack. He was very young to be an admiral, but Jack was brilliant in all his studies and rapier-quick in learning. In retrospect, his silent distance and unbreakable mystery could have told me he was not here to make friends but to observe the enemy (us). How did anything so beautiful as Jack

Matsumoto and his watercolors turn into spreading blood and gore and the horrendous death of so many young men?

Only yesterday a World War II hero and a friend of my cousin Dickie's listened to all this from me about Jack and said peevishly, "Oh, Carol, that's too bad. I shot him, the dirty bastard." So there you are.

My parents came and gave me a way out of my marriage with Ted. They gave me support and guidance, even after I cut myself off from them. My father had me write a loving note to the Naidish family thanking them for everything they did to help me. To this day I am grateful for the experience of being part of their traditions.

Barbara Walters said to me when I told her I learned to speak Yiddish, "Oh, Carol, I'll bet you found those years exotic, safe, and exciting." How did she know me so well? Well, that's one of her gifts. She knows how to get to the essence of people. It's what makes her our lifelong Barbara Walters. And she has been my unwavering friend since, as she says, "forever." I always know she's there if I need her, and even if I don't need her. She is a giver, not a taker. Months can go by, and still she remains my constant friend.

*M*y father's itinerary was for train travel for one person, just him. Instead, he must have decided to take the car, bring my mother along, hope to pick me up in New York, and drive as fast as a train, sometimes all night long, getting to the next town just in time for a noon lecture.

I traveled with my parents on my father's lecture tour to San Francisco, which was home again for the three of us. I worked in I. Magnin's exclusive clothing store as a model because I was still so thin, for the only time in my life. I got a divorce, saved my salary money, and from there I moved to Los Angeles and lived in a room for ten dollars a week in the family home of the Los Angeles chief of police—his last name was Steckel—a friend of a friend of my parents.

The best times were with my dear cousin Dickie, who was living in Whittier, California, in a small G.I.-loan house with his then wife. I went to see them on some weekends, and it certainly eased the loneliness. I loved being with them. Dickie tried hard to help me by calling friends.

There wasn't an inch of the entertainment field I didn't investigate. I auditioned for anyone who would look. I was surprised and grateful that people I auditioned for all tried to help me. Finally, I auditioned for a man named Johnnie Walsh, who owned a restaurant with a small stage. Every place I auditioned they gave me the name of someone they thought might use me. Johnnie Walsh's restaurant was precisely where the original Spago is now. The floor leaned exactly at the angle it slid to. Strange it never slid the rest of the way down the hill, isn't it? Except for Wolfgang Puck and Barbara Lazaroff having added another room to it up the hill, all is the same. The wooden stairs are there. The windows overlooking Sunset Boulevard are like my memory of them.

Every time I go there for dinner, I see Johnnie Walsh in my mind, giving me his entire afternoon and trying to figure out who in Hollywood would be interested in a girl who did a speech of Uta Hagen's in *The Seagull* or Ethel Waters singing "Supper Time" or the Orestes Funeral Chant in French, Gertrude Lawrence doing a speech from *Susan and God*, Marlene Dietrich in *Blaue Engel* singing in German "Un Suntz Garnicht," and Sophie Tucker singing "Yiddishe Mama," in Yiddish, of course. So then, so that Mr. Lastfogel didn't waste *his* time with me (he suggested I do someone better known than Orestes, like Carmen Miranda, who was only as far as the two songs in a musical in New York at the time, so no one on the West Coast really knew who she was yet).

Maybe it comes from growing up in an exciting seaport, but anything that wasn't ordinary American magnetized me, in fact blinded me to the fact that most Americans don't give a fig about foreign languages. They don't believe it's all that thrilling just to hear a song in a language they don't understand. What, please, is wrong with me? I'm not clear what the songs mean either. They just sound so good.

My son, Chan, is the same about languages and food. We don't know what forebear is responsible for it. For his personally cooked Thanksgiving dinner, he served lamb marinated in a seven-year-old fish oil . . . a recipe that descended from the Ming dynasty. One tastes it on one's tongue for three days after. His breakfast is a muffin made of mili flour from Lebanon, et cetera. I keep wondering if Wheaties would taste just as ordinary to him if they came from, say, the Aborigine tribes in New Zealand. Certainly Kiri Te Kanawa's voice excites him far more than Marilyn Horne's. No . . . for me, from the cradle on, it's the formation with your own vocal cords and your tongue to make glorious sounds that no one who speaks English has ever heard before that totally sends me. But for the listener it sends no one else but *me*. Same thrill to make my American neck and head slide from side to side so as to look and feel as if I were Uday Shan Kar. I'll have to ask Eartha Kitt about this. Where does *she* get all those sounds in songs no one ever heard before? She has the same problem Chan and I have.

Anyway, Johnnie Walsh sent me to Cupid Ainsworth and Queenie Smith, whose offices were in the Lyons Agency in Beverly Hills. Cupid was a much-respected agent. Everyone I asked knew who she was, and Queenie was a fine stage actress . . . actually an actor's actress. So, to an actor, of course that meant they were the best! They were happy to audition me. They said they never missed my father's lectures. Wasn't that convenient for me? At the end of it they said to one another, "Marge Champion would be interested in her." Marge's husband, Gower, was directing a little revue called *Lend an Ear*.

Marge just told me how she was already there in the Lyons's office when they asked her to come right in. She did. I did everything all over again for Marge and Cupid and Queenie.

Now Marge and Gower had only been married for three weeks, so Gower had to do whatever Marge wanted because she was so very cute looking and because she was Marge, who had an extra antenna for spotting talent. Well, she thought I had it, didn't she? Talent? I decided she must be a most astute and penetrating mind. She also thought when Liza Minnelli was a child that she would grow up to be a great star and that Lee Remick was going to be a fine actress.

She explained that this little revue, *Lend an Ear*, was all cast and Gower was already working with the company. But another divine quality about Marge is that if she believes in something she is a force like Niagara Falls. She wouldn't like that description of herself, but what can she do? She just is like that. She set up this audition for me with Gower.

She says I began by asking Gower if I could take off my shoes. If she says so, I must have done it, because it would indeed be difficult to get the heavy, earthy quality of Ethel Waters's body if one were wearing dainty high-heeled pumps. Gower explained to me, checking his watch, that he had only a minute and a half to be with me. I told him that was unfortunate because he couldn't possibly know what I was about without seeing all twelve of my songs, sketches, and dances. Marge jumped right in from the back of the studio with "Do Gertrude Lawrence." Apparently she kept her eye on Gower and interrupted me whenever he lost interest.

"Now do Ethel Merman."

I obeyed her without hesitation from the start.

"Now Lynn Fontanne."

I did.

"Do Fanny Brice."

I danced her and sang her with "I'm an Indian, Too."

"Now Libby Holman."

After Marge had me do twelve numbers, Gower said, "Go on, what else?"

I said: I haven't got any more.

Gower: Then go back and start again.

I did just that. When I saw Marge on my way out, her silent, smiling face looked as though she had just delivered the healthiest baby in the hospital.

That evening Gordon Giffin, the stage manager, rang the chief of police's home phone, and I heard he said to the chief, "Well, I'm sorry, sir, but I just *have* to speak with Miss Channing." I'll never forget that call.

"Miss Channing," Giffin said, "Mr. Champion wants you to start rehearsals tomorrow morning at nine o'clock at the Masonic Temple on Hollywood Boulevard."

To this day when I pass that very same Masonic Temple (fifty-eight years later), I get a reflex action of stage fright mixed with euphoria.

Several people have told me, "Carol, you seem to feel that your entire life and every problem you have will be solved if you just get a job in the theatre." Well, that is the unexaggerated truth. Most actors from the first rehearsal on are hitting on all cylinders, and every sinew of their body and brain is used to its capacity. When I run into other actors who look as if they're blushing with being in love, I ask, "What show are you rehearsing or in now?"

Other Actors: Oh! How did you know?

Me: It's obvious. I'm happy for you.

Lend an Ear was written by a composer-lyricist–sketch writer named Charles Gaynor. It was in the manner of the little English revue traditional in the West End in London and was superbly written, I thought. So did the critics. After we opened it had its own cult of movie stars who came again and again to see it at the little Las Palmas Theatre, just south of Hollywood Boulevard. William Eythe, a movie star himself, coproduced it and played in it. I never saw it from the audience, but in Los Angeles people told me it was unusually and perfectly charming.

We rehearsed all day and every day in the theatre of the Masonic Temple. We all received thirty-four dollars and ten cents a week after we opened, and I was in bliss. One of the first things I had to do was have a talk with my father about getting transportation. No bus or streetcar went from the chief of police's house to rehearsal. I got a secondhand rumble-seat Ford that lost its brakes every time it rained, but I was able to get around that by removing my foot from the accelerator and calculating it to run down to a stop by the next signal. It got me there and back and helped some members of the cast to a bus stop.

When we moved to the Las Palmas Theatre for the opening, our first big step was to remove one seat from the last row of the 300-seat house. With this 299-seat capacity, we came under a different Equity jurisdiction, which meant we didn't have to be paid actors' minimum. Also, once we were open we could schedule more matinees if necessary. I was euphoric about that because I didn't have to wait twenty-four hours to fix what I did wrong on the previous show.

Gower was our director. The director has to demand that everyone get behind the director's own eyeballs, look at this project and see only what he, the director, sees. I remember reading in our history books in school about a string of "benevolent despots" in the history of France, beginning with Charles somebody . . . was it Charles the Great? I never met a benevolent despot until Gower Champion, and after working with him two days in that little revue, I couldn't keep from calling him that. "Dear Benevolent Despot," I would say from the rehearsal stage, "should I go upstage or down?" He didn't seem to mind that title, so it stuck.

As you know, there are so many elements involved in getting all those tremendous creative forces to go in one direction, but that's the thrill of musical theatre . . . the teamwork. The composer, the costume designer, the music arranger, the choreographer, the set designer, the book writer, the orchestra conductor . . . each one of them is a star unto himself, and his work could stand up alone at the box office. Can you imagine what a powerful, clear-minded force the amalgamator of all this has to be? That's the director. Gower was ideal for me as a director. Years later, while casting *Hello, Dolly!* he said to me, "I am not a choreographer. I am not a director. I'm a showman. I have to choose people who can handle themselves on dialogue."

Gower not only sized up his company's limitations and worked around them but worked around his own. To me it was apparent the first day of rehearsal on *Lend an Ear* that he was a man hell-bent for success, because he was egoless enough to face what wasn't his territory. He stated so out loud, at least to me, and for every other department of his show he became "Benevolent Despot" because he knew that he knew exactly what he was doing within his territory. I was completely comfortable with his despotism. We all worked well under that. I also always knew that revues were my native habitat, so I fit right into that slot in which Gower didn't fit, and he supplied me with what character he wanted from me.

Charles Gaynor was the first to dig up and satirize the twenties era with his mini-musical "The Gladiola Girl" in this same little revue. Next came me in *Gentlemen Prefer Blondes* and then Julie Andrews in *The Boy Friend* and lots of twenties on TV. In *Lend an Ear* we started a fad. We honestly did. We advertised in the *L.A. Times* want ads for any hats or dresses or jewelry that people might have in their attics left over from the twenties. They sent things. Gower and Raoul Pene du Bois (costumer and set designer) picked out a faded yellow satin cloche hat, for instance, for me that had a hole worn out of its lavender veil right where the eyes came through. Later, when we could afford to have new hats, mine was never as funny as the limp, tired old fecrumpft thing that my merry, eager character of Pru never knew was fecrumpft.

See, we were Sue, Lou, Pru, and Boo—the chorus of the lost road company that just turned up tonight (every night of course for the run of the show). I was Pru (for Prudence). I adored the name alone. We wore high-heeled silver pumps traditional for choruses of the twenties. That made me over six feet tall, which for my generation was not a normal height. The other girls were five feet to five foot three. Gower's direction for me was "I want you, Carol, to play Dottie Babbs standing next to you."

Dottie was the prettiest four foot eight you ever saw. The audience fell in love with her right from the opening. Gower framed her fabulously, too. So, in one flash, I turned into Dottie for him. I could do it in one flash because I, too, thought she was adorable. Gower tried to hide his laugh when he looked at me being as dainty and pretty as Dottie, and I knew then that this characterization he gave me was going to stick for Gaynor's divine sketch. I knew the twenties well. My grandmother taught me, when I was three, the Charleston, the Black Bottom, and Ballin' the Jack. We saw movie after movie, beginning before I was three, while most American children were raised with such classics as *Mrs. Wiggs of the Cabbage Patch* on up to *Oliver Twist* or some such British tradition that didn't relate to our culture or times at all. Clara Bow and Toby Wing were my heroines, so I was completely at home in "The Gladiola Girl," the first-act finale mini-musical of *Lend an Ear.*

Now this was the character Anita Loos and Jule Styne, the great composer, saw in New York and Anita said, "There's my Lorelei."

I was on top of the world with *Lend an Ear.*

Bill Eythe was also happy for me and proud, the sure sign of his star status. He would often escort me to his movie star friends' homes after they had seen the show for about the fourth or fifth time.

The one and only Josh Logan, who seemed to have a monopoly on directing and producing Broadway shows, came to the little Las Palmas Theatre to see *Lend an Ear.* After one of the shows Bill Eythe called the company onstage and said, "Joshua Logan is buying the show for thirty thousand dollars. Josh says we couldn't afford him as a director, so he [Josh] will have to buy it and bring it back to New York." We all cheered, including Gower, and couldn't wait to meet him. Gower being Gower and, as I said hell-bent for success, knew that having Josh as director would take care of everything that wasn't Gower's native territory. So he welcomed Josh Logan.

Before we went to New York to meet Mr. Logan, another girl from the show, let's call her Yenta, a protégée of Charles Gaynor's who was also represented by the Lyons Agency, was given feature billing. When we opened in New York, the marquee in front of the National Theatre (now the Nederlander) would read: "William Eythe presents *Lend an Ear,* featuring Yenta." Later we moved to the Broadhurst.

I raised holy ned with Cupid and Queenie, my agents from the Lyons office, to protest but to no avail.

One night after the show, Anne Baxter and her husband, John Hodiak, invited Bill and me to their home. Ann Sothern, a big movie star, later a giant TV comedy star, was there along with others. I told them about our show going to New York, about the other girl's billing, about her raise in salary and how I didn't want to go under those circumstances.

The movie stars all *yelled* at me. Ann Sothern said, "Are you nuts? Don't you know what's going to happen to you in New York? *I'll* pay your extra salary. How much do you want?"

They all pitched in and said, "We'll all pay it! Go! Take our advice." I looked at Bill. He had the same proud parental grin Marge Champion had after my audition. Ann Sothern said, "Go, you fool!" I went.

Ann Sothern was right. The feature billing only threw all the rest of the company into the spotlight. Don't you admire really talented people like Ann Sothern, Anne Baxter, John Hodiak, and William Eythe? They get inspired by and are happy for other talent (me) like most actors do for each other.

The first day of rehearsal onstage in New York, Mr. Logan appeared to us from stage left. Through my myopic eye, he had the size and bearing of my father . . . a big, tall man with an equally big nature and an aura around him of possessing a touch of greatness. As he moved toward us, he appeared even more like my father. Because Mr. Logan seemed to be familiar territory, and because he was walking straight toward me, I threw my arms around his ample middle and settled into his all-enveloping arms. I was home! He didn't seem to mind at all and took it as naturally as I did.

I have never been an aggressor. That's my problem. I don't know how I had the nerve to do this, but I never met anyone like my father before because he was unique. So was Mr. Logan, and in the same way unique. I knew one could never get into trouble with my father if one were letting him know that one loved him. My cousin Dickie tells me now that Daddy was a strict disciplinarian, but I didn't know it. I just did anything he said and was grateful for his guidance. Well, it has kept me afloat for a very long time now.

Onward with Mr. Logan's first meeting. Mr. Logan dismissed the rest of the company to Gower Champion. Gower, as I say, was after success more than personal aggrandizement. Mr. Logan said that he (Josh) would start with the sketches and wanted to work with Bill Eythe, Charlie Gaynor, and me. He said to them, "First, Carol has to be given at least two sketches in order to establish her before "Gladiola Girl." She is so believable as a big girl who thinks she is tiny that the audience thinks that's Carol."

"It's Dottie Babbs," I said.

Mr. Logan: It doesn't matter. It's hilarious.

Wow! Can you believe what he said? I took it in stride, as my father would have wanted me to.

Mr. Logan gave me all three of the Gaynor sketches that were done by Eythe . . . but previously with three different girls in the company. Logan took over directing the sketches from the author (Charles Gaynor), and Gower stayed where he was in the choreography. Mr. Logan bought two more sketches for me from Joseph Stein and Will Glickman. One was a satire on Dorothy Kilgallen, a tight-lipped, cruel syndicated columnist of the forties. I played that with Bill Eythe again. For some strange reason I always hear more laughs when I play cruel women than when I play Christian Scientists or people of any religion. The other sketch I played was a robot wheeled onstage on a platform with roller skates under it. We finally had to cut it on our pre-Broadway run in Boston because it was so dangerous. There was no one in the scene, including Yenta, who could keep me from rolling into the orchestra pit. Dumb me! I never tried to roll her to her destruction, even though she had all the best comedy material in the show.

Well, Mr. Logan plowed on and gave me the role of the mother in a beautiful Gaynor musical number called "Friday Dancing Class." It was a tiny role, but this character had the majesty of Marian Anderson (great contralto opera and concert singer for those too young) mixed with Deborah Kerr in Robert Anderson's *Tea and Sympathy*. Mr. Logan approved of my thoughts.

Now for by far one of the happiest times in my life. Mr. Logan asked Bill and me to come and rehearse the sketches with him all night long. He explained why. He was directing *Mr. Roberts* all day, *South Pacific* all afternoon and evening, and something else . . . I can't remember . . . and so it was necessary for us to work with him after our rehearsals till dawn. It was rumored Josh was a manic-depressive. Manic schmanic. He seemed absolutely normal to Bill and me. Either you want something or you don't. There's no in between. He wanted us and our show. I was only happy with him and Bill.

We went that night to the top floor of a storage and warehouse building by way of a superintendent-run freight elevator. It was next to the *New York Times* building. We worked on the three Gaynor sketches that Bill had already been doing at the Las Palmas. The English one came easily to me . . . most Christian Scientists that were guests in our home were English. I could do the accents and personalities of people from any part of the British Isles that visited my parents. Josh chose the one he wanted.

After many nights of perfecting all the sketches, the American one never really had a brilliant ending. Josh wisely said, "When this happens, go for a soft ending and don't try to top any of them."

Us: How do we do that?

Josh: We can try simply turning your backs to the audience, holding each other's hands, walking slowly upstage toward the back wall into the sunset together.

The French sketch, we decided, was Vivienne Romance. She was the reigning movie queen of French movies at this time, before Brigitte Bardot. The three of us were soul mates the moment we were

together. The air around us crackled with creative energy, especially
when all this pulled the Jean Gabin out of Bill Eythe. I had a very long
speech in French that I learned in one endless walk home alone at
dawn from Forty-fourth Street down Broadway to my fifth-floor
walk-up on Canal Street, almost skipping all the way because my
tongue and larynx were caressing all that gorgeous Montmartre
French so gloriously. This heavenly speech was written by Charlie
Gaynor. With my high school French I had a vague idea what I was
saying, but I had my usual clear idea of how it was pronounced. As I
say, I cherished it, so naturally, I learned it all in one walk.

The next night, after rehearsing *Lend an Ear* all day and Josh rehearsing his other shows, the three of us walked to the warehouse. I
did the speech for Josh and Bill. They were entranced with it as much
as I was, and then it came to Josh. This Jean Gabin (Bill) is begging
Vivienne Romance (me) to go to bed with him. Josh said, "Carol, build
the passion of your speech in French as high as possible. Stop. Turn to
the audience to translate it, (beat) just say, 'Yes.' " We tried it. We suspected it was divine.

We rang the freight elevator bell, which clanged piercingly
through the night. The overalled superintendent arrived. We begged
him to sit down and watch this sketch. We swung ourselves into it, and
when the end came with our newfound "Yes," the super howled with
laughter.

We grabbed him by the hand, one of us on each side of him, and
danced Ring Around the Rosies with him. The four of us had each finally met three others of us, who were just like each one of us. We
cried and laughed and hugged and threw ourselves on the floor with
fatigue since we hadn't slept for nights. We, including the superintendent, were the happiest people in Manhattan, which proves manic
depression is indeed contagious.

Have you ever noticed that many great men have a wide streak of
childlikeness running through their greatness? Well, anyway, Josh
Logan certainly had it. We heard from some of the *South Pacific* company that in his enthusiasm he talked about Bill and me to them. Now
Mary (Martin) I'm sure was happy for us. But her husband, Dick Halliday, didn't know what she knew, and that's that there's room for all of
us. Dick wanted Josh exclusively for Mary, apparently.

So he enlisted Josh's devoted wife, Nedda, to share his feelings.

Now Anita Loos told me again and again that Nedda Logan was a living saint. Everyone who knew her thought she was. I never saw that side of her. But when a brilliantly wily man like Dick Halliday gets ahold of you, you find yourself sharing his viewpoint. If Nedda was what everyone said she was, she would have been so at ease to observe that Josh was completely soul-fed from using every valve in his brain. She would have known his brain was well oiled by the adoration of two people who truly adored him. The *South Pacific* company *must* have adored him as much as we did, and they certainly turned out to be the biggest hit musical, with most critics' awards going to them. So what was Dick so frightened of? I can say this because we didn't open in the same season as *South Pacific*, so we weren't in competition. We opened the season before, so when we did open, we got all the awards we needed, but I was "Most Promising Young" so often I thought I'd never come to fruition.

Suddenly we ceased to see Josh Logan again, but he had already passed some of his knowledge on to us.

Working with Josh revealed to us that his intelligence was indeed a neat filing cabinet of what he had gleaned from his longer-than-our experience in the theatre. He said, "When you're creating a sketch, start with the ending and then go back to the beginning and work up to that ending."

I told this to Tommy Tune. He put it into his marvelous and honest book *Footnotes* and said that I said it. I forgot to tell him it was Josh who said it. How would I know anything that helpful at that young age?

I never saw Mr. Logan again until New Year's Eve 1949, two weeks after *Gentlemen Prefer Blondes*, my first starring part, opened. The opening night critics' reviews on *Blondes* were more than sensational. As it turned into 1950, Mr. Logan asked me to dance with him. In his manic nature he read me the riot act. He said I had no idea what constituted a star. "I'm not a star. I haven't got star billing," I said. (Herman Levin gave it to me after the critics bombarded him weekly in their papers with "Blaze Those Star Lights!" I loved it.)

Josh said: You don't know half of what you should know. You should study the choreography, the sets. You don't even know what the orchestra is doing.

I was in a flood of tears in the middle of the Rainbow Room dance floor and probably making a spectacle of myself. I didn't care. The real reason I couldn't stop crying was because he was on such a pedestal.

He went on to say: Mary knows every detail of a musical show. You don't know a flute from a bugle.

I tried to tell him: Mr. Logan, if I know what the flutes are doing or notice anything but my own job, that is my danger signal that I'm giving a very bad performance.

But I couldn't get the sentence out without choking every other word. However, whoever worked Josh up didn't win.

Years later I saw Mr. Logan in Jurgensen's Gourmet Grocery Store in Beverly Hills. He came over. I stayed quiet. He was so kind. No fancy sentences . . . just quiet understanding of one another. I could tell he remembered only the good things and the deep happiness.

*T*he heaven part about being nearsighted is it doesn't interest you whether anyone else sees you or not. You can't see *them*. I figure if the crew is a blur to *me*, then we can do our fast changes anyplace we want to. None of them ever objected and they seemed to understand that I had to get back on that stage changed. It really doesn't matter how you got there as long as you got there on time and with no bras or things accidentally hooked on your costumes trailing off you.

Forgive me for dwelling on *Lend an Ear* for so long, but it is my very most favorite show until *Sugar Babies. Lend an Ear* had a pre-

Broadway run at the Wilbur Theatre in Boston. The mayor came to it. The governor came. It was a smash hit. Even Jean Kerr came from New York to see it when she was first married to Walter Kerr . . . need I repeat who he was? I'm sure not. Jean writes me now that she called Walter after seeing *Lend an Ear* and said, "Boy, have I got a girl for you!" I believe her. Jean is incapable of lying.

Anyway, we brought our New York crew with us to the Wilbur, naturally. All shows do. This was in 1947. We had the A men in their union: Red Walters, Petey Joe Smith, Artie Sicardi (pronounced "Ardie Sa*gar*di"). He, years later, invented the potato puffs for Dolly to stuff into herself in the eating scene. I saw some of their names on programs, but less and less. Artie was still on them. Whenever I'd go backstage, he had already gone home. Artie must be 102 years old now. These men formed and built their union, IATSE. I can understand why they're hated by the managements of Broadway shows, but let me tell you, they cared deeply about our little *Lend an Ear*. Red Walters used to run out front to see who in the audience was enjoying it the most.

"Listen, Doll," he'd say to me, "the women like you. That's important. They're the ones who decide where their husbands or family are going for a show."

Petey Joe was married to a beautiful Ziegfeld Girl . . . you'd never guess it from how he looked backstage.

Petey Joe: I've crewed dozens of shows. This show is a hit. They're talkin' about you, Doll.

Spotlight Man: I put an extra carbon in your spot, baby.

I used to wonder why people came backstage and said to me, "I can't take my eyes off you." Of course not, with my extra carbon. These men were pulling hard for us to the point of being emotionally involved with this show. They had tears over standing ovations. They simply loved theatre and nurtured it. Who in their union raised their benefits and salaries so high that they can all retire at a young age? The crewmen I knew wanted to be in the theatre, not out of it. I know they don't want to annihilate the power of live theatre by raising the price of tickets to such a level that only a few can afford to attend.

The nucleus of a live theatre audience across the country is now the wealthy . . . retired. Sometimes, like opening nights in Birmingham or Pittsburgh, the audience must be mainly inherited wealth, I'm sure, because they don't understand the give-and-take of life. George Burns played to university audiences after Gracie left us, and they were screaming with approval. When those students graduated he had a whole new generation who adored him until he died. Whenever I lecture to a college or university, suddenly entertainment is what it was meant to be. Life, endurance, strength, and sex are ignited by their youth, and the give-and-take begins. In Mr. Schwartz's chemistry class it was called anodes and cathodes. They breathe their own energy back to what they receive from the performer. As a result they and the performers get a hundredfold what they give, and *that's* show business! Not passive dignity, where electricity has been unplugged. However, these young students can't afford tickets to live theatre. Please, IATSE, what can we do about this? Theatre people aren't about the price of refrigerators or automobiles. We're all dedicated people who come to life when we're working, just like you.

On pack-out night in Boston for New York, I couldn't possibly go to bed. I had to be at the railroad station to help them load the show. I kept the big coffeepot sitting right in the middle of the tracks, on a wood-burning stove. I had each of their mugs lined up with donuts and stuff. We ate all night long. I saw how they loaded the huge wooden upright boxes of costumes. I saw the derrick lift Raoul Pène du Bois's scenery into the longest freight car. I felt responsible for Raoul's costumes because of the thrilling times we'd had planning them. For the opera number we found two inner tubes to make my bust and hips look as big as those of Kirsten Flagstad, the Wagnerian opera singer of that day. I was big enough already, I thought, but Raoul decided to overdo it. No wonder Raoul held the monopoly on set designing and costuming for almost every Broadway show at the time.

I kept the script in my hand because Stein and Glickman were constantly changing the new sketches. This was indeed "the whole gaudy legend of show business," and I was a part of it. We all loved each other because we suspected we'd made each other a hit. I was in love with Raoul from the first costume fitting back at the Las Palmas, or was I in love with his experienced knowledge of the live theatre?

About a month after we opened in New York, Al Hirschfeld, the mainspring in giving *The New York Times* its enduring individuality, drew a huge caricature that spread across the front page of the Sunday theatre section. It was entitled "Supporting Actors Who Are Stopping

Their Shows." There were three or four of us. Lisa Kirk singing "True to You in My Fashion" in *Kiss Me, Kate*, Bambi Lynn leaping floorless with her partner, and me in that cloche hat and fringe dress daintily clinging to knock-knees. I had no idea the character was coming through so extremely funny. How did the great Hirschfeld know precisely what I was thinking? How fetching little Pru thought she was. How happy she was to have such a pretty little face (*my* face was not little), and how eager she was to celebrate it with the audience. I didn't realize these thoughts were so apparent. Well, they were to Hirschfeld. To be Hirschfelded is an eerie experience. You better not have anything to hide, because he'll expose it like a neon sign.

Because of this drawing people told me they had to get a ticket to *Lend an Ear* to find out who this overweight klutz was. Cole Porter got a ticket and offered me the role of Juno in *Out of This World*. George S. Kaufman bought a ticket also, and said he was writing a musical version of *Dulcy* (Lynn Fontanne's first American Broadway play) for me. Noël Coward came backstage to my dressing room, got down on one knee, looked up at me with his handsomely craggy face, then kissed my hands! We talked after that matinee till a half hour to the evening show. I am being very careful now not to exaggerate. If I do, then I'm wasting not only your time but my own, at the expense of what's left of my unbelievably caring family, with whom I'm now living. I cannot do that to them or to you. Why were tears streaking down Noël's face when he looked up at me? What did he see onstage?

He confided to me what to do when you feel no response from an audience. "Put me in your audience when you think you're losing them," he said. "You'll see. It will work. We all do that, you know. In your mind, put someone you love and someone who loves you out there and play it to them. But it only works if that person truly loves you. It's a very good way to find out who your friends are. When it doesn't work, they never really loved you. It will always work with me."

I let him hold my hands as long as he wanted to. I just stayed still, filled with gratitude and healing from all the rejection wounds over the years.

Later Noël gave me a script he wrote. I couldn't see how I could do that character. It was too straight or something. Isn't that youth for you? I was dumber than anyone in my youth. I still am. I was about twenty-six when I thought I had lost Noël Coward's friendship. How dare I not at least *try* to make that play work! So Noël wrote in an autobiography of his, "But Carol Channing turned my play down—the silly ox." I laughed at "silly ox" because that's exactly what the great Hirschfeld made little Prudence look like, a newborn baby ox whose knees kept giving out from under her. I loved her, not me, I loved *her.* If I were aware of me or ever thought of me, it never would have been funny somehow. Besides, none of us has perspective on ourselves anyway. The moment we do, we become a formula, which is immediately boring and unattractive and, most of all, not true.

-I still put Noël in the audience sometimes, like he said, and it does indeed work, so beyond his own deep hurt of my turning down his script and my ingratitude, he still had to understand me or it would never work. Sometimes I'm with someone who entrances me and I think, Oh! I just treasure her, I'll put her mentally in the matinee audience today. And when I do I find out she didn't treasure *me.* The reason this is so important is that no emotion can affect an audience that doesn't flow through the performer to them with complete ease. Even if one is playing nervousness or tension, its source has to be sure and untentative or the emotion won't flow through. It becomes like a kink in a hose. It gets bottlenecked and never gets to the audience. There is only one way to achieve that ease, for me anyway. Play it to an understanding heart.

For me, putting my father in the audience is infallible, because he was never any pushover for me. Well, he's gone, too, but it seems to me he never left me, especially when I need him. It helps to play to someone who won't tolerate anything second best from you but who wants to hear this story because he cares a lot about you. Your being will relax, and suddenly there's no effort to any emotion. Also, the entire audience slowly comes to understand this character you're playing as well as your caring one does.

I found this out when Daddy died in 1956, and I had to open at the Tropicana in Las Vegas. I knew my father so well that I knew if he thought his death had interfered with that opening performance he would not have been happy with me at all. Of course his death absorbed all my feelings, so I played every character I portrayed in this revue-type show to him. I wanted him to laugh and cry and be thoroughly entertained (in my mind). Again, the obstacle to overcome of his death crystallized my thought concerning each of the characters.

Also, acting or performing is emotion *remembered*, not emotion you are experiencing yourself at the moment. So cry your eyes out or laugh your head off *before* you go onstage. If you're experiencing personally what your character is experiencing, that also won't reach the audience. *They* are the ones who must feel it. The old adage "If you're listening to the sound of your own voice, you can bet nobody else is" seems to me to apply to everything in the theatre. If this scene seems touching to the performer while he's doing it, it's touching only to the performer. Of course we all know this, so we don't let anyone *see* that it's touching, but simply being aware of it without showing it kills the scene dead too. Audiences know what you're thinking. Just hand the scene over to your "understanding heart" out there, and it's not nearly so complicated as I keep repeating, drumming it into the ground here. When Charlie Gaynor first wrote the whistling silent film star Cecilia Sisson, I couldn't stop laughing. It took me days of doing her for any audience every night before I didn't even *think* she was funny. Then, for the first time, the laughs started coming.

It's a privilege to play a show over five thousand times. You learn things you'd never learn otherwise. How do you get *the audience* to cry? How do you trigger *their* emotions? They paid for the tickets, not you. Answer: Don't feel it *for* them. If you do, there's nothing left for them to feel. You did all the work. Of course you conjure up as accurately as possible the memory of the emotion, but from then on hand it to *them*. Most all actors know, to achieve this delicate balance you must respect and trust the script. Gower, in his divine sense of showmanship, built Dolly's entrance down the red stairs so that, as Charles always said, "Your mother could come down that stairway and they'd cry."

Behind the red door curtain at the top of the stairs, before Dolly enters, I used to say to myself, "I am an abalone. I'll hit myself once (mentally) in the center of my emotions, and then all of my reflexes will relax as a result. Just float down those stairs, Dolly, slowly. You *have* no feelings now."

After my having toured *Dolly* to so many cities, the TV and press interviewers have often asked me, "What are you thinking when you come down that red stairway?"

"Nothing! It's not easy, but I am thinking *nothing*."

Charles told me not to say that. It disappoints the listeners, so I have to tell them that it's really Gower's setup that makes it happen, and it is. George Burns used to say, "Never have two jokes going at once. One kills the other." And I have found: never have two good cries going at once. Then again, it may also be that Gower built the focus on Dolly to tears at that point and the wisest thing I could do was not mess with Gower's handiwork. Don't do anything, Carol. Don't interfere with Gower's great gift. If I think something is up to me to think at that moment, it ruins everything, including my own slow, low, sparsely orchestrated first chorus: "Hello, Harry, hello, Louie, Manny, Danny," et cetera.

I never did sing "Hello, Dolly!" and every drunk in every bar demands I sing it. I guess it's taken the place of "Melancholy Baby." When I am only passing by a bar, why do I keep standing there trying to explain that it was sung *to* me, I never did sing it? I *was* Dolly, so how could I sing it? George Burns used to cut me off and say, "Just say, Thank you, I have to catch a plane."

Why do I hate to leave them feeling as if I have refused them? It didn't bother George at all to pull me away. I keep trying to get through to those total strangers. What is my problem? I am going to stop explaining if it's the last thing I do.

I have found in creating a character or a portrait painting that it has to be done with total approval or nobody recognizes it as a person. If it's done with any criticism at all, then nobody ever met anybody like that and they don't relate to it. Jean Kerr once said to me, "I never saw Sophie Tucker, but that woman you do that you call Sophie Tucker is very recognizable to me."

People have said to me, "Why don't you make fun of the Gabors . . . how untalented they are? It'll be hilarious!"

Nobody can do that. Just be crazy about them (which I always was), and the satire will take care of itself. I am sure it's the same in every business. You can't create an elevator that you haven't fallen in love with. Maybe you can copy one. That's how I know for sure there's a God and it's a good God. We had to all have been created with total affection, and all we have to do is see it and re-create it. Otherwise, somehow there's no creation there at all. He, She, or It had to be crazy about every single one of us, because we exist, don't we? This isn't *my* theory. This is what the audience tells *me* are the facts of life. *They* tell *me*.

Aren't we in the live theatre lucky? The live audience is a constant barometer and lets us know how close to or how far from accuracy we are. When I'm acting in a movie, it's necessary for me to draw on the memory of having an audience. I never can imagine how those marvelous movie stars can do such believable work without an audience. But then few of them are doing comedy. Maybe the audience is only necessary for comedy. If it's actually happening for the first time in the actor's mind, they laugh.

I wasn't crazy about myself in *Thoroughly Modern Millie*. In my mind I was the cutest little flapper since June Knight in that bathtub in a movie my grandmother and I went to. When I saw myself up on that *Millie* screen, I saw a girl who looked a lot like my father only in a hat of egrets. The movies are a more literal medium than the stage, aren't they? That's because what an actor is thinking is far more powerful than any physical means of expression he may have. That is, provided the actor is live and in the same theatre with you. Even when Gower has told me to put my back to the audience and not to move, if I'm really thinking this character's thoughts, the audience lets us know they heard every one of the thoughts. As George Burns always said, "The acrobats are the lowest-paid people on the bill. They're tear-assing unthinkingly all over the stage."

He was so right. Henry Fonda in *The Grapes of Wrath* hardly moved when the great 1929 depression was destroying his dignity and pride. We all cried and cried. His thoughts were excruciating and, to me, that's the same reason it's not necessary to miss a show just because you're sick or incapacitated, like having a broken arm or no voice at all or even being in a wheelchair. Have you noticed that—no matter what business you're in—when you have something to overcome in the process of getting to your goal, it is a much finer piece of work than if you didn't have something to overcome? Yes, you have. I have too. It helps of course to believe in the project you're in. But there is a mood, a message, a reason why our playwright had to write this play. It is so strong that nothing can destroy it. The mind that stuck to writing this play is more powerful than any physical ailment.

Richard Coe, the critic emeritus on *The Washington Post*, was in the audience for *Hello, Dolly!* in Charlotte, North Carolina, when I had severe laryngitis (eight shows a week of singing like the character, rather than in your own voice, will get you in the end I want you to know). Anyway, he got the message and the character of Dolly clearer than ever before. By the way, six different southern remedies were sent backstage to me by 7:30 P.M. for the evening show by those caring Charlotte matinee ladies. One had a candle under a Pyrex cup of caramel syrup and leaves from up in the mountains for my dresser, Tiv, to spoon into me while it was hot. Another was herbs grown in the woman's kitchen and simmered overnight, and so on. In desperation I devoured every one of them. One of them worked. If I only knew which one, I'd have the answer to live show business for all performers for all time.

But those matinee ladies were one of the best audiences we ever had. They kept applauding to let me know they could hear my whisperings. Our soundmen working for Peter Fitzgerald surely were artists at their craft. I pity my fellow actors. They said they couldn't hear me at all, but then, we're all in this together. I'd try to do it for *them*. The important thing for them and for the audience is that they not miss the show or they surely will miss one of their own best performances.

John Latouche

 o let you know how miserable opening nights are, there was a Bennington girl named Patricia Morand who wrote plays. It was her play's opening night on Broadway. I can't find the name of it on the Internet. The composer John Latouche and I escorted her to it. Before the curtain, her nerves couldn't take it another second, so we took her to Sardi's and John ordered a triple bourbon on the rocks for her. She took it back to the theatre and sat down near the critics with it. Finally, the curtain went up. The first act was almost over. As intermission drew closer—you're way ahead of me, I'm sure—yes, her nervous, shaking hand spilled the ice down the open-backed dress of the lady sitting in front of her. She clasped her hand firmly over the lady's mouth and held her into the back of the lady's seat. Then Patricia whispered in her ear, "Don't scream. Don't move, we're sitting near the critics. This first act will be over shortly. Then I'll let loose of you, and during intermission you can scream, you can take me out in the theatre alley, you can beat me, call the police, do anything you want to me, but I will have to hold you still until the curtain. Please! It's only a half a minute more, only a few more lines, now! Curtain! Shoot me if you want."

During intermission John and Pat took the lady out for air. She couldn't speak at all. I got a napkin from the bar to dry her off and try to shake out the unmelted ice from under her dress.

Having been raised in an atmosphere that gave no importance to the idea of physical discomfort (not unimportant because of my religion but because of the basic masochism of ballet training), I ignored the lady's temporary apoplexy and wanted to see the rest of the play. The last I saw of Patricia and John, one on each side of the poor woman's staggering, limp body, John was hailing a cab for her. The play didn't make it, I'm sorry to report, especially after all that trouble.

Speaking of John Latouche, he was for years my dear confidant. He wrote the songs "Ballad for Americans" and "Taking a Chance on Love," as well as all the lyrics for the musicals *The Golden Apples*, *Cabin in the Sky*, and *The Vamp*. If we could have just made a concert of his songs, *The Vamp* might have been fine, or at least more tolerable.

On another subject, John had a childlike belief in elves, Irish lore, magic, and otherworld manipulations. When he was very little, his tiny Irish mother, Effie, with her white Irish lace collar and cuffs, told me he drew a magic circle on the kitchen floor. He announced that anyone who stepped inside that circle would be cursed with demons, have Lucifer on his tail and bad luck for the rest of his life.

I said, "Oh, Effie, you must have laughed him right out of that one."

"Of course," said Effie. "I told him I didn't believe him for a second."

John (listening): But you never stepped in the circle. You walked around it, even with big dinner plates.

Me: Effie! You didn't? Why not?

Effie: Well, just to be sure.

nce you are in a hit show, you love everyone with the show as if they were family. Or at least almost everyone.

"Yenta," the girl who'd gotten the feature billing, came to me in the Broadhurst Theatre when our dressing room was empty and said, "I told everyone some lies about you. I want you to know I was told they were true. I didn't know they weren't true." I was so concentrated on the show that I forgot to even ask her what the lies were. I think about her so often. When *South Pacific* opened at the Majestic Theatre next door, we all leaned out our windows in our little makeup smocks to watch the icons of Broadway entering to see Mary Martin. I remember something or someone pushing me further out, so I had to grab the sides of the window for safety. I always wondered if it was Yenta.

After we were established in the Broadhurst, Yenta took to moving on all my laughs in "The Opera Company That Lost Its Orchestra" sketch. We were onstage at the same time. My biggest laugh was my entrance, looking recognizably like Kirsten Flagstad . . . long blond braids, two inner tubes around the middle, and heavy Teutonic warriors' bracelets. Yenta concocted so much business to do on that entrance that I finally completely lost the laugh. The next biggest laugh was when I said, "Farewell, you-all"—lifting both breasts and placing them down still inside my dress on the other side of an armrest—"I die." I died catching up with them. Well, I warned Yenta and I warned her. She threw her feet in the air, her head back and forth, anything to distract. When she finally succeeded in killing the bit dead, I brought my wrist down on her head with the weight of one of those huge brass bracelets. As I say, I warned her. She phoned our stage manager from a doctor's office, saying she had a concussion. When Actors' Equity officials asked me about it, I told them, "Now you know as actors that when you finally find the perfect timing of a laugh, it's as if the heavens opened up and this blessing descends upon you. For Yenta to interfere with this blessing is a criminal act or, more accurately, . . . murder." Only to a fellow Equity member would what I did to Yenta be labeled self-defense. Left to civilians, I probably would have been sent to jail. The Equity members didn't write anything down, and I never heard any repercussions from the incident. Eddie Weston, the fabulous Equity arbiter, tells me there was no report on this. We have a great union in our Actors' Equity, where only justice prevails.

We had a reunion of the original *Lend an Ear* cast in Hollywood only about eight years ago. Someone had Yenta's phone number at her home in Connecticut. I wanted to phone her, because that conversation we had about her lies had taken courage on her part and she had cared about my opinion of her. She told me she was now a dental assistant. I would rather have died than become a dental assistant in Connecticut, but it could have happened to any of us. How hard to take! What a cruel business we're in. She was a talent, that's the tragedy of it. It could have happened to me, except that I haven't got the kind of brains to be a dental assistant, let alone a good one. I didn't ask about her head. She was warm and poised with me. Some people seem to have more respect for you once you've put a hole in their head, don't they?

id you know that very small people play with us as if *we* are the dolls? At least Anita Loos did. Wasn't I fortunate? She was four feet nine inches of lithe, slender, dramatic chic. We often wore the same outfits on the same day, usually sailors' middies. Anita was known for wearing those. As I say, I was over six feet tall in high heels. I never saw us together and never asked. She wore massive Aztec jewelry that looked perfectly in proportion to her because her little face was so theatrically carved. Once Anita said, "There's my Lorelei," referring to the main character who wrote her book, I wanted badly to become her spiritual daughter and, of course, I adored her, as did the entire fashion and literary world.

Her *Gentlemen Prefer Blondes* book, which she wrote in 1921 as Lorelei Lee's diary, was hailed by *The New York Times*, book reviewers worldwide, and *Vogue* magazine as "the Great American Novel." Even though it was high comedy and a brilliant satire on Americans, it was, in the twenties, what the rest of the world thought of us . . . that we were uneducated, powerful, manipulators, inexperienced, childlike, irresistible, and gangsters, all at once. Each of these qualities was embodied in Anita's tremendous creation Lorelei Lee.

When the original book came out in 1925, it truly electrified the world. I was born in 1921, so I became aware of its impact through my mother when I was around six years old. I cut Lorelei's "boy's bob" on myself after trying it out on my grandmother first, so with Onna's three-way mirror I was able to correct on me what I did wrong on her. I thought it looked jazzy. I should have done hers second, it took quite a long while for it to grow out.

Little did I know that twenty-four years later Anita Loos herself would take me to a leading New York hairdresser (Michel) for precisely the same boy's bob, only she had my hair bleached white because of the title of the show. Anita was famous for her own flapper's wind-blown bob, but I was twice the size of Anita all the way around, including, of course, my head. So I had this tee-tiny haircut on top of all of me. One of the reviewers said, "Channing has the strangest large build that goes up into a pin-head." But my father kept reminding me that the critic's headline was "A Triumph of Miscasting."

"Don't you see, Tootsie?" he would say, "it's not 'A *Failure* of Miscasting,' it's 'A Triumph.' "

Of course it was miscasting! It was supposed to be a *satire* on a Jean Harlow or Ruth Taylor type, not the real thing. Marilyn Monroe was far from appearing on the horizon yet. Anita always said, "You can cast Lorelei two ways, with the cutest, littlest, prettiest girl in town, or with a comedienne's comedy comment on the cutest, littlest, prettiest girl in town. I wrote her as a comedy, and Broadway is attuned to satire."

As I said, Pru from *Lend an Ear* was the character Anita Loos and Jule Styne, the great composer, saw in New York when Anita said, "There's my Lorelei." They brought in Leo Robin, the brilliant lyricist, who captured the nature of Lorelei's diary in one song, "A Little Girl from Little Rock," and then they promptly went home to write, as Ethel Waters called it, "Carol's 'Battle Hymn of the Republic,' 'Diamonds Are a Girl's Best Friend.' " Since then Marilyn Monroe and Nicole Kidman have sung it in movies. Apparently if you are that beautiful and sexy it isn't necessary to keep the song uniquely a stand-up comedy routine set to music. But Milt Rosenstock, our conductor, was miraculous at holding thirty-six men in midair until the crux of the laugh before he continued the music.

*M*y first vision of Jule Styne was when he opened his front door to welcome me into his apartment. He had fluorescent-red colored hair, cut in a "slitzie," like the Nazis. He was wearing a chrome yellow satin pugilist's robe with purple satin collar and cuffs, and when he turned around to go to his upright piano, the back of him had ASCAP in purple satin letters from shoulder to shoulder. (ASCAP stands for the union American Society of Composers, Authors, and Publishers.) It was noticeable that boxing gloves were the only things missing from the ensemble, but then they would have interfered with playing the as-yet-unfinished score for me. He introduced me to Leo Robin, sitting in an easy chair with scraps of lyrics all around him and on him. Jule (pronounced "Julie") looked like no one else I'd ever seen on earth, except maybe Jiggs of the funny papers' *Maggie and Jiggs*. Leo (who asked me right away to call him Uncle Leo because, as he explained it, "I saw you in *Lend an Ear* and I want you to call me Uncle Leo") had one of the kindest, sweetest male faces I'd ever seen, shining through a sharp bone structure that revealed the other side of his nature—focused discipline.

I was playing the usual eight shows a week in *Lend an Ear*, so I went to Jule's in the afternoon. These two titans of Broadway and Hollywood swung immediately into asking me to sing certain lyrics they'd just written for Lorelei. Jule demonstrated them to me. I sang them back to his powerful Ozark piano beat. I say "Ozark" because that's where Lorelei was born and raised . . . a barefoot bumpkin at the foot of the Ozarks. They said, "Try this lyric. Try that." I did.

Uncle Leo: I think Carol's Lorelei is funniest when she's grateful like the Little Match Girl, grateful for the bones they threw to her on Thanksgiving.

I wasn't clear on the story of the Little Match Girl, but I knew how

Lorelei felt when she was grateful. So he gave me the lyric that he had written right at that very moment, all about thanking "the one who done me wrong."

I knew Lorelei enjoyed being "done wrong by" to the bottom of her being (or her bottom), so we did a forward "bump" to be sure it was apparent. Later, in our pre-Broadway tryout in Philadelphia, it had to be censored to a sideways bump because the original was considered too suggestive. Can you imagine how times have changed? Leo and Jule said, "Keep it in."

I felt they were maybe the sculptor Rodin and I was the statue *The Thinker.*

On this first day together, the phone rang. It was the show's coproducer, Herman Levin. Jule answered: "I don't care that her contract isn't signed. I don't care how little you want to pay her. If we can't go on writing with her here, then I quit! Get that contract signed no matter what." Then he threw himself on the sofa and kicked his feet in the air insanely. Uncle Leo went right on calmly concentrating on what he had just written. I could see he was used to Jule. Then Anita phoned, and I heard Jule thanking her for telling Herman the same thing he had.

For some strange reason I wasn't the least bit flattered by all this. I felt like Uncle Leo did. I just wanted to get on with moving this character from the printed page to the live, wild world of musical theatre.

At 7:00 P.M. I left for the Broadhurst Theatre to do *Lend an Ear*, promising them I'd return right after the performance. I did. When I returned, Leo and Jule were knee-deep in "Diamonds Are a Girl's Best Friend." Uncle Leo was trying all kinds of introductory verses. Again he moved toward me to try a sentence, then moved back as far as he could to survey what he did, like a portrait painter.

Leo: No. That's not right. Forget it.

Jule: Try singing like those French Apaches.

Me: Yes! With a long cigarette holder and lighting the cigarette.

Jule: Wait! We'll start with the Marseillaise.

Leo and Me: Yes. Get back to the piano, let's try it! Stop talking, Jule, let's try it.

It worked! For us it worked!

Jule's brain functioned so much faster than he could possibly talk that he was frequently unintelligible. His speech was constantly racing to try to catch up with his thoughts ahead that he hadn't yet said. The result was that he would often forget he hadn't even told us the subject he was talking about. When it was hopeless to decipher so much as the song to which he was referring, we would tell him to "go back to the piano and play it. Stop talking and play it." Why couldn't such a brilliant brain realize that nobody could understand him? He would stand helplessly in the middle of the room and *yell* what his current inspiration was, apparently thinking the problem was that we were both deaf. But when we demanded that he play it, he would obediently march back to the piano and play it. Someone before us must have told him he didn't talk like most other people, so he would obey us immediately.

The reason for relating to you how superhumanly fast Jule's brain worked is because, one day in rehearsal, Agnes de Mille chirped in to say that we didn't have a title song. So Jule took Leo to the deli across the street from the Ziegfeld for lunch, and in exactly half an hour they returned with "Gentlemen Prefer Blondes—Like I" (Lorelei's impression of upper-crust English).

Jule also had a habit of pushing his index finger into his listener's chest to emphasize his speaking point. If you're a female, you could get cancer of the breast from that. I somehow didn't, but he never thought of that. With all his hyper heterosexual sex appeal, which he had bountifully, it never entered his mind that he might be doing harm to my mammary glands. I learned to fold my arms over my chest and go in a corner whenever he got excited with a new idea and started toward me to describe it.

Another habit Jule had was throwing his "epileptic fit," especially when a lot of people were around. Of course, it wasn't an epileptic fit, but it was attention getting. I can't remember the name of the famous man who did the orchestrations for the show. It's hard to remember the name of anyone who didn't do what you told him to do. We told him what we wanted was music that had the quality of blue smoke coming up out of the log cabin chimneys deep in the Ozark Mountains. We also wanted the first note of "Turkey in the Straw" to sound like a broken rubber band whistling as it was shot through the air. This would send Lorelei shooting through the air right on her first skip. Jule told me to demonstrate for the orchestrator physically what he wanted to achieve orchestrally. He also wanted to contrast the "Turkey in the Straw" country music that would introduce the song with the way the music would sound when she got rich and elegant. To achieve that he wanted violins on the lyric "Now that I'm known in the biggest banks," et cetera.

Jule specified clearly what he wanted throughout the song, and the well-known orchestrator gave us nothing of the kind, not one thing. The day the orchestra came in and played the orchestrator's work on "Little Rock," it was the stock fox-trot, dance-band version you could buy of any song at G. Schirmer's music store for ten cents. So Jule threw himself onto the rehearsal stage floor and went into his "epileptic fit" . . . screams, crying, rapid foot kicking in the air . . . the usual. The entire company was there, along with all the creative forces. They hadn't seen this demonstration before. It got their attention. The orchestrator ran up the aisle and out of the Ziegfeld Theatre, never to be seen again. But the result was Jule finally got what he wanted. Milt Rosenstock, Jule's personally owned conductor, worked and worked until he satisfied all Jule's wishes.

Now! "Speaking of China," Leo and Jule told me to be with them whenever they wanted to try something new on me. Naturally, once I heard that you couldn't get me to be anywhere else in the world. Jule had a street-level apartment with a back patio of inlaid bricks. I remember I'd been learning the score by coming in after performances of *Lend an Ear* and working till about 4:00 every morning. All three of us were energized by it. We tried the songs this way and that and got new ideas every eight bars. One night the doorbell rang. It was the police. They told us we had to be quiet. They looked surprised to find us sober and apologetic, so they left.

Jule (whispered to me): Can you hit a high A?

Me (quietly): You play one and let's see.

It was now around 3:00 A.M.

Jule (softly singing the last line of "Diamonds"): Diamonds are a girl's best friend ("*friend*" being the high A).

Me (I took a deep breath and hit square on): Best friend (high A).

Beer bottles and opened cans came raining down from the upper floors of the apartments all around us.

"We've had enough!" "Shut up!" "Don't you ever sleep?"

So the three of us put fingers to our lips and whispered, "Shhhhh," to each other. We were finally forced to leave the apartment, but Jule held the sheet music as we sat on the front steps and agreed that we didn't mind. "Look at this score and lyrics! Whaddo we care?" We were euphoric!

The apartment was in Jule's name, but since few people knew my name, we put it in my name and I moved in with Ax Carson, my pro-football-playing husband, who was seldom with me anyway. That way we went on rehearsing in the daytime, and Jule could bang away on or caress his upright all day.

erman Levin and Oliver Smith, the producers of *Gentlemen Prefer Blondes,* had reached an impasse in getting backers for the show. No one wanted to risk all that responsibility and money on a comparative unknown (me). In those days, theatre people invested in other theatre people's shows. Nowadays the investors are companies like Coca-Cola, the Sony Corporation, for a while the Japanese government, automobile manufacturers, et cetera, and now they even name the Broadway theatres after their products.

So, canny little Anita Loos, who wrote a play called *Happy Birthday* for Helen Hayes, got Helen to bring the Lunts to the home of their director, John C. Wilson, in Fairfield, Connecticut. We all went, including Tallulah Bankhead, who was swimming in the pool when we arrived. I told her I wished I could get a good night's sleep before the Lunts arrived the next day (I'd had rehearsals and excitement with Jule and Leo all night).

Talloo: Take a sleeping pill.

Me: I would, but I don't want to start that mess of being addicted.

Talloo: Don't be ridiculous. They're not addictive. I ought to know. I've taken them every night of my life for thirty-six years.

Richard Rodgers was there. I was surprised to find my faults were perfectly excusable among these people, yet I could never seem to correct them when I was with civilians. For instance, I can never seem to stop plunging directly into the misery or the happiness (or whatever) of the emotion that's consuming me at the moment and confiding it to a total stranger. I can't hold it in—to a fault. Richard Rodgers, instead of saying "Hello" or "Glad to meet you," took me aside and his first words were "Carol, why lately does my daughter reject my affection and suddenly doesn't even want me to tuck her in bed at night like always?"

I had to give his question every bit of my attention, since he seemed so anguished.

Me: Well, I remember in *my* teens I couldn't let *any* adult come near me. If my grandfather hugged me, it upset me at that age. Not like when I was littler. Could that be?

Him (after some thought): No, Carol. I don't think she likes me anymore.

Me: Oh, that *can't* be true. Girls are sometimes funny when they first start to become women. Please know that. I hope I didn't hurt *my* father.

I surmised that he asked me because I was nearer his daughter's age than anyone else there. I didn't think there was anything strange about it.

Later he said: "Please don't let them make you lose weight. That's the first thing they do to make you look like everybody else. You look fine." (He was underweight, and I guess couldn't gain it, so he thought I looked fine.)

Leo, Oliver Smith, and Anita must have already told him they were settled on me for Lorelei. But what a lovely man, Richard Rodgers. I wanted to help him. I think I know now what the trouble was with his daughter, but maybe you want to know what happened that weekend instead.

Before the Lunts arrived the next day, Anita fixed my hair so it was just like hers (Anita's). Her famous hairstyle was a frame of little spit curls going forward, all around her face. The crown of her head was parted into a square. The hair within that square was gathered together in a ribbon that left it geysering straight up. On Anita it was oddly chic. On me it was ridiculously alarming. She would tie the same small red bow to gather my boy's bob together at the crown that she wore. I don't know what visual effect our being dressed like twins had on any other people.

After they arrived, the Lunts asked if they could go alone with me into another room to question me about Lorelei's character. They had previously told Helen Hayes it might be demeaning for me to audition for them, when really I was so full of Lorelei I would have auditioned her for the garbageman. Truthfully, I *wanted* to audition for them. I wanted their affirmation, and I knew that if they gave it, it had come from on high. Lynn was always my favorite legit actress because of her ability to completely change her character for each new play. I naturally learned a lot about that just from watching her. I learned that it is possible to sustain for two and one-half hours in a character that isn't your own. She never allowed playing her characters to be merely acting who they are. People don't act who they are. They *are* who they are, with no effort. She knew that. I watched her as I was growing up, and I saw her step into a character like Irene in *Idiot's Delight*, a phony Russian princess, then a Greek goddess in *Amphitryon 38*, next a quiet, introverted, untheatrical housewife . . . lovely in her support of her husband in *There Shall Be No Night*. She was sexy in *The Pirate* and impossible in *The Taming of the Shrew* and, finally, mesmerizing as the mysterious and glamorous Mrs. Zachanassian in *The Visit*. She was frightening and sinfully attractive.

Studs Terkel, who is no slouch as a critic, considers Alfred Lunt *the* world's all-time greatest actor and says so in his book on the greats of the theatre, *The Spectator.* Indeed, when Alfred died, they dimmed the lights in theatres all over the world for two whole minutes just before the curtains went up. Lynnie always told me, "Alfred would have been amazed at that." It seems they never, either of them, had the time or energy to do anything more than cope with the next audience and communicate to them the glories of the play they were performing at the moment.

When I was alone with them for the first time, they treated me with the same respect they themselves commanded. They looked at me through their own clean windows, and they both brought out the best in me.

Lynnie spoke first: Tell me about Lorelei. What was her mother like?

Then Alfred joined in: And what was her father like?

What penetrating questions! Neither of Lorelei's parents was in Anita's original diary, but they knew my answers would reveal to what extent I had been living with and dreaming of and understanding Lorelei.

Me: She was born into poverty, otherwise she wouldn't have discovered so soon the unchanging, worldwide security of diamonds. Her mother tried to make a home, which prompted Lorelei to say to a judge, "I enrolled in beauty college . . . so I could help Mama out? And then a man named Mr. Jennings came to our class. He looked over all we college girls and he picked me out." Her father was probably full of moonshine, so he felt free to terrorize any passerby with his backwoods rifle. You see, it's possible when Lorelei didn't get the diamond Mr. Jennings promised her, she shot him. She said in court, "The bullet only went in one hip and it came right out again. But he called me names I couldn't repeat."

Lynn: Yes, I surmise that he did. Did she have overwhelming physical appeal?

Me: Probably more of a lost orphan baby quality, although displayed only when she needed it to clinch her deal. As I say, she could shoot to kill if that didn't work.

Alfred: Would you say she was intelligent?

Me: Certainly not about constructing a sentence or spelling. She had no ear whatsoever. Because she was ignorant, she assumed everyone else was as well, and that they needed to be patiently instructed. But she could count money and tabulated the value of diamonds faster than Mr. de Beers! She also knew how to make men laugh and how to play with them by teasing with her physical attraction.

Lynn and Alfred and I were in the library of Jack and Natasha Wilson's home. Natasha was once the Princess Paley of all the Russias. I wish I could tell you more about her because, to my thinking, she looked like, and had the presence of a Titania in *A Midsummer Night's Dream*. She was a favorite subject in *Vogue* and *Harper's Bazaar* and of the photographer Margaret Bourke-White and all that crowd during

I cut the "boy's bob." *Ruth Taylor crossed her legs in the part talkie silent film of* Gentlemen Prefer Blondes. *Do you think this is another case of "Be careful what you set your heart upon for you shall surely get it?" I thought I was Ruth Taylor.*
(Author's collection)

With Anita Loos on our London and Paris trip. (Paul Hesse/MPTV)

*Tallulah Bankhead with a tiny diamond for one of our birthdays.
(Sammy Siegel)*

With Armina Marshall and her son, Phillip Languer, discussing the G. B. Shaw script. (Sammy Siegel)

At Disneyland with Maurice Chevalier and Walt Disney. (Author's collection)

With the great George Burns. (Author's collection)

On opening night on Broadway, this photo was taken just after reading the reviews of Dolly. Here with Gower Champion, Marge Champion, and the fabulous David Burns who played Vandergelder. (Sammy Siegel)

In my dressing room with Jack Lemmon. (Sammy Siegel)

Backstage with Bobby Kennedy. (Sammy Siegel)

Gower and Jerry's kisses were heaven for me, but somebody touched up my face so they look like they're an inch from me. They weren't. This sensational memory is still with me.

With the great Ethel Waters, Chan's adopted grandmother, which she took very seriously. Chan was three when this was taken. Is this another case of "Be careful what you set your heart upon for you shall surely get it"? (Sammy Siegel)

Here I am at a Chicago White Sox/Boston Red Sox game in 1964 with Senator Ted Kennedy, Attorney General Bobby Kennedy, Stan Musial, Jean Smith, and Pat Lawford. (Bettman/CORBIS)

With Barbra Streisand after Dolly's Actors Fund Benefit in 1964. (Sammy Siegel)

With Neil Simon. (Sammy Siegel)

my growing-up years, when those magazines set the standard for modern photography. I never asked Anita about Natasha's history, for obvious reasons. Who could care about anybody but the Lunts when they were around? I only had eyes for them. Natasha never captivated an audience and lifted them to the heavens the way the Lunts did. She wasn't even in show business. However, I got used to her incredibly delicate beauty being around a lot after the play opened. (Jack Wilson was also Noël Coward's director.) Besides directing the Lunts and *Gentlemen Prefer Blondes*, Jack and I never got close, but we drained each other's talents dry.

His and Natasha's great bond was their sharing of impeccably fine and aristocratic taste, to the exclusion of all other kinds of good taste. I remember Jack saying to me as he lifted his Marlboro cigarette (no cowboys in the ads then, and a pack cost four cents more than any other) from the silver case inscribed from Noël (I never read what it said), "You know, Carol, I can live without anything except luxury." I suppose you'd *better* marry the Princess Paley of all the Russias if you feel that way.

That's another thing I have to admire Alfred for. Even with all the Anna Moffo performances he directed at the Metropolitan Opera, he considered gutbucket vaudeville just as much of an art form, and was equally thrilled by both. I remember years later he and Lynn came to the Wisconsin State Fair, where I was doing a full concert in their huge outdoor theatre. He came backstage laughing and said, "That 'Diamonds' number is religious, altruistic pornography. It's heaven."

Jack Wilson really did have great taste. He staged "A Little Girl from Little Rock" and "Bye, Bye, Baby" and "Diamonds" and all my songs. Agnes de Mille said she wouldn't touch them. She was right. A choreographer shouldn't touch them; only a director should. Jack Cole's choreography in the movie was so busy it kept you from hearing any one word of Leo's lyrics. Scrambling Leo's lyrics allowed the greatness of the show to go right down the drain. Certainly the dialogue never captured the comedy of Anita's novel. Only Jule's music with Milt Rosenstock conducting it and Leo's lyrics equaled the novel but, of course, I would think that. You see, Jack Wilson insisted they buy a black velvet curtain to go behind me in "Diamonds." They originally had a busy ocean liner scene. Well, it made every thought, every flicker of an eyelash stand out like a neon sign. I could feel the focus from that black all around me. Same principle as Ethel Waters's "Supper Time" in *As Thousands Cheer*. I wish I had told John C. Wilson how I appreciated him, and how I felt he helped the audience appreciate the show.

Three-quarters of an hour of "audition" went on in that library. I was able, as we talked, to quote Lorelei exactly in the character I eventually played her, without the formality of reading a script. They were so wise in not wanting an audition from me. They knew Anita's work. What they wanted to know was how *my* mind worked. Lorelei would tell them, "Oh, Daddy, you're sending me out all alone on the great big oshin (ocean)?" I had to find some way to indicate in speech Lorelei's misspelling . . . like Bosting, Massachussetts. I just raised my voice an octave or two to say these things and it sounded right to me; what I mean is it sounded like Lorelei. Lynn and Alfred were totally focused on everything I said, but Alfred elicited one "hah," and Lynnie couldn't erase a smile. I felt it. I knew it was all falling on very attentive ears. Finally after much talk that I couldn't let up on because it was my whole life at that time . . . finally we all three decided to go back into the living room to be with everybody else.

Alfred announced: Lynn has something to tell you.

Lynnie: I will put my financial interest into *Gentlemen Prefer Blondes*.

Alfred: I will contribute mine. (Alfred was proud of their having separate bank accounts and even separate banks.)

Both said: We want very much to support this project.

I was sitting next to Oliver Smith. I don't think anyone saw him squeeze my hand because it was already hidden under his. I put it there myself for support.

As I told you, Oliver was the coproducer of the show with Herman Levin. He was the first to come to me to talk about Lorelei; it was at an outdoor Long Island summer theatre during the intermission of *South Pacific*. I had come to see Ethel Waters as Bloody Mary. While I was watching her, I felt a big surge of affectionate envelopment coming from behind me. My father was alive then. I thought it might be he . . . him . . . whatever. It was that caliber of affection. I looked behind me but couldn't see anyone I knew. At intermission this startlingly elegant and immaculately clothed gentleman of tall and slender male grace approached and introduced himself as Oliver Smith. I knew who he was, having written a thesis while at Bennington on his sets and their contribution to the ballet and Broadway theatre. Oliver was only two years older than I, but he was a rising star then, and gradually breaking the monopoly Raoul Pene du Bois held over the design of Broadway shows. Oliver said, "I'm about to coproduce a new musical, *Gentlemen Prefer Blondes*, and I think you should play Lorelei." I said, "I do too, Mr. Smith. I've been reading the original book for weeks."

He had no doubt come to see Lenore Lonergan (her musical, a different one, had just closed on Broadway). Here she was playing Nellie Forbush, better known as the Mary Martin role in *South Pacific*, but his fix was on the back of me for the entire first act, no one could ever tell me it wasn't. What a penetrating mind and feelings Oliver had! Later he invited me to his Ninth Street apartment off Fifth Avenue for lunch with David Ffolkes, another theatre set designer. I was still playing *Lend an Ear*, so it had to be lunch. I told them I'd written my theses on them. They both seemed to be delighted with me. I guess *so*. They didn't know there was a Bennington college where students could write their theses on such young and as yet inexperienced set designers as themselves. I chose to study them for Arch Lauterer's theatre classes. Lauterer was Martha Graham's set designer, as I told you. It makes a tremendous difference if a teacher is *practicing* his subject. Otherwise he's got a case of the Maria Callases (as she was depicted in Terrence McNally's play *Master Class*). We'll have to go into this later, because I'm off my subject again. And this human phenomenon should be pointed out.

Now, what was our subject? Oh yes, getting investors for *Blondes* with only me to hold the entire show together. Well, once the Lunts invested in it, Rodgers and Hammerstein, Leland Hayward, Joshua Logan, Billy Rose, and many more came swiftly in. That's the way it used to be. I never saw the list of backers, but wasn't Anita brilliant to intrigue Lynn and Alfred? And, most remarkably of all, to trust *me* to such an extent? Why didn't someone tell me what an all-important day that was? I might have taken one of Tallulah's sleeping pills the night before and been as incoherent as Talloo. Nobody ever told me anything. I never knew why we had to go there, really, but I was totally aware of what a privilege it was to be treated with respect by such luminaries. Every one of them had a nature that was vulnerable and not sure of itself, like so many highly intelligent people, and so they were innately kind people. I was very grateful and not as frightened as I would have been with lesser talents.

n opening night for *Blondes,* I don't remember applause. I don't remember laughter. I only remember a reflex action that enabled me to time the applause and laughter. I was clinging with all my being to Anita's character of Lorelei Lee. I was in love with Lorelei Lee, and that must have had something to do with sustaining me. Being in love is stronger than any other human emotion, I have just decided. Stronger than panic or fear or the possibility of certain death. This was my first time up at bat with the responsibility of the entire production resting on me.

After the show, I could not leave my dressing room until Anita, Jule, Oliver, Miles White (costume designer), Agnes de Mille, Herman Levin, and all the powers that be had advance notice from the newspapers that we were a hit. They came running back to tell me, and I could hear them through the intercom as they rushed across the stage calling, "Carol, we're a hit!" When they finally got upstairs to me, I was halfway down yelling, "You don't mean unanimous notices?" Anita explained, "Carol, you will never get unanimous notices. The fact that it thrilled most people has to mean that it irritated some. If it stirred up the air at all, it has to run smack against somebody."

And, sure enough, the next morning, the leading columnist for the

Hearst Syndicate wrote for her headline, "Gentlemen Must Prefer Amazons." Well, she was right. In Lorelei's spike heels I was still over six feet tall and built strong, and it *was* a funny headline.

Many people have asked me if one knows a show is going to be a hit before it opens. I always say no but, just between us, there *is* a strange phenomenon that comes just before the opening of a show like *Gentlemen Prefer Blondes*. As you know, there are weeks of rehearsal, with each section of the show centered in a different place. You go to this room to learn your dances, to that room to put them with the chorus, to this room to learn the songs, to the stage for the dialogue. There is a full company run-through every week. And then—it happened, at the final run-through without scenery or costumes. There, standing in the middle of all this entire company, I suddenly felt and saw the aura of our show for the first time, and it was a beautiful, laughing aura. I felt I knew the level of it. I knew where my character fit in. I do not know how the rest of the company felt, but I suspect that at that moment we all knew. It was a vision—"the holy city new Jerusalem descending out of heaven like unto a cloud." It was a pat on all our heads and a blessing. I almost cried.

I shall never cease to be grateful for the opening night newspaper critics' reviews. The second night the magazine reviewers came to *Blondes*. In those days *Time* magazine openly ignored stage or movie actors, but they put me on the cover! The second actor ever on its cover. (Tallulah was the first, many years before.) Did you think I would leave *that* unsaid? And for the second time in this book? I want to be sure you caught it.

In *Lend an Ear*, little Pru (my character in the "Gladiola Girl" sketch) had something of the same problem. My own godfather came to *Lend an Ear* in L.A. before Josh Logan gave me two characters to do before the "Gladiola Girl" sketch. He came backstage all distraught and said to me, "Carol, don't ever try to dance in a show again. It's embarrassing to watch you. Take it from someone who loves you, and don't be hurt. You're a born klutz." Isn't that a compliment? That little Pru actually existed on that stage and was so real to him? That's why Josh Logan insisted on giving me a chic and sophisticated woman (Dorothy Kilgallen) and a robot to do before doing Prudence.

Did my godfather think the rest of the audience was laughing at the scenery or the chandelier? Al Hirschfeld drew caricatures of Pru and

Lorelei that were hilarious. As I said, I did not know the characters were that funny. I only hoped. But I could hear the audience laughing, for God's sake. My dear godfather was a brilliant businessman who built Shreve's jewelers in San Francisco . . . no dummkopf. It shows you how oppositely different people's minds do work. Lorelei wasn't a klutz by any means, but in a childlike way she sweetly manipulated men as knowledgeably as Attila the Hun. I do wish someone had told me, though, that I was going to shrink two inches all the way around. We all do, it seems. I would have been so heartened. I'm now at least passable.

I'm trying to tell you about the Lunts. I'll try again. When they came to see *Blondes* months after we opened, because they were still playing in *Shrew* or *The Pirate*, they dressed as if it were opening night. That was a lesson to me. It showed such respect for us. I have adhered to that ever since. If I'm going to wear the wrong outfit, which seems to be my proclivity—but then we all think that about ourselves—be sure it's because of overdressing not underdressing.

One of my favorite experiences with the Lunts happened at the Wisconsin State Fair years later. As I say, it was outdoors and, on the first matinee, with the Lunts in the audience, it rained buckets. No one in the audience, it seemed to me, wanted to leave. I had nine costumes to change into right onstage, behind two screens, while I just kept talking. I was halfway through my show when the cloudburst came. I knew the audience couldn't get its money back for the tickets and, besides, the management was depending on me to keep them afloat financially. So I asked my accompanist, Robert Hunter, to cover the piano with a canvas. He did, but canvas isn't waterproof. The orchestra got under an awning, and we finished in a blaze of fun and glory. My wig was drenched.

At the end the Lunts came backstage to my dressing room. Alfred was still laughing at the "Diamonds" number but asking for a big towel so he could dry off the piano. Lynn wanted my drenched wig immediately. She asked for hair rollers and a dryer. Then she said to my dresser, "No! Do not put heat on those wet costumes, it will shrink them." She asked the stage manager for a big electric fan. She got it and lay the heavy costumes on the floor, so they wouldn't stretch on hangers while wet, and moved the fan back and forth over them. She told me to lie down—that I had an evening show to do—and to drink hot tea. I found through years of friendship after that, that very strong hot tea with lots of sugar was her panacea for everything. I drank it without question.

She had to work fast, but she got everything done. The costumes were immaculately ironed by the evening show. Of course, I had a wardrobe dresser, but she had never coped with a crisis like this. They were both undaunted. Now, how many people could ever afford the Lunts as wardrobe, hair, and stage manager assistants? It was even more dramatic than I'm telling you. Alfred was giving orders to the stage crew on how to dry the screens, shoes, and stage floor. I was busy regluing my false eyelashes, which had started to slide down my face. Everybody backstage snapped into line and did everything the Lunts ordered as if it were D-Day (in World War II). You see, Wisconsin was the Lunts' state. Their home Ten Chimneys in Genesee Depot, Wisconsin, was as revered as the White House by the entire state. Alfred was their president, and Lynn was their First Lady.

I was asking Frank Langella, to me one of the finest and greatest of Broadway stars of my time anyway, "Do you think we could be great dressers and great stage managers, too . . . just because we know what the star needs?" "Absolutely," he said. "I think, as a matter of fact, we should place an ad in the paper and rent ourselves out between shows as a couple." Well, I know I could do it. The fascinating thing was how accurately Lynn knew where to put the rollers in my wig in order to make it look precisely the way I had it before the rain. She noticed. I always had to set it myself until the wee small hours because no professional hairdresser can do that. They don't notice the way she did. She must, like me, have had a grandmother she practiced on all her growing-up years.

ow! After the reviews on *Blondes*, Twentieth Century–Fox purchased tickets for Marilyn Monroe in our third-row center for exactly one month. Our orchestra never ever saw anyone that beautiful before. For the first time they were all looking at Marilyn instead of our conductor, Milt Rosenstock. The only one not looking was Bus Davis on piano. They were all begging him to look. Finally Bus did and said, "Ask her does she have a brother." Well, you had to have known Bus.

I do think it was one of her best movies. Not funny, however. They didn't use one word of Anita's original book, which was hilarious and which was what constantly kept the stage musical on a higher level. Anita didn't write the musical's book. So where they didn't insert her original book it was mundane. It was the stock formula for a dated Broadway musical. I followed Anita's original Lorelei character ferociously. Uncle Leo was able, as I say, with his lyrics to condense her plot wittily and probingly into this amazing Arkansas child. Agnes de Mille, our choreographer, refused to touch anything to do with me. She always sat in the audience section of the Ziegfeld Theatre with my father during rehearsal. She said to Jack Wilson, "Anyone who tinkers with Carol's concept of Lorelei's walk, talk, dance, song, or pantomime, is a fool."

Somehow, anyone who ever got to know my father well thinks that much of me. The same thing happened with Leonard Bernstein's tender and lovely wife, Felicia. Bernstein wrote the music for *Wonderful Town*, but he got adjusted to the only way I could play Ruth Sherwood sooner than anyone else because his wife and my father became friends. At his first meeting with her in my dressing room, Daddy opened his arms to Felicia. She did exactly what I did with Josh Logan.

She nestled into his arms and wanted to stay safely there. Daddy said, "What does it feel like to be married to a genius?" She looked at him straight in the eye, realized she trusted him, and said, "It's just beautiful," smiling relaxedly. Then she put her head right back under his chin. How did you know, Daddy, on the first moment of meeting her that she needed safety and affection and the knowledge that she was lovely? Tallulah was the same way with my father. I'll tell you later.

Robert Fryer, the prestigious Broadway and movie producer, and I were touring his Broadway musical *Wonderful Town* when a wire came from Sol Siegel inviting me to the world premiere in New York of the *Gentlemen Prefer Blondes* movie. He said he thought my appearance would help put it over . . . no doubt thinking he was complimenting me. I was heartsick about the whole thing, of course. Even Jack Cole's movie choreography completely upstaged and clouded Uncle Leo's valuable lyrics and laughs. Jule Styne's blue smoke wasn't anywhere to be heard.

Bobby took right over. He said, "We'll send Siegel a two-hundred-and-fifty-word collect wire [those were the days of telegrams at three dollars a word] telling him why you're so heartbroken that you can't be there. Say, 'You see, Mr. Siegel, I am touring at the moment with *Wonderful Town*, which must not be as important to you as to Robert Fryer and me, you have so many things on your mind, but my mother is coming to Pittsburgh, where we are en route right now. Stop. She wants to see it because she read the Chicago Claudia Cassidy reviews that meant it ran for over a year to packed houses at the huge Shubert Theatre. Stop. I'm so sorry you weren't aware that I'm all tied up. Stop. To me, *Wonderful Town* is the story of a female Mark Twain who captured for all time the lives of two sisters growing up in the Middle West. Stop. Cassidy said and I quote, "Whereas Rosalind Russell played it for intelligence, Channing plays it for genius." Stop. I'm so sorry you missed that. Stop. Few people in Chicago did. Stop.' "

It went on for all the two hundred and fifty collect words. As you've probably sensed, Bobby can be a bitch, but only when protecting his friends. We laughed till we fell asleep in our shared stateroom with separate bunks. That sounds provocative, but nothing seems to be provocative with me, especially with eight shows a week and traveling by train and constant press conferences. Anyway, Bobby and I enjoyed the wire, and I truly enjoyed Bobby's friendship, right up until yesterday. Today I read his obituary in the *L.A. Times.* The same happened with Mr. Merrick. I phoned him at David Merrick Productions in New York at the end of writing in this book about him. They said he was in London but they would relay how I treasured working with him. He died two days later. What with Ethel Merman, Mary Martin, Alfred Lunt, Lynn Fontanne, Yul Brynner, et cetera, it has just occurred to me, I do hope I'm not writing next about any of you.

Louie Armstrong

I've told many interviewers that after I first heard the score of *Hello, Dolly!* I phoned my friend Louie Armstrong and asked him, "Louie, do you think I am up to singing a tremendous score like *Hello, Dolly?*"

George Burns told me to say Louie had said: "Carol, what are you worried about? Your voice is as good as mine." I wish Louie *had* said that, but isn't that a true George Burns retort? I had to tell you, it's so good.

When we were together, we would also dress together in the locker room. "Dressing" means making up, warming up, and fixing up hair, not undressing clothes. Anyway, we were once in the Kiel auditorium in St. Louis, and the last time was at the Washington, D.C., Armory for John F. Kennedy and his presidential campaign. Louie's brown skin made him look all covered up instead of having on only his immaculate white shorts to the knees and white handkerchief on his head. There he sat, looking like a baby cherub ready to sprout wings. We automatically sat right next to each other, even though we had a half a city block of locker room to spread out in . . . so that we could talk and warm up together. We warmed up from middle C on down, and whenever making up Louie always wore this handkerchief on his head with a knot on each of the four corners. Why, I don't know. Something to do with setting his hair, but the knots looked like tiny wings ready to lift him off and fly him somewhere.

It was easy to be around Louie. The first time we met, I thought I must always have known him. In Vegas we spent every supper together in my suite after his two shows at the Flamingo and my two shows at the Riviera. Charles always went immediately to sleep in the bedroom right after shows. One time Louie put me on his own diet, giving me some green chopped up leaves to chew on before meals. For a week, all food went straight through me. Louie lost weight. I just got wan looking.

He had a natural dignity. He knew he was abused when he had to go to sleep in a broken down motor court across the strip. He looked at me with a hurt expression that said, Why is this? Do I deserve this? I worked hard all my life so as not to be treated like this. It hurt him because his sweet kindness *didn't* deserve this. He mentioned it every night to me before leaving. I didn't know how to give him an answer without going into a psychological history of the ignorant element of our United States society. Of course I didn't have that in my pocket, but racial prejudice is, indeed, a yardstick for measuring who is truly ignorant. We'll all be café au lait colored one day soon (hopefully something like Tiger Woods in looks and discipline), and then we'll have to find something else to be irrational about. Oh shut up, Carol. I found out everybody talks this way, but they don't really feel this way or act accordingly. Why do I tell you? You know it, and there's nothing we can do about it.

Lady Astor

*T*here are "reformed whores" in every religion, I'm sure. Lady Astor, my parents told me, was known to knock the crutches out from under cripples, tell them God would hold them up, and leave them sprawled on the sidewalk. They told me this just before we three went to dinner at her London estate, where years later part of the Profumo scandal took place. If you don't know the Profumo case, ask anyone who's seventy years old or older now. I don't want to go into it because it's off the subject I'm on, which is Lady Astor. But it was very jazzy and it was right under Lady Astor's nose and she never suspected a thing. Well, now you're more curious about the Profumo case than you are about Lady Astor. I'm not. I never was. Lady Astor is far more alarming to me and, as we agreed in the beginning, this is *my book*. If you want to know more, ask somebody who's fascinated with trivialities, like dirt and gossip that is very possibly not true.

Now for the true issue . . . Lady Astor. She was an overzealous Christian Scientist and came to all my father's lectures in London. That's why my mother and I were invited. I can't remember why I was in London, but I was surprised to learn how the cover of *Time* magazine makes one more widely known than one would realize.

Yes! That crutches story was true. The first thing Lady Astor did was take off my glasses and say, "Tell your father to heal you." She went right on talking with "Now! Let me show you the paintings of all the Astors ever since the first." I missed the whole thing. I couldn't see one Astor. I missed seeing her handsome sons, who later were involved in the Profumo case. I missed everything except her sitting next to me (within my range of vision) at the dinner table, and a Sir Benjamin Harrison immediately on my left. My father whispered to me, "I wish she'd get off of our side."

As we sat down at the long banquet table, some of her guests mentioned, in passing, issues that led me to realize Lady Astor held a seat in Parliament and spent most every Sunday marching through Hyde Park holding high in the air large signs on sticks that advocated political issues she believed in. Then she called down to the other end of the banquet table to one of her sons, "Leonard! You *are* Leonard, aren't you?" She went on: "There was a marvelous speech made in Parliament today. (She was unraveling a piece of paper.) It shall be indelibly imprinted on my mind let me read it to you." Well, that's all *I* heard right there. I don't remember the speech.

As we shared our lives with one another at our end of the table, she asked me how I could so clearly remember every city I played in. I explained that the easiest way for me was to remember what I ate in each one. For instance, in Sioux City, Iowa, they serve three eggs for breakfast wherever you eat. They don't ask. They just serve them to you. Now in Ada, Oklahoma, for lunch they have cold whole hominy balls in lettuce for your salad. In Dallas, Texas, there are tamales—

Lady Astor: What's a tamale?

Me: Oh, a real Texas tamale is more than just a food, it's an experience. I always feel you can tell more about the people in each place by the food they eat and their music and singing and dancing than by history books, don't you agree?

Lady Astor: I asked you what a tamale was.

Me: Yes, well, a tamale on the outside is sun-bleached, sun-nurtured corn, beaten into a husk wrapping. You can sense the Indians' strong, sinewed, copper-colored thighs that they beat the earth-flavored corn against. The taste of the meat in the center reveals the wild, cruel, warlike, bareback Indian horse riders as they charge into battle.

Lady Astor (coldly): You can be healed of that.

I sensed that she was through with me for a while. Now the gentleman on my left, Sir Benjamin Harrison, had what is known as a Mayfair accent. What it amounts to is you can understand only about every fifth word. In the Mayfair section of London, I notice they often have those long British teeth slightly bucked, that interfere with the consonants. However, I told him, "When I finish my show here, I'd like to go to Istanbul."

Sir Benjamin: "Aaahahhhh. Whe' you get to Istanbul, you mus' tase the chaz thaz big'z golf balls." (Big smile.)

Me: "I beg your pardon."

Sir Benjamin: "I say, when you . . ."

and he repeated the entire sentence twice, slower each time, which only exaggerated that there were no consonants. Finally I turned to Lady Astor and asked, "What is Sir Benjamin saying?"

Lady Astor (high, clear, and without interest): "Oh. He's saying: When you get to Istanbul, you must taste the cherries. They're as big as golf balls."

Me: "How do *you* know what he just said?"

Lady Astor: "Oh, that's what they always say when you're on your way to Istanbul."

When it was time to leave, she had a hard task finding my eyeglasses, but I wouldn't leave till we found them. We made it back to my parents' hotel, where I stayed the night with them. I was so glad to be with them again. Besides, my mother had told me the next day the hotel was serving eel for high tea in the lobby. On the big silver serving platter it looked exactly like one very long, slender snake curving back and forth to the edges of the plate. It was more exciting than any of the paintings I couldn't see at Lady Astor's.

I finally did make it to Istanbul as well. Hedda Hopper was leaving Hollywood on a press junket to open the Istanbul Hilton. I told her I had always wanted to visit Istanbul. She got me on the trip. They picked me up at Orly Airport in France, and I joined the press plane. It was fabulous! Bill Eythe and Lon McAllister were on the plane, thank God. The ruling class of the press can be awing if you don't know them. By the time we were on our way back, we were all friends, helping each other with luggage and passports. Hedda Hopper and Louella Parsons sat together on the plane, obviously enjoying one another all the way there and all the way back to their homes in Hollywood. Abel Green, the creator and editor in chief of *Variety*, Mary Lee Logan Leatherbee of *Life* magazine (Josh Logan's sister), Tom Prideaux (*Life* magazine's entertainment editor), Art Buchwald of *The Washington Post*—these are the only ones I can remember, because they were people who were excited with their jobs and every statistic and story they could collect in Istanbul.

Also on the junket was Sonja Henie, the movie star, ice skater, and diamond collector. I had just finished the entire tour of *Gentlemen Pre-*

fer Blondes, the score for which included "Diamonds Are a Girl's Best Friend," so she took it for granted she and I were soul mates. Earl Wilson, the New York columnist, and so many others wrote fascinating stories of the trip. Art Buchwald and I borrowed the pilot's microphone and sang a song from the cockpit that Art wrote while we were there.

Art and I had two pairs of those huge brass cymbals that punctuate the Ottoman Turkish Army's march. By the way, the army was spectacular! Robin's egg blue and cream colored striped shirts with huge balloon sleeves coming out of turkey red vests lengthened to the ground. Big black handlebar mustaches and two black eyebrows on every one of their olive-skinned faces. Turkey red pillbox hats with gold embroidery and gold earrings to match the big brass cymbals. The energy of all of Islam was inside their every marching step. Art and I sounded almost like them when we sang his song.

We watched them together. Art thought I was physically attracted to all of them. That wasn't it at all. He misunderstood. It was just that they were dressed so beautifully, with the sun glistening on their oily black hair peeking out from under the rich red and gold pillboxes, and they all looked like Elia Kazan. Oh, Art! How could you miss the glory of all that?

And the belly dancers were a religious experience, too. I always thought they meant to be doing a sexual dance. No! To watch them is a spiritual enlightenment.

But the most unusual sight of all was Irene Dunne and Merle Oberon looking precisely like themselves standing on the dusty dirt sidewalk of a main street trying to hail a cab. Not one of the cabs would stop for them. However, Leo Carrillo, remember him? Well, I do. Not a good-looking leading man type at all. Simply an eccentric and very funny. He was standing two blocks away from them and caused a terrible gridlock of cabs and private cars as drivers recognized him (he was the most popular movie star in Turkey). They began yelling to him, trying to coax him to get into their cars. They actually fought over him. I think the problem with the two girls was that their movies didn't get sent to Istanbul.

I saw all of this from a bus. Art, Bill Eythe, and Lon McAllister kept telling me, "Carol, there's that same woman again in black chiffon.

Now she's on this corner." Her face was always covered. Of course, it was the traditional garb for women left over from Constantine's reign, when Istanbul was named Constantinople, which had been until only a few years before. So it wasn't the same woman at all, but you knew that. Art tried to convince me the woman was running alongside our bus, so every time we stopped, there she was again. It took me only a split second not to believe him, although you'd be surprised how convincing he can be.

hen I finally finished the tremendous tour of *Blondes*, I was still married to the Canadian pro football player, who decided to come along. After the tour, Herman Levin was bringing *Blondes* to London. The scenery and costumes and all went on ahead, until I discovered that Chan was on his way. My then husband's family told him, If you don't give her a baby, she'll leave you.

I carried Chan for almost ten months before he was born. I learned after his delivery that often happens with one's first child. In those days we had no way of knowing prior to birth whether he was a girl or a boy, so Gant Gaither and some friends decided it would be named Channing, after my father, no matter what. Chan reeked of ether when they first brought him in to me. The doctor who was supposed to deliver him wasn't there, so somebody very kind, a man in a white jacket

like a student doctor or intern, gave us both ether. I was afraid I was crushing the baby's skull when the ether took over. I saw a deep sink above each of Chan's ears that were scalpel indentations. It must have been painful for him too, but I could feel his will to live. He was the most gorgeous baby born that day in Women's Hospital, New York City. My parents thought so too, so I'm right. Well, you see, the other babies behind the glass weren't fully formed like Channing. Just little ex-ectoplasms or embryos. But Chan was, as I said, weeks overdue. They can tell to the minute by the optic nerves. Isn't that marvelous?

George Kleinsinger, who wrote a great score for the album *Archy and Mehitabel*, and Joe Darion, who wrote equally great lyrics, and Columbia Records, who was going to record it all, waited patiently for Chan to arrive. I wanted to do that album as much as I ever wanted to do anything. Columbia Records was holding its biggest orchestra and studio and cast until I could be there. Therefore Chan and I couldn't relax. So we all decided to go ahead and make this fabulous album and let him be born after it. Chan apparently agreed too, because he kicked happily in time to the music. Eddie Bracken sang the role of Archy, the legendary cockroach who was dreamed up by Don Marquis, a newspaperman dear to my father and all press members. I sang the part of Mehitabel and reveled in it to the skies. She was a rotten, low-down, oversexed alley cat who had litters of kittens and drowned them all. Chan thought she was funny, too. I could tell from his uncontrollable kicks. My opening song was a gutbucket blues with no less than a tympani drum to supply the Ethel Waters *auschpannen*. We (Chan and I) thought she was uncivilizedly laughable.

I asked Eddie, who had already had five children, to feel my tummy where Chan was. Chan was utterly poised and quiet until the big orchestra started the music again. On the downbeat, Chan came in again.

Eddie: That's a very strong kick that child has and precisely on the beat! This is unusual.

Me: Maybe your and Connie's children didn't have an awe-inspiring seventy-five-piece orchestra at the time they kicked.

I felt then what might have been the first labor pain, but then Chan and I decided it wasn't.

When we finally finished this album, I thought it was the best recording I had ever made. Chan thought so too. The moral of this story is: Don't ever put anything off just because you're in the last stages of pregnancy. It'll all turn out splendidly. By the way, a day after this I was sitting in the audience at Harry Belafonte's one-man show at the Palace Theatre. I was particularly thrilled with Harry when the second labor pain struck me. To this day Chan is carried away by Belafonte's voice; he has told me so many times. Chan was born in 1953. I think the American Medical Association has discovered since then that babies do indeed know what's going on before they are born. Do they get it from their mother's emotions? Wouldn't you love to know?

I had to ask Chan's father's mother if she could take Chan until I finished a TV special. It was called "Svengali and the Blonde," and I appeared in it with Ethel Barrymore. I was to play Trilby and didn't know at the time what typecasting it was for me. Basil Rathbone played Svengali, his character hypnotizing me through most of it. Perfect! Du Maurier (the author) was Ethel Barrymore's lover for their fifteen-year live-in affair, so she was the narrator.

To prepare for the role, I went alone to Paris to stay opposite the Left Bank, where the cathedral of Notre Dame stands. I wanted to stay in a place like the one where Trilby lived. Earl Blackwell, through his Celebrity Service, found a room for me on the fifth floor of the Hôtel Bisson. It had two of those famous Parisian windows that lean every

which way because of centuries of people sitting on the windowsills to watch the goings-on in the street. I did the same and felt, I thought, just like Trilby.

Fern Bedeaux, my love-aunt, lived in the Château de Candé where the monks developed the first gunpowder. She lent me her young assistant as a guide. I don't know how I thought I was going to accomplish this research without him. He took me to the Comédie-Française, interpreting what was said, and to the Place Pigalle to drag shows and to the Grand Vafour Restaurant, where two cold poached eggs *en gelée* stared up at you as you came in the door. He took me everywhere that Trilby went.

Joan Crawford may have been difficult with children (Bruce Vilanch's telephone message machine answers: "The Joan Crawford Day Care Clinic"), but she had a soft spot for Broadway people. I got in on that.

When Joan heard I was heading for Paris, she asked me to sing at her wedding, the one in which she was marrying the board chairman of Pepsi-Cola, Alfred Steele, which was to take place at Maxim's in Paris.

It seems Joan had a Dictaphone that she spoke into, and someone who typed out everything she said. This machine was right by her bed, so she spoke to many of her acquaintances before going to sleep. Obviously she enjoyed playing with it a lot.

At Christmastime I sent her a card. She and her machine answered with a friendly thank-you note. Then came a Christmas card from her. I sent her a thank-you note. She thanked me with a thank-you note so, of course I was touched by her warmth and friendship. I sent her a thank-you note for her thank-you note. The exchange continued throughout the run of *Blondes*, but *I* didn't have a machine or a typist. Now you know, anyone who asks *me* to sing at her wedding deserves what she gets, right? In Paris I went to Edition Salabert, which was like G. Schirmer's music store in New York—it had everything musical. I picked out a song, "Voulez-vous de la Canne à Sucre?" My memory of high school French was that it meant "Would you like some sugarcane?" A charming choice for a wedding, wouldn't you think? So I bought a record of it with the sheet music and thoroughly enjoyed learning it.

I was never so Gallic as at Maxim's, doing it in a sort of Maurice Chevalier, Josephine Baker influence. But do you know, it turned out it embarrassed even the French? It had a triple meaning, not just a double, I was told later. I emptied out the wedding reception. The lyrics must have been horrendous, because people who understand French get very angry at me when I sing it, and it sounded so divine. I adored doing it.

I want to apologize to anyone still alive after Joan's wedding in 1956. No one believes me that I didn't know what the lyrics meant. What I did understand seemed appropriate. Thank God, for years afterward, Joan didn't even remember the incident, or celebrating her marriage to a roomful of empty chairs. The whole thing was a total blank to her.

Since it was her wedding day, I think she had something a little stronger to drink than Mr. Steele's Pepsi-Cola, so I'm grateful for that because it made it possible for us to remain friends.

Anyway, back to Los Angeles and the filming of "Svengali and the Blonde." Charles Gaynor wrote the adaptation for TV. Remember he created and wrote *Lend an Ear?*

Charlie kept after me in Los Angeles, "You've got to come to dinner with Charles Lowe and me. He insists on meeting you."

How could I? I had to learn lines and think incessantly about this character Trilby, but he also invited the director, the producer, and the writer, so if it was business I had to go.

Coincidentally, Charles Lowe's great friend "Willie" had been on the Istanbul trip with Hedda Hopper, and he was still abroad on that junket. I wasn't attracted to Charles at all then, but he was very hospitable in his apartment at the Chateau Marmont. He just found out it was my birthday. At the last minute he had his cook put one candle on a cupcake. I didn't even know it was my birthday. Wasn't that thoughtful of him?

It surprised me when I got a call on the set just days later from Charles telling me to go immediately to the hospital because Bill Eythe, my close strong champion, the producer of *Lend an Ear*, was dying. Somehow Bill's dear friend Lon "Bud" McAllister contacted Charles to find me. I'm not sure how it all came to be, but as soon as I got the call I dropped everything . . . even Ethel Barrymore . . . to be with Bill. Long after *Lend an Ear* we stayed close. For me, it was through *Blondes*, Chan's arrival, and *Pygmalion*. During that period Bill had several times predicted the scene of his own death to me, even the room he would be in. Now, years after that prediction, when the doctor told me, "He's not going to make it," I was stunned to see the exact room Bill had described. He said, "The room is all white. There's a window to my right, almost behind me. The sheer white curtains are billowing. The head of my bed is wrought iron. You're there, Carol, sitting next to my bed holding my hand."

Indeed, when the moment came, I was the only one with him. The next day in all the papers they said I was the only one with Bill when he died. Bud (Lon McAllister) was nowhere around when Bill died, and I know he wanted to be. Bill and I worked beautifully together, as I told you, and we had shared with Josh Logan a theatre experience which amounted to a spiritual journey, or so it seemed to us. I wanted to sustain Bill, but I don't know whether he knew I was there or not. I didn't know I was being used as a "beard" for him and Bud, but it doesn't matter, because Bill and I instinctively protected each other. He was an excitable child at heart. That heart was pure. He was so proud of every last person involved with his *Lend an Ear*, including me.

Milt Rosenstock

*A*fter finishing Trilby, I did our final performances of *Wonderful Town* at the Greek Theatre for a few weeks' run, then returned to New York for *The Vamp* rehearsal and the security of John Latouche and Milt Rosenstock.

Milt was known as the greatest of all Broadway conductors by other theatre conductors and by classical ones, including Arthur Fiedler, John Williams, and Kitty Dukakis's father, Harry Ellis Dickson, who was the founder and musical director of the Boston Pops. He changed his name from three Russian Jewish names just like Michael Tilson Thomas did. When your work is that great, why do you have to change your name? Only they know. Harry Ellis Dickson was ninety-two years old when I met him (I was conducting the Boston Pops), and he had as much sex appeal as George Burns, which is saying a terrific amount. When George and I worked together for two years in theatres across the country, I was told I was standing too close to him. But moving away from him was for me like trying to pull the big round rubber stopper off the sink drain.

We had Milt Rosenstock all during the run of *Blondes* and on the national tour. I had him on *The Vamp*, and later on the national tour of *Lorelei* and when it opened in the Palace Theatre on Broadway. Again, I would have died for Milt. For every single show he always put himself emotionally inside the performer. Then he'd come back to the performer's dressing room and check to see if he'd gotten it right. Of course, it was right! He was uncanny. I don't have to tell you I was in love with him, too. I even loved his wife and son, George. But Milt was busy scoring with the most attractive females in the company.

It's vaguely possible that Milton came on to me too, although he must not have because it's unbelievable that I would never realize it. I get sex all mixed up with eternal understanding of one another and dedication to our mutual work and stuff, which is a big mistake. I was completely aware of male electricity running through me simply because he was in the room or the orchestra pit. I just think you're never supposed to sleep together because of it. That electricity is the divine blessing that descends on both of us, giving us this great contact in order to get this show on. It's thrilling what happens to the music and to my performance when this connection happens. But I never thought of giving in to it. I thought it was supposed to be saved for the show.

The cast members of all musical shows, during their run, rehearse with the orchestra once a week. Milton told me in Chicago, "When you, Miss C, walk on that stage for rehearsal, you're so fucking elegant—" I stopped him to correct him. "Milt," I said. "That's a dichotomy. You can't be fucking and elegant at the same time."

Milt: Well, you *can*.

Me: No, you see . . .

Milt: Oh, forget it.

This was long before Whoopi Goldberg, Billy Crystal, and Robin Williams all made *fucking* almost the only adjective in our language. It's a reflection of our times, so don't knock it. These are our great comedians, to me and to most everyone.

When I read over this exact conversation as I remember it, I realize now he could have been coming on to me. What a compliment! I should have been honored, even though Milt had a wife and I had a husband, and they weren't in Chicago with us. My husband, Alexander Carson, was called the Murderous Ax, center on the Ottawa Rough Riders; he was Chan's father.

Milt used to tell me how proud he was of his wife's intelligence. She was the editor of some intellectual magazine. And his son, George, was going to be a brilliant lawyer, he was sure. He told me he never could understand why his wife later divorced him. I decided not to give him any clues. Let him figure it out for himself.

In Seattle at the Fifth Avenue Theatre, my dressing room always looked out on a known gay bar called Sonya's. I've played that theatre four times, and each time the fleet happened to be in simultaneously. So I asked Milt, "Milt, how is it that there is a steady stream of uniformed Navy men going directly from all those submarines and battleships into Sonya's Gay Bar?" "Well," said Milt, "it was a long war."

The Vamp was my only flop, so of course I learned more from that show than any other. Isn't that always the case? We learn more from failure than from success!

If Milt Rosenstock was your friend, he never left you when you needed him. Now with me, he supported, sustained, and laughed me back to life through the whole lying mess of *The Vamp*.

No one with the show would ever listen to any of the reasons why *I* wanted to do the story of Theda Bara. A flop show is always the star's fault. It should be. I should have walked out. But that's another story, and I'm certainly not a musical comedy book writer. That's a tricky art in itself. Of course, the script of *The Vamp* had to be changed every day . . . to no avail, because the entire show was basically not well thought out. In Washington, D.C., at the National Theatre, again Milt stayed with me in my dressing room before each show. I was cramming the new lines into myself. Milt finally said, "You listen to me, schvester [sister]. You can't go out onstage in this frightened *cronkite* [sickness] *ziddling* [shaking] like palsy."

Me: Then will you hold the script and throw me the new lines if I need them?

Milton: Yes. Now let me tell you a joke. It'll relax you. Ready? This man died. He saw God. Then he came back to life. Everyone heard he had seen God. Every TV channel, newspaper, and magazine came to interview him. "All right. Now, tell us, what is God like?" The man replied: "Well, first off, She's black."

This joke sent me onstage still laughing. I was doing better than I thought I would until my first song. Suddenly one whole line escaped me. I hummed it to keep with the orchestra. But the next line wouldn't come to me. I just stood there. Milton had to hold thirty-six musicians in midair. He stopped the orchestra. Silence.

Milt (in his Brooklyn accent): You didn't mind the Schmitchet (baton).

Because the microphones were in the footlights in those days, his ad-lib rang out over the audience.

Me: Milton, what is the next line?

Milt picked up the script, thumbed the pages, and read the lyric "But when I growl and howl and chew the scenery."

Me: No, Milt. The lyric after that.

He threw one white typewritten page high up into the beam of the spotlight and yelled, "Oh, here. I'm everybody's baby."

Me: No. No. That's the title of the song. We all know that by now. Please, go back one more line.

Milt: I can't go back, Bubeleh! I just threw those lyrics away. You want this? No? This? No? This?

We got into a "fight." We were both embarrassed, but the audience seemed to be eating it up. Milt built the velocity of the fight like a great cantor. This sort of exchange went on all through the matinee. Finally, he fanned all the pages into the air, pointed straight up, and said, "Ask Her."

Just before the evening show a straight wire came for me. It was from Tom Prideaux, the one-man theatre editorialist of *Life* magazine. It said,

> 23 Skiddoo, we love you.
> You're on the cover of Life in three weeks!

We had no idea he was out there for that matinee, along with Mary Lee Logan Leatherbee.

Tom told somebody, who told me, that he thought it was a terrific refreshing idea to costar the conductor and the star. I said, "Did he actually *like* this show?" He only said, "He thought you and Milton were marvelous together."

By the time we got to New York, the show was frozen (no more changes). So we got to secure our lines and all. Milton didn't have to cue me. Opening night it rained heavily. I couldn't hear a peep out of the audience, but I remember instinct telling me not to force it: Don't press. You can't make them like this show. Just let it slide through your fingers into failure, like a muddy rainstorm on your prom dress. There's nothing you can do to stop it, so just let it die. If it won't hold up without your forcing it, it won't hold up anyway. It was difficult to do, of course, but at least I didn't insult anyone's intelligence.

The main thing I learned from this experience was: If there is no "benevolent despot" at the head, then the book writer thinks the show is about *this* plot, the choreographer thinks it's about the dances, the composer, about the music, the costumer and set designer man, how it looks, the lyricist, the lighting man, yet another. And I'm sure *I* thought it was about something nobody else thought of. No "holy city" ever descended on that show, and by the time it didn't, it was too late.

In the first edition of Walter Kerr's review of *The Vamp*, in the first paragraph he said, "Miss Channing is the victim of gangsters." He was so accurate. At that time, Kerr wrote for the *Herald Tribune*, and they took that immediately out of all following editions. How I wish I had it. The script wasn't anything like what I told them I thought it should be, and when I said I wanted to leave, Marty Cohen insisted that it would be criminal of me to desert them after all the work and money they'd put in. All I had to do was say, "You aren't doing anything I ask you to do, so I owe you nothing." But I didn't say it, because without asking me they had published for months before that I was committed only to their show when I carefully wasn't.

Life's cover, however, came out, so the darned show wouldn't close for weeks.

People were confused by poor Tom Prideaux and his *Life* article. Greer Garson came backstage to see me opening night, which was brave of her. I asked her, "Was it all that bad?"

"Yes," she said. "But I want you to know I had *six* flops in a row in London before I got *Mrs. Miniver* and the sequels. Don't you forget that. It won't be the last of you." I've loved her and the memory of her ever since.

Later, when George Burns and I played the Majestic Theatre in Dallas with our two-man show, Greer Garson was married to Buddy Fogelson, who was the main support for building the gorgeous Dallas Symphony Hall. She came to see us every single performance and brought us home with her one night. George whispered to me, "Do you think she misses show business?"

I personally think (although I could tell how much she cared for her husband) that she would have traded places with me even after my flop and everything embarrassing and horrible about it.

George Burns phoned me as soon as he read the bad reviews on *The Vamp*. I learned then, by the way, that's when you need people. So, in memory of George, I phone other theatre people when their show gets panned.

George Burns wasn't the only one to call me after the show got panned. Charles Lowe also called, and without saying hello or anything said, "Now there's nothing older than last week's *Life* cover, so we've got to get to work." I thought he was funny at the time.

Charles told me he would see to it I could get Chan from his paternal grandmother in Canada and fly to Las Vegas so that I could establish residency and get a divorce from my football-playing husband. Within six weeks I had my divorce, Charles and I were married, and he legally became Chan's father.

The first year of our marriage, Charles was still employed by Erwin Wasey, the advertising agency. His job was to represent the sponsor Carnation milk to Burns and Allen. That first year, Erwin Wasey made a big merger with the Ruthrauff and Ryan Agency. They held a huge tea so that wives of men in both companies could meet and perhaps eventually become one big happy family. When I arrived at this tea, they asked me to pour. Now anyone who asks me to pour tea deserves what he or she gets, right? I mean, wouldn't you guess that unless an actor has had a scene that involved pouring tea graciously, how would she ever know the little tricks of making it all go smoothly?

I was wearing one contact lens at a time, shifting it from one eye to the other every two hours so that I could be only half as uncomfortable as with both. The result was that I often saw two teacups where there was only one, so I poured the tea carefully onto the tablecloth or the rug. Howard Williams, the big boss (Charles told me beforehand), had a warm and friendly wife, Catherine Williams, who tried to help me but turned out to be no help at all because she disintegrated into a fit of the giggles. Another Mrs. Williams, Deedie (same family), who was born with quiet, chiseled, obvious aristocracy, at least was able to stop me from scalding ladies' hands. My gratitude to her was so deep that Deedie Williams and I remained friends over a lifetime, or at least for as long as Charles lived.

She wanted to go to the Lenox Avenue Ballroom in Harlem with me to dance and learn the latest steps. I truly adored the Lenox Ballroom because I didn't have to waste time with anyone white who asked me to dance with him since I was usually the only white person there and everyone was very kind. Once, when I went there alone, an excellent dancer escorted me to the nearest bus stop and waited for it with me to be sure I was safe. I realized, though, that what my mother told me about my heritage must be true, because Deedie did not cotton to the Lindy, or Peckin, or sliding through people's legs like I did. Of course, I had gone there alone for years before, since I couldn't miss Fats Waller at the piano singing "Your Feet's Too Big," or little Maxine Sullivan doing "Loch Lomond," or Chick Webb and His Orchestra playing "A-Tisket, A-Tasket" sung by his adopted daughter Ella Fitzgerald . . . so young and skinny then.

Deedie enjoyed seeing the fabulous shows at the Apollo Theatre. The great tap dancer Honi Coles was the manager of it then. I was in *Blondes* with him and his tap dancing partner, Cholly Atkins. We toured the show together, too, doing hospital shows on the side all along the way because Honi had contracted malaria in World War II and it reinfected him whenever it wanted to. He wanted the three of us to entertain the permanently disabled veterans, so we did. Tommy Tune later used Honi as a dancing partner in his terrific Broadway musical *My One and Only*. Honi was without a doubt the most elegant, cool, smooth African-American in show business. I thought he was highly intelligent, mainly because I learned so much from him. He was born with a certain ease. He was sophisticated yet uncritical. In Chicago they took me often to the South Side to the Grand Ballroom, where I could learn more of the latest steps. I wasn't married to Charles yet, so they adopted me. I had a truly great time with them.

Honi is the one who told me about Dr. Loyal Davis and the interns at Loyal's hospital. I must digress here and tell you about Dr. Loyal Davis and his wife, Dee Dee, spelled differently.

Following the *Blondes* tour, the next time I played Chicago was with *Wonderful Town* at the Shubert Theatre. I lived in an apartment building right next to the Davises. She was president of the Sarah Siddons Award committee, and when I won the prestigious award that year, everyone told me I couldn't possibly have won it if I weren't Dee Dee's friend. I didn't agree; I thought I deserved it. "It doesn't matter," they said. "If you were Dame Sybil Thorndike still playing Juliet, you couldn't have won it without Dee Dee's personal decision that it go to you." She surely was good to me.

Chan was two years old then. I took his nanny with me, but Dee Dee saw to it he had a playground right near us with children his age to play with and all the activities two-year-olds need. I went to her apartment every Sunday for dinner. Actually, Mary Martin prepared me for her friend Dee Dee and her husband, who was the renowned brain surgeon. Mary told me their daughter, Nancy Davis, married the movie star Ronald Reagan. Sometimes Nancy was there.

Now one day Eartha Kitt phoned me to say she was in Chicago to break in a play for Broadway called *Mrs. Patterson*, which, by the way, turned out to be well approved by the New York critics. This was around 1954. Eartha said, "Carol, would you believe it, every hotel in Chicago has told me they're all full when they see me, even the one where I had a reservation. We're rehearsing day and night with changes and I haven't time to commute all the way from the South Side." I said, "Eartha, today is Sunday. Come with me to the home of the lady who runs *every*thing in Chicago. She can pull anything off. It's always a buffet dinner, so one more won't matter to her." We went right over together. Idiot me! Why didn't I phone first?

We arrived. Dee Dee was indeed welcoming to Eartha. Loyal began talking at the table, saying, "You know, when these gangsters come into my office wanting a bullet removed from someone's head, I refuse them." Loyal was the type of man with whom you want to agree. So I said, "Yes, I can understand that. You don't want to get involved with the Mafia." Loyal said, "Mafia, forget it! They're Italians." Then he started on the Polacks and every group he could think of. In hindsight he was, I suppose, building to the blacks.

Dee Dee took Eartha and me by the hand into the kitchen and said, "Oh, Loyal's on his ethnic speech again. Tell me, what can I do for you?" We told her Eartha was in trouble. Dee Dee got right on the kitchen phone and called the Allerton House on the next street behind her apartment building. She told them she wanted their red carpet rolled out for Eartha and that she'd be phoning every couple of days to find out how they were treating her. Then she gave Eartha her car and driver so she was able to get her luggage at her theatre and check in at the Allerton.

I have to tell this story because in Kitty Kelley's scandalous book about Nancy Reagan, Kitty told this same story, only she said Dee Dee berated me for bringing "that woman" into her home. Kitty Kelley phoned me often when she was in the process of writing her Nancy book. I never took the calls. Neither did Charles. Would you? No! So Kitty must have settled for interviewing someone who wasn't there that night at all, and this is my chance to erase a total untruth. Dee Dee was a magnificent lady, as you can tell from this true story.

allulah Bankhead and I had the same birthday. Also, we were both born at 8:30 at night, only she was in Alabama and I was in Washington State, so there had to be a three-hour time discrepancy. The difference of the year we were born she utterly ignored.

As I've told you, Tallulah was the first actress to appear on the cover of *Time* magazine. I was the second, we surmised. At least we were the only two *we* remembered. In those days *Time* put only world leaders, politicians, financial figures, sports champions, that sort of thing on its cover. Today it often has performers, but at the time we were quite tickled with ourselves.

Later we appeared at the *Time* magazine celebration party for all the people who had been on the cover. This was before I met Charles, so I came alone. It was hosted by Henry Luce, who personally met all the guests, and Clare Boothe Luce, who was the warmest, most devastatingly feminine lady ever . . . and pretty! Well, we all knew that from her pictures. But she was laughing for some unknown reason as she stood at the door of the Waldorf's Grand Ballroom greeting her guests. I looked behind me; there was no one, so I decided t'was I. I couldn't stop laughing *with* her; she was so contagious. It was indeed I she was laughing at, I found out, but she never told me and we celebrated our first meeting right there. This was just after the *Blondes* opening.

I've often asked, and especially after meeting Mrs. Luce, "Why are pretty girls almost always so sweet and friendly?" Finally, after I met Charles years later, I got an answer. "Because you're not in competition with them." And do you know, I married him anyway after that? Well, I thought it was funny then.

There were place cards at the dinner tables for us all, with four at each table. I had Donald Budge, the great tennis champion, on my left; Cardinal Spellman in his little costume on my right; and across from me was Jean Kerr, the finest comedy book writer, to me, since Clarence Day or Woody Allen. I knew, of course, the name Don Budge, but Tommy Tune and I think it's a tennis course and possibly a golf court that he played on. So I couldn't ask him, "What did you win, Mr. Budge, and when and where?" You see, by the time everyone concerned with a Broadway show gets it to look as if it could be a hit, they have no idea what Donald Budge or even O. J. Simpson ever did.

I tried to talk with Cardinal Spellman, but Betty Beale, at the table behind me, whispered, "He's known for being extremely taciturn." She was right. He never ever answered me. So finally Jean Kerr said to him hopefully, "I met the Pope." It got a nod of his head. But it didn't trigger any mutual acquaintance whatsoever. The cardinal never said a word, not even to a devout Catholic like Jean.

Well! Talloo and I celebrated all the birthdays we could together. She took home the booze, I took home the birthday cakes, and I *looked* it, but most women think themselves to be overweight I found out. The first mutual birthday party was when I was one of twenty unknowns in *Lend an Ear* running in Los Angeles and she was also in Hollywood to finish the movie *Lifeboat*. Out of *Lifeboat* came the oft-told story of what to do about her not wearing any panties under that mink coat. They didn't know which department's problem it was. Who was going to tell her? Makeup, Hair, or Wardrobe?

At another mutual birthday she informed me, "Listen, dahling, everybody great was born on our birthday. Franklin Roosevelt was born on our birthday." (No, he was one day earlier.) "Julius Caesar was born on our birthday." (How could she have known that?) "Napoleon Bonaparte" (now I knew this was all what she preferred to believe) "was born on our birthday."

Me: And Eddie Cantor.

Talloo (thundering): Oh, now you've completely destroyed my point! Don't interrupt me. Napoleon, even Jesus Christ almighty was born on our birthday, and don't let those Romannnnn . . . calendars fool you.

Another very important element Tallulah and I had in common: Richard Maney. He was always her personal publicist. My father used to point out to my mother and me, when I was in junior high school, "That takes courage to offer the press the whole truth of an episode with which someone is trying to blackmail Tallulah."

I remember the newspapers said her secretary, who made out her checks, had Tallulah sign them and then added hundreds of dollars in front of the figures after that.

When she was discovered, the secretary tried to blackmail her boss with incidents Tallulah didn't want made public. No newspaper mentioned anything she tried to use for blackmail. That had to be Dick Maney at work. His charisma, like my father's, was enormous. As I said in my introduction, This is *my* book, so I can write anything I want to. If it's annoying you're free to skip it. If it's not annoying to you, then you might as well go along with me that everybody great was like my father, okay?

Again, Dick Maney and my father were molded out of the same clay, cut from the same cloth, wallowing in the enjoyment of their self-earned education that had opened them up to the big, wide, wonderful world of poetry, essays, and the onomatopoeia of the English language.

My third meeting with Tallulah was when we were both guests on the Jimmy Durante TV show. She, Jimmy, and I had a song together. On the day of the live broadcast she came bursting into my dressing room yelling, "Oh my God, I've got laryngitis."

I reacted as you would have. I was perplexed and calmly said, "Well, Tallulah, who's going to know the difference?" I shouldn't have said that.

She lunged on me. Her voice dropped two more octaves. "Can't you hear it, you fool?" She shook me. "Tell your father to pray for me. Pleeeeeeese! Do it now." It always amazed me that she knew so much about my background.

Just then Daddy walked in. She didn't even let him take off his coat. She threw her arms around his neck and hung there like a bib. She was surprisingly small. "Oh, dear Mr. Channing, please help me. Do something! I've got laryngitis. Make it go away."

Daddy put his arm around her and sat her down. She was like a little girl. I never saw her like that. She listened. She cried. They whispered, so I don't know just what he said. My father didn't find her eccentric at all. He seemed to know all she needed was a little understanding. We're all wired for love, and I guess Talloo needed it as much as the most starved of us. Her automatic security and sweetness with Daddy made me suddenly wonder if she wasn't in love with Dick Maney all the years of their association. She seemed to know my father well. I was happy for her. I knew she had stage fright.

Tallulah spent a lot of the week of rehearsal for Jimmy's show saying to me, "Just because your father's a newspaperman, Dick Maney is partial to you," or "Dick was born in Seattle and so were you and he loves publicizing it." How did she know so much about me? Maybe Dick Maney.

Anyway, she did a terrific Durante show. I don't know, as I said, what Daddy and Talloo talked about, but she wanted me to be with her for her opening night of Noël Coward's *Private Lives* on Broadway. She sent me into the audience to watch her perform Noël's character Amanda and then report to her at intermission.

"I know, but dahling," she'd ask, "is it Amanda?"

Me: Oh, Tallulah, this audience couldn't be happier. Why shouldn't Amanda be you? They bought their tickets to see *you*, and they're getting *you*, every nuance. They don't know Noël Coward wrote it for Gertrude Lawrence. I'm thrilled with you as Amanda, and so are they.

She let out that terrible bleat that was her version of crying. (Some idiot must have insisted she play it like Gertrude Lawrence, the original. *Why?*)

Thank you, my father, for another soul-fulfilling friendship.

An interesting quirk of Talloo's was one that I suspect very few people have. Some people love to appear in the nude . . . for anything from auspicious occasions to just putting the garbage out in the hall. Sue Mengers appears to be such a person. She was the personality agent who helped put Streisand in the *Hello, Dolly!* movie. They don't appear in that condition in order to be lewd or even sexy. They don't seem to be showing off, either. Now Sue, for instance, is pear-shaped. I know because I spent a weekend with her at Jerry Herman's house on Fire Island. As each of Jerry's guests awakened in the morning and came into the kitchen, we would find one part or another of Sue left out in the breeze. Later, when she entered Jerry's pool, all of her was out. Many of Jerry's neighbors were around the pool watching her swim.

They'd say: Are you in show business, honey?

Sue: No, only sort of.

Boys: What business are you in?

Sue: I'm a literary agent and also a writer myself.

Boys: Oh, what's your name, sweetie?

Sue: Audrey Wood.

Boys: Audrey Wood! You're a well-known name in the literary world.

Sue: Yes.

(Actually Audrey Wood was a *great* name to be conjured with in the book world, but then you knew that.)

As plethoric as Sue's figure was, she used her pudgy little fingers in a very dainty manner, often with each of her pinkies held out. As she got slowly out of the pool and put on her cotton sweater, it was noticeable that the sweater ended where the bottoms of two soft pink cheeks peeked out. She made a few delicate efforts to pull it down in the front, but it snapped right back up again. I never met Audrey Wood, but her reputation is that of a woman of integrity and, of course, impeccable literary taste. I imagine her office being besieged by summer habitués of Fire Island and Miss Wood finally announcing: "I was never in Jerry Herman's pool. I've never even seen Fire Island. Why am I plagued by this irritating identification?" Sue must savor that thought, too.

Sue especially enjoyed putting her little garbage pail out in the hallway of her New York apartment building each night wondering if she could make it back inside before her heavy kitchen door would close behind her nudity, leaving her locked out. One night it finally did close. She told us she had no recourse but to knock on the apartment door across the hall, which a nice young man opened. While she explained what had happened, she could see a gray-haired lady, perhaps his mother, sitting behind him. The man quickly closed his door, leaving her in the hall again. She was therefore forced to ring the elevator button. Of course the elevator had people in it, staring at her while she slowly explained to the elevator boy her labyrinthine tale.

Jerry Herman and all of us made up the rest for her. We told her, "Of course you asked him if you could ride down with all of them to the lobby. You crossed the lobby to the concierge's desk, only to find there was no other key, so you went round with the glass revolving door to hail a cab back to your office for the other key." She cut us off because she felt we were just making fun of her. We were. I do not know if Sue's story was true or not, but I suspect most of it was. Tallulah could easily have done the same thing.

Years later, Orry-Kelly, who created movie gowns that were works of art, was fitting me. He had a mouth full of straight pins to pin the dress on me but went right on with his steady stream of talk.

Orry: I don't know why Tallulah does that all the time.

Me: Does what, Orry?

Orry: She gives these grand cocktail parties, invites the finest people, and then when she opens the door to usher them in, she's wearing a large black garden hat, a strand of pearls, and her black pumps. That is all. And, you know, it isn't pretty.

Me: What isn't, Orry?

Orry: It looks like an old Chinaman's mustache. . . . It's food stained . . . and it's on the bias. It has a sneer.

To drop two names and a place, I was first introduced to Marlene Dietrich by Tallulah in the lobby of the Desert Inn in Las Vegas. Is that a good drop? However, what usually happens when I'm with two celebrities is they're so entranced with one another, they leave me with nothing to do but count the diamonds in my bracelet while I pretend to be happy. Does that happen to you, too? I'm invisible in a three-way conversation. Not with you would I be. We're only invisible when we're in between two Greek gods, even though they're both dear, kind people, as vulnerable as you and I. Have you found that? Let's not dwell on it. That's their problem, not ours.

My second encounter with Marlene was when her daughter, Maria Riva, was playing in Chicago at the Drury Lane Theatre and I was in *Wonderful Town* at the Shubert. I met Maria in 1949 on the Milton Berle TV show. We've enjoyed a heavenly friendship ever since. Maria and I made a date to meet Mama Marlene after our shows. Dietrich was arriving on the Twentieth Century Limited train and was to go straight to her old hangout Gibby's Bar and Grill in Shubert Alley to meet her daughter.

Prior to Mama's arrival, Maria and I were trying to save a table for the three of us. The circus was also in town. Two members of its audience sat down with us uninvited saying, "Ain't you Maria Riva?" and "You're not Carol Channing!" Stupidly I said, "I'm not?" I wasn't thinking because I was trying to figure out how to keep the seat ready for La Dietrich. They were firmly immovable. So I beckoned Maria to come with me to the bar to the safety of the *Wonderful Town* chorus (now called the ensemble). A touring company is like a family. We're protective of one another. Just as they were squeezing to make room for us, the two circus attendees were on our tails.

Maria and I ran back to our table, dragging two chorus members to sit with us. Too late! The two civilians sat down just before us and almost got in a verbal fight with the ensemble. They went on asking Maria and me questions until Dietrich appeared. She came straight to our table, and stood to dictate to us: "Maria, you sit here. Carol, you sit there. I will sit in this chair, and you two, out." They ran like bunnies. It was as simple as that. Sprung and leaping with fright over Mama is what they were. Will Maria and I ever garner that kind of respect from two beer-guzzling strangers?

Marlene, lowering her famous heavy eyelids, said to the waiting waiter, "The usual." It arrived almost immediately . . . little squares of assorted cheeses. She started in without bothering with any grand greetings, or even small greetings, to her daughter, yet they seemed to me to be so close they didn't have to bother with that rot. She'd come from L.A. by train, it had to have been a while since they saw each other, but Maria appeared securely and contentedly used to this. Good.

Even though the cheeses were in very small squares, from the first bite on Marlene had rapid-fire bite-bite-bite-bite-bites with only her front teeth, like a rabbit. It was startling, she made no attempt to hide it. I realized she didn't have any back teeth. She must have had them pulled after *Der blaue Engel*. She was, by the way, dynamite in *The Blue Angel*, her first movie from Berlin that Americans know of. It's what caused all the Sturm und Drang about Dietrich. Through her then round face and unstudied brunette hair came waves of concentrated thoughts of sex, with no seeming awareness of her own face or body at all, only cleanly mental hypnosis and an underlying good nature that must have disappeared with the teeth. She was powerful in that subtitled movie. Over my lifetime, for one, unforgettable. Until she came to Hollywood, she was the only human being before or since her who had a healthy, joy-of-living energy underneath relaxed, sinful sex. At least she made sex seem sinful.

See, what angers me is there is a stock European female sexpot. To Americans they seem phony, because in comparison we're steak fed and athletic and usually unaware of ourselves. These European dime a dozens are mysterious, silent, thin, more of a presence than human beings—faces in the passing train. Utterly no sense of humor, especially about themselves. But Dietrich in *Blue Angel* was far from ordinary, like those women. I read in Maria's biography of her mother that Josef von Sternberg was stipulated in her contract to be her only director in Hollywood. He made her a walking Hurrell still photo.

Remember Hurrell? He was great, but he made all his subjects look alike when they were important enough to have their own individual dynamics. He made them all look as if they had no back teeth and no interest in anyone but themselves. Oh well, I'm mad at von Sternberg. He had an assembly-line mind, and Marlene did not. I'm mad because such a talent shouldn't have handed herself over to someone else. This is probably the answer to why brilliant minds like Barbara Walters say, "Never mix business with sex." Instinctively I agree. The man you're attracted to is the man who owns you. Dangerous when it comes to your work. Your work is *you*, with no other influences. Your boss or director can order you around all he wants. You can follow him implicitly provided you're not in love with him.

Well, according to Maria, von Sternberg and Dietrich was one hot affair for years. The moment he went back to Germany she became the one and only great Dietrich, not a second Garbo, not a second anybody, I thought. There was a scene with John Wayne in a Hollywood movie of her descending a stairway in a white-and-gold Navy officer's uniform and cap, all her hair scooped up under the cap, one hand in her pocket, and John Wayne laughing at her. Maria told me that scene was made while Wayne had made up his mind he was not going to let her get into bed with him. She never made it. She was at top pitch, pulling every color of herself out on camera, but looking at him. Wow! It's true. Don't dissipate the attraction off camera or offstage. The audience gets the impact instead. On second thought, how should I know? I never had an affair. I keep telling myself the deep grooves of Puritanism in me surely have some payoff.

So! One night in Vegas, Lucille Ball and Desi Arnaz brought Dietrich to the show. I prayed to do her accurately. That was before I found out the last person to know what your victim is like is the victim herself. There were seven boys doing me in Vegas at the time, all acting exactly alike, with not one tiny thing that resembled me, I felt. However, George Burns laughed his head off at them. All I could see on a couple of them was five o'clock shadow, but how come they all assumed exactly the same weird mannerisms? Then I knew anyone who knows what he himself acts like is totally phony and therefore a bloody bore. Well, even Dietrich, whose greatest creation was herself, didn't really know how she looked and sounded when she did what she did. She was busy thinking great thoughts, though, or we women wouldn't all have worn men's pantsuits for the first time in history hoping we looked something like her. I did, anyway, wear men's suits . . . hoping . . . something like . . . maybe.

Oh! Lucy, Desi, and Marlene! I forgot. So I did George's Dietrich number, ending with "you dunderblitzen dummkopf (spotlight man)" (you see, I rehearsed him to keep moving it off her). I got up off the floor and explained to the audience (as me) that the great lady herself was in the audience and would the spotlight man please move my spot to her. He did. Where we knew she was sitting before was an empty chair! She was nowhere to be found. The maître d' said she didn't pass him on her way out, that she must have gone down the laundry chute. Even Lucy and Desi didn't see her leave, and they were sitting with her. Lots of national press came that night to see her reaction. They caught up with her at the Desert Inn, where she announced, "They don't want stars anymore in Las Vegas—only this cheap clop-throp like Carol Channing."

After finishing my act I was in misery over her. Charles said he was leaving to get the press back. "Just keep crying like that and don't stop." I, of course, couldn't stop. It was a reaction to being nervous about her, and why wouldn't I be? She's not a barrel of laughs about other people's acts to begin with, let alone that she herself should emerge as laughable to an audience. He returned saying, "This is the best thing that could have happened to you. The more questions the press asks her, the madder she gets." Her remarks went all over the world. The immortal Hirschfeld did a brilliant caricature of Dietrich and me facing forward, seated on twin wooden *Blue Angel* chairs, the only difference being our faces. It was blown up in *The New York Times* the very next Sunday. Charles was right. Mary Martin told me she was in Siam when our interviews were in the *International Herald Tribune*. I was not aware that I was that well-known at the time, but I was *now*!

The press asked Dietrich if she thought some of the lines were funny, like asking a man at the first table to come back to her dressing room for "a little Schnitzel à la Holstein mit an egg on the top? Hah? We'll talk about *you* for a while. How did *you* like my performance?" It was all very true to her nature and the audience knew it, but it obviously fell on her ears and eyes with a dull Teutonic thud. Noël Coward, her dear friend, for a while, told me I dropped twenty pounds as I turned into her, and he said my facial bone structure became fragile. "It was extremely accurate," he said. Yes. That's show business. That's our job.

But wait! Desi and Lucy came backstage to scold me. Lucy said, "Oh, Carol, you don't have fun with icons like that. It's almost sacrilege." So this noble speech to me was in deference to their friendship. You see, Marlene had made it her business to become Lucy's and Desi's closest family friend. Whoever the top names—"Papa" Hemingway, Noël, Jean Gabin, Yul, Orson Welles—were at the time, she glued herself to them, for only as long as they were at the very top! And do you know, in two weeks Lucy was doing Dietrich on her *I Love Lucy* TV show? Talk about sacrilegious! She must have been laughing at the idea while she was scolding me. Then she did me! I was so pleased to be done by an attractive, feminine woman for the first time. It's always these bass-voiced laryngitic men, as I say. It makes one wonder if one has a glandular imbalance of some sort that no one ventures to tell one about. However, the last line of Lucy's sketch on me was "Oh, officer, I didn't mean any harm."

Officer: Harm? Look what you just did to Marlene Dietrich and Carol Channing.

I love being grouped with Marlene Dietrich and Lucille Ball. Nice company, don't you think?

*A*fter Las Vegas, Herman Levin (coproducer of *Gentlemen Prefer Blondes* and the sole producer of *My Fair Lady*) and Anita Loos were organizing a musical for me. Charles heard about this, and he told me precisely what to say to them. I memorized it, said it, and after I said it to them, Anita was alone with me. She said, "Well, you certainly killed that proposition dead, right in the beginning, before you even heard all of the proposal." Besides Anita, I had eliminated Herman as well. I adored Herman as a producer of *Blondes*, but Charles told me that what he had me say to Herman and Anita was very good business and that I couldn't possibly understand. He was right. I didn't understand. Charles produced *Showgirl* instead on Broadway, which was largely the Las Vegas act. You don't do nightclub acts on Broadway.

In the photo insert, you'll find a picture of Queen Elizabeth and me at my third command performance. I began to sink into the deep curtsy Yul Brynner taught me. Queen Elizabeth said, "Oh, please, that's not necessary for you at all. You are an American." Isn't that interesting? We must all remember that in case we run into the Queen.

Yul was just off camera on my left, making sure to be next to me for nudges, kicks, and moral support. The Queen was saying, "You have done me a great honor, bringing your magnificent Broadway musical shows to the British Isles. I consider it a personal favor. We are most grateful."

Me: We are most grateful for this welcome you've given us.

The Queen: I want to be sure you understand that I am welcoming you at this moment. I want you to know how welcome you personally are.

I remembered she refers to herself as "we," as in "we are most grateful." And I'd gone and said, "We are most grateful for this welcome you've given *us*." Did she think I suddenly decided I was plural, too? In order to be certain, I stood corrected and from then on referred to myself in the singular.

Yul told me later, "No, she wasn't correcting you, she was having one of her rare good times with you."

Me: Oh.

To continue with the Queen, she had memorized the titles of eleven Broadway shows I had done, two Theatre Guild tours, and a national symphony concert tour. I heard Prince Philip was a great theatre buff. Later, thinking back on the conversation, I imagined Philip standing at the foot of their bed saying to his be-pillowed, sleepy wife, "And then what show did she do? No, no, no, do get it right."

Of course, I wound up crazy about the Queen. What a bother she had gone to, to get all that correctly! To me there couldn't be a finer public relations representative for England. No pretension. Dead on for real. She'd never say anything just to be courteous. She'd only say the truth. She wound up with me with "You've honored us." She went on to Yul, then suddenly returned to me and said, "I meant that, most sincerely." With Yul she didn't try to make every thought so important. She treated him as if she had said enough of all this to him before and was glad to see him again. Of course, as I say, I was gone over the Queen. With apologies to Joan Rivers, I think she's a living doll, and she works like a chain-gang member on her job.

I especially remembered what Queen Elizabeth said to me because a part of this command performance was a girl named Janet Brown, who was popular in London for doing imitations. She did one of me at that performance that was apparently hilarious. I, of course, adored it. She made me an eccentric American who sold her own show by repeating my opening speech, "Matinees Wednesdays and Saturdays, with convenient parking facilities immediately adjacent to the Drury Lane Theatre in Soldiers' Field" (big laugh, because Soldiers' Field is almost in Ireland). I was delighted that the British audience responded to Janet's jokes about me. I didn't realize they noticed me that carefully. I suspect they enjoy teasing Americans. Many English actors like Maggie Smith and Rex Harrison wouldn't stoop to such flagrant public relations, but with me, and I think with most Americans, it's just genuine enthusiasm for the show we're in at the moment. Maggie refused to let a photographer take her picture with me in my dressing room after my show. I've been hurt ever since. What's wrong with it? Oh well, someday we'll laugh about it.

On this same subject, one night my phone rang where I was staying in London, in a carriage house, if you please. Charming! It was "Rafe" Richardson as they called him. Do you believe it? *Sir* Ralph Richardson, one of the three greatest actors in the history of the British theatre. Well, I knew him—that's why he called. We did a television special in London together with John Gielgud doing a tap dance with me, and I found them to be two of the funniest people ever. Ralph could do an asthmatic cough that sounded like his last long wheeze. I don't know how he did it, when he himself actually hadn't a sign of asthma. How could he make near death so hysterically funny? But that was his magic. Well, this time he was on my phone one night after both our shows. He had got home on his motorcycle with his helmet, leather jacket, and goggles, as usual.

"Caddol (Carol)," he said, "I've found the secret to a full house for as long as we wish."

Me: Oh? Please, Ralph, tell me.

Ralph: I've just opened in Chekhov's *The Seagull*.

Me: Yes. How is it going?

Ralph: It's long. Veddy lonnnngg. I don't enter until the third act, and that goes on even longer. But, Caddol, no one knows where we're playing or that we're playing at all, it's become such a guarded secret. When finally one man who combed London came up with a ticket he shouted, "Ahaaaa! I've got a ticket. I've found the theatre. What a prize!"

"No one knows how to get one." Ralph continued, "It's become a big treasure hunt. Caddol, you must paint your *Hallo Dawly* sign black. They don't particularly want to see *The Seagull* again, but they think they've won the game just to find where it is. It's the most coveted ticket in London. *Your* show would run forever. Take my advice."

He was probably quite right. The British don't seem to understand cheap, American publicity, but they forgive you if you're a comic, I've noticed.

What Charles and I did create together was a circle of friends, including truly wonderful people like George Burns and Gracie Allen. As I've said, Charles represented their sponsor, Carnation milk, to Burns and Allen. He became one of Gracie's close friends by reading the Dailies (that's *Variety* and *The Hollywood Reporter*) every weekday morning to her. They were both Irish, so they had that same Jean Kerr, Helen Hayes, Orry-Kelly flash of wit. He used to insert items like this as he read to Gracie: "We're sorry to report that at seventy-eight Louella Parsons has experienced a miscarriage." Charles told me his own news bits would help waken Gracie if she dozed in her makeup chair. By now you don't give a fig how I happen to be close to Burns and Allen. So I can tell you about them here.

The Lunts and The Burnses

N *ow!* Did you know that for thirty-six years the Lunts and the Burnses wrote each other fan letters of the highest praise? But they never, ever met. George could show me anything Alfred did onstage while giggling to himself at the deftness and subtlety of it. Alfred felt George was a master creator of a platform for Gracie and himself.

It was stunning how alike Lynn and Gracie were offstage. They even looked alike. Both George and Alfred married women who were their dreams of lovely ladies, of aristocracy, of integrity, intelligence, femininity and, of course, of high comedy. Then they proceeded to build dynasties around them.

Both these men had poverty-stricken lives as children. George danced and sang for pennies on the street corners of the Lower East Side. His father was in temple praying every day, all day, so George was the one money earner in his family. There were eleven children who slept in George's one bed. He gave his mother every last cent he earned, including a Bulova watch from the Presbyterians. George told me he said, "Mama, the Presbyterians gave me a Bulova watch. I think I'd like to become a Presbyterian." She said, "First you'll help me hang up the washing, and *then* you'll become a Presbyterian." George and Alfred and their backgrounds were extremely similar.

Alfred was the eldest son in his family. His father died when he was young, so his mother gave him the responsibilities of the father of the family. Anita Loos told me his mother didn't care for any girls Alfred showed interest in, but when his mother died she asked on her deathbed for Lynnie, not Alfred! Growing up, Alfred delivered newspapers before school. He thought the most beautiful house he delivered to or maybe in the whole world was Ten Chimneys. Lynn saw to it they could buy that house with their savings when they married.

They added a new wing with each show they toured and a guesthouse. Their set designer did his only job as an interior decorator on Ten Chimneys.

During the Los Angeles run of *The Visit*, Charles must have suggested to Gracie that she invite them to her house for dinner. I don't know how it happened because, I repeat, nobody ever tells me anything. Why don't they? Is it because I don't ask about anything? Anyway, we were driving to downtown Los Angeles to the Biltmore Hotel to pick them up. This was after several visits to Genesee Depot and Gracie Square, New York, and one in Milwaukee, when I was playing my London Drury Lane show. We four stayed in Milwaukee for dinner together. So I was totally at home with them. Well, I always was at home with them; they made you feel that way. I played the Biltmore Theatre three different shows and never knew the Biltmore Hotel grew right up out of the roof of the Biltmore Theatre. Well, it does, and the Lunts stayed right there, which confirmed my suspicion that they were two people after my own heart. Touring is no time for luxury. Both of the Lunts' homes were jewels, but the Biltmore Hotel was a typical downtown plebeian setup. However, it got the show on with far more efficiency. They invited us up to their suite, where Alfred said, "Lynnie has been dressing for this dinner since eleven o'clock this morning and she's still not ready. Lynnie!"

Lynn: Hello! I've got too much rouge on, haven't I?

Alfred: She's been putting on rouge and taking it off all day . . . changing her dress, her hair . . . Lynnie! Just have a big slug of scotch for your nerves and come on. You look fine, and don't look in a different mirror. You'll decide to put more rouge *on*. Now, doesn't that scotch make you feel better?

Lynn: No. I can't remember being more nervous than this.

She took my arm for strength, pulled herself up, and walked majestically to the elevator and then through the garage. I was so happy to return to her some of the security she gave me on that first "audition." I naturally would never admit it even to myself, but I sensed Lynnie wanted a strong American daughter. However, I'm sure if any actor knew them they would feel that way about both the Lunts. No! I'm not sure of that at all. At the risk of aggravating you, reader, with such egocentricity, I have to tell you the absolute truth. I wonder if other people have ever felt with certain people what I felt in their home and then every time I was with them, and that is: I finally must have done something right. I've died and returned to where I was born and raised, in harmony, in the abode of these two people, and I'm with them now again and all pieced together. Have you ever felt that? It was always so strong, this feeling with them, that I had to tell you.

When we arrived at the Burnses' house in Beverly Hills, I remember Alfred deliberately going ahead of any of us to greet Gracie, who was simultaneously opening the front door.

Alfred to Gracie: I'm glad I'm dizzy, because boys like dizzy girls and I like boys.

Gracie: Oh! Oh! I haven't thought of that line for thirty-six years.

It was Gracie's line from George and Gracie's first vaudeville sketch that George wrote for the two of them, and Alfred was in the audience.

Gracie screamed with surprise and laughter, and they hugged and hugged, while George ran down his little path to Lynn to help her out of the car and kiss her. Lynn stayed with George, adoring him. Gracie and Alfred seemed to be finishing the "Dizzy" sketch together. The famous two-way timing the two couples had with each other was every bit as exciting when they switched mates. I heard George say to Lynn: "You know, I have a new nephew who weighs five pounds without his dickie and eight pounds with . . ."

Lynn (joining George on "with"): . . . *with* his dickie, yes, yes, ah ha ha, of course.

Now that was the signature stamp of the Lunts' unique craft together. She would join Alfred on the last three or four words at the end of his sentence and they would enjoy it together. But she did it perfectly with George.

The chatter between the four of them built and went faster and faster. Four happier people you could never find. When we went in to sit down for dinner, Gracie suddenly realized that she'd been so nervous when she was setting the table, she forgot to set herself at the other end from George. She stood at her place while Daniel and Arlette (their couple) came in with a chair and a setting. The Lunts and Burnses were all already so giggly it didn't matter. What a historic evening! You, patient one, reading this, are the first person to share it with me. Well, besides Michael Korda and Chuck Adams, who decided to print all this chozzerai.

The Lunts played their last show, Dürrenmatt's *The Visit*, to great success on Broadway. I myself thought it was their finest.

They told us they decided to rent a Swiss chalet with the Dürrenmatts and discovered after they moved in together that the Dürrenmatts did not speak one word of English and the Lunts did not speak Swiss French. But they pantomimed and got through to one another completely successfully. Alfred was so proud of this that he didn't like admitting they did have a translator. He said the translator really wasn't necessary until typing the final script into English.

The Lunts were always at their most memorable in every play, but the older I get, the more the memory of *The Visit* rings a resounding bell of the truth about our lives, at least mine. More and more circumstances remind me that this already happened in *The Visit*, and the knowledge you gain from watching this play is the same knowledge you gain if you live long enough. To me it's saying, "If you have a little money or a lot, the world seems to revolve not around kindness and respect for one but around money. If you never pulled yourself together enough to make a little money, it often revolves around people being caring and loving to one another, otherwise the whole world seems to want your money and not want *you*. According to Dürrenmatt, when love goes awry, it's a violation against the divine powers that be."

In the process of watching Alfred Lunt become annihilated before our eyes I realized Studs Terkel could be right. He may indeed be the world's finest actor. In watching Lynn as Mrs. Zachanassian, I realized it's possible there is a very much alive Satan, and we'd better all watch out because its revenge is deadly. Well, if you didn't see it, then you *shoulda*. It might have changed your life, as it did mine.

There was a simple, sweet scene in a forest of both of them watching the birds as they talked old times. It was important for the audience to see their forever young romance in contrast to the rest of the story. Lynnie entered carried on a litter in a vermilion chiffon turban, a fire engine red wool suit with slightly darker big red cape, that good-taste Nancy Reagan red. Then sheer burgundy stockings right down to her garnet suede shoes. Dynamite! Obviously, the Lunts never minced around about who their characters were. Lynn's entrance was as totally "theatre" as when she took her bows from the audience (at least when I introduced them in the audience at the end of any show I was in). She bowed right, left, and center to the back of the house. Then regally raised her arm to all balconies, to right and left boxes, and took the house down for as long as she chose. Her final gesture was a queen's bow to me center stage, and I felt knighted in St. James's Court.

Alfred always took a very American relaxed bow, but never forgetting he had a great lady for a wife, so he did it slowly. Weren't we lucky to be within their life span? If you're going to bow, take stage and *do* it. Don't fool around with it. If you're absolutely honest with your grateful feelings, it becomes your own individual bow, and the audience knows it is true to your nature. Lynn's thoughts were I am upholding Ellen Terry's choice of me as her protégée, I am upholding the British Empire, and I hereby give you my love in return because this bow to you is very important to me."

Alfred had a slight glamour-boy slouch, but his thoughts were more how magnetized he was by all of us he was bowing to. His bow's sex appeal came from never forgetting the importance of Lynnie. Women (including me) loved that. Men, too, I guess, since all the world loves a lover. But he *did* love her, and that's why it affected us so. He genuinely never took his mind off her, onstage or off.

My bow is simply a celebration that all of us were uplifted for the last two and a half hours and now it's over and we're free to openly, unstintingly hug and kiss each other. We can laugh together on this bow because I and maybe you have been healed of whatever we came in with. My bow becomes abandoned because I'm so glad to be this healthy from doing this show just now.

I've seen some actors imitate someone else's bow, and it doesn't build the applause because, as I say, it's not true to their nature. It's difficult to find your true self, much easier to find the character you're playing but, as I say, just hand yourself to your understanding heart, and there you are, for better or for worse, but it's you.

The Lunts would often lock up playwrights in their guesthouse until they finished their work. With *Idiot's Delight* Robert Sherwood was locked up in the guesthouse and they did not let him out until he finished the play. That's exactly what they did! He got to go to their dining room for each meal but had to answer to how much he wrote at each meal.

One morning at breakfast Sherwood announced that he had just altered Lynn's character to being a former Russian princess. It's most likely he knew Natasha Wilson. It easily could be. Lynn said, "I can't do a good Russian accent, so could you make her a phony Russian princess?" And that's how the classic Irene (pronounced "Ea*ra*yna") was born.

They also locked Noël Coward up until he wrote *Design for Living*. Noël got a terrible cold. Could not get out of bed. So Lynnie put on a rubber apron, took a large baby bathtub of soap and water, and went into the guesthouse to bathe him. When finished, she turned around and made one of her grand exits, and Alfred heard Noël let out a huge screech of laughter. It seemed she had only the apron on, and her bare bottom was out in the back.

We did not stay in the guesthouse but in the guest room just below their master bedroom because Alfred had done a mural in the guest-house and it wasn't dry yet. He wanted scenes of the Garden of Eden. He had no one else to pose for him in the buff, so Lynnie had to pose for both Adam and Eve, and it just looked like two women. One of the walls had an extra rib on one of the women. It somehow simply changed the entire plot. I don't know how to explain it, but there was this rib that one woman was handing the other woman. Now, would you have recognized the oldest story known to Christianity? I wonder if this mural is still there. It is inspiring that Alfred, in all his wisdom and mental precision, could gum up a story as easily as any of the rest of us.

One time at breakfast, I sat listening to Lynnie's rendition of how she tried to help her friend Helen Hayes. I sensed the superiority in the tone of Lynnie's voice as she said, "I had to tell Helen, 'You must take diction lessons, Helen' " (reader, I must repeat that Helen Hayes was the First Lady of the American Theatre to many people). "Alfred, *do* help Helen." Oh, she was lofty as all get out, but only about Helen. There wasn't a sign of loftiness about anything or anyone else ever that I saw. She was all gentle, womanly safety and security.

Ten Chimneys seemed to be buzzing happily with both their hobbies. While Alfred was cooking, Lynnie was upstairs designing her next evening gown. I watched her execute it herself. The next morning at breakfast Alfred complained. He said he had again slept in a scattering of straight pins. They had a bed so narrow that they couldn't turn over in it. They slept like sardines in a can. All their lives they had this bed that was the width of an army cot. Lynnie would lay the dress on it to pin it.

Alfred and Lynn had nightly vigils in their kitchen, where Alfred was so at peace with the world that he would open up and tell the answers to the universe or show business. To an actor, the universe and show business are synonymous. As Ethel Merman cracked, "Sure, I know there's a war on, I read *Variety*."

They took that line out when other people, who didn't give it a comedy delivery, played *Gypsy*. Tyne Daly kept it in. She was heaven as Rose. Ethel would have approved of her.

Alfred said informative things like "If your show is enough of a hit in New York, then you can tour with it."

Lynnie: Of course you treasure it, and the way you treasure your show is you bring it on tour and treat it carefully, remembering which theatre is best for this particular show. Yes, love. It's your duty to the theatre to take it to the provinces.

Alfred: And it pays off on your next show. The New Yorkers have tickets for the first three months. After that it's your road audience of tourists that keeps it going on Broadway.

Lynnie: We found that out with Noël Coward's *Point Valaine*. We couldn't believe that Noël could possibly write a flop, but it was. However, tourists to New York would say, "Oh, look. There's Lynn and Alfred playing. Let's go there."

Alfred: They felt we had been their houseguests simply because we had played their town. We were family friends, and they kept buying tickets. We wanted it to close but it wouldn't.

More kitchen talk was:

Lynn: You love Mr. Gaynor.

Me: I do?

Lynn: Oh yes, you love him, he's your writer. You never stop loving him.

Me: No?

Lynn: No. You adore him.

And I certainly did.

Opening night in Las Vegas with my father dead only a few days, Gaynor said to me, "I'll be your father, Carol. Please let me be your father. I'll help you."

Kind, quiet, delicate-natured Charlie Gaynor couldn't have been more opposite to my father, but yes, Lynnie, I loved Charles Gaynor.

Alfred even scolded me like a caring father one night during a stay at Ten Chimneys when I had to go to the nearest television station to do the weather report for my show for the Middle West. The weather was new to me then. They watched it on their set. When we got "home," Alfred said, "You came through as nervous because you were unsure of your lines." He waited for my answer. I didn't answer because I didn't know it then. I know now, in retrospect: I was afraid of Charles and of forgetting the lines he gave me to say. Now, I can ad-lib my way out of anything, but Charles would be very upset at my ad-libs if he were still with us. I was always surprised to find that my words got the laughs, though, because my words were naturally true to me and everyone watching knew it. I didn't. They did.

Everybody, including the Lunts, seemed to like Charles very much, though, so I guess I just should have played Birdie in *The Little Foxes* and gotten all this aggravating timidity out of my system. It's also aggravating to everyone around me. Why can't she speak up for herself? Because I sensed then, but didn't know then, that I had no one else to turn to but Charles, and he planned it that way. Charles cut Dickie off from me first (Dickie is a tough cookie when it comes to protecting his family), then my mother, then Chan. However, from the fourth grade on, I was high, wide, and handsome *onstage*.

Nothing can touch you when you're trying to help other people and, in my case, lift their lives. That's why creative work heals everything, including cancer and AIDS, that I know of. Apparently the Great Creative Force is still creating, and as long as *we* are creating (anything) we latch on to the power that heals and gives us more than human strength. So when we create, even (as Bill Moyers said) a sand castle, we are closer to being whole and well. You got it, I'm sure, long ago.

One morning at around four o'clock at Ten Chimneys, I awoke as usual and had to get to the refrigerator for an apple. Out of a sound sleep I remembered to go down one flight of steps, then across the dining room and into their kitchen. Whenever I used to travel, it always registered deep into my brain where the refrigerator was and what was in it. Even to this day in my cousin's home no one ever has to return home to make a list for food shopping. I *know* what food is left, what day it arrived, and what we need. I can't understand why no one else in the house, including the housekeeper, seems to know. However, we all have different interests in life.

Now, at Ten Chimneys I made it to the fridge, got my apple, and suddenly a screeching, nerve-shattering alarm went off. I then heard sirens, saw yellow and blue lights circling the dining room from the tops of police cars, heard fire engines clanging and voices from people marching up from two different roads. I looked out; they had long rifles pointed toward the house. I was sure I heard a gun go off outside. I swung flat to the floor under the dining room table. I looked up, and there at the top of the stairway stood Lynnie in a long, white flannel, Shakespearean nightgown, a ruffle high around the neck, and a red-and-white-striped nightcap that came to a tall point at the crown of her head. It was tied under her chin. Over the din soared Lynnie's voice. In clarion tones she almost sang on one note:

Lynn: Jules, to your post! Robert (chauffeur), to your post! Do not let anyone open the garage door, Robert. Margaret (hairdresser and Robert's wife), to your post. Alfred, open the secret passage! Seize Ellen Terry's acting notes to me. Then to the kitchen for your recipe book!

Finally, Alfred, on his way to the kitchen, caught my face under the table in his flashlight beam and called out, "Carol!" I didn't realize I was still holding the apple till I could stand up and face him.

Alfred: Lynn. Stop. I've found the culprit.

Lynn: Stand still, everyone. We've trapped the burglar.

The house was suddenly devoid of heavy footsteps. Alfred took my hand and brought me to the third step up to show me where I had stepped on the alarm.

Lynn was laughing her famous musical laugh, but it was genuine and abandoned on her. "We've been rehearsing this regularly for fifty years," she said, "and we never had a chance to find out if it worked. It works! Beautifully!" More musical laughter.

I don't know how long Charles had been up there standing sleepily on the first landing, but he pointed accusingly at me.

Charles: Let this be a lesson to you, Baby Lowe. No more sleep-time trips to the refrigerator.

Me: Yes. I'm so very sorry.

I was apologizing to every official I could get to. One large, distinguished-looking man in his bathrobe could have been the mayor.

He: Not at all. Nothing is a bother to protect the Lunts.

Both the Lunts seemed to be enjoying the whole thing or she, with her Anglo-Saxon etiquette, pretended she did, like the queen breaking another teacup. Just the same, they couldn't seem to stop laughing.

Another evening, after Lynnie and I ended our rides on her stationary bicycle in their master bedroom, I left her finishing pinning her self-designed and self-cut pattern onto a bolt of antique gold fabric to go downstairs and see what Alfred was doing in the kitchen. He and Jules, his chief cook and bottle washer, were re-creating one of their Cordon Bleu lessons. Alfred, you know, was a Cordon Bleu chef. Very few actually graduate from the school. Alfred did. I don't think Jules ever made it. Every weekday they walked to it together, Jules and Alfred, schoolbooks under arms, in their little Swiss shorts and Tyrolean shoulder straps. Jules was black then, now African-American. Lynnie said they looked darling as she waved them good-bye each morning. Well, they were making some kind of apple pfannkuchen, and Alfred sat down with me to talk to me again about his diseases. I dearly loved to talk with Alfred about his illnesses. First, because he had more than any other human on record ever had, I'm sure, and, second, because of my being raised in Christian Science, I believed it was best not to make a reality out of any illness by talking about it. "No, Tootsie, you don't have a cold. You have a *claim* of a cold, and it has no power over you."

I think this is a good rule, myself, but Alfred never heard of it. However, I ferociously swung into these discussions because, for me, they were like necking, or cutting classes in school. It was forbidden. Well, Alfred and I sat up in that kitchen (Jules and Charles each went to bed long before) and went into the intricacies of Alfred's pancreas, his liver, his digestive tract, his spleen, his left eye drift, the hole in his esophagus. I was in bliss! I think Alfred was, too. No one ever listened that attentively, he said, not even his caring Dr. Bigg of Passavant Hospital in Chicago. Dr. Bigg didn't have the passionate enjoyment of the details, Alfred told me. Well, as I say, it was "forbidden fruit" for me. The pfannkuchen got better and better as he took each tray out.

We looked forward to these late-night kitchen vigils, and when we ran out of his illnesses, we started on Lynnie's diverticulitis and what berry seeds did to it. Also when she broke her arm, and then a wound in her right calf that simply would not heal. Alfred said he finally told her, "If it never heals, Lynn, you'll carry off a walking stick even more elegantly than Sarah Bernhardt." But it finally did heal, after eighteen months.

As a matter of fact, years later, in my final conversation with Alfred, in a phone call that I made to him in Passavant Hospital during a break in my *Dolly* rehearsal for the second road tour, he seemed on his deathbed funnier than ever. He said, "Oh, Carol. You'll be so interested in this. They've operated on me here for four things. I left my liver on the fifth floor, my colon on the third, oh, and something new has turned up, kidney stones! I've been all over this hospital, and I've been thinking . . . I do hope I get the chance to tell Carol all about this. I'm so happy you called."

We both laughed till we cried. The entire *Dolly* company was waiting to rehearse the second act, and I forgot all about it, I was so glad to hear Alfred laughing so. I wish I could remember all he said, but he was truly the funniest and wittiest I'd ever heard him.

Lynn called a day or so later to tell us of his death. Later she said, "I was able to get through his funeral, Carol. I didn't think I'd make it when they brought his casket in. It came over me . . . Alfred is in there. And I held my breath and did not break down. I made it. Somehow I made it."

For some television guest shot Charles and I had to go to New York, so we asked them to book the flight to Chicago and then we drove to Genesee Depot. Lynn and Charles and I visited a long time. She never motioned for us to leave, but we had to in order to board the plane at O'Hare. She was stoic and very affectionate. All the way in the car back to Chicago I cried steadily for her. I couldn't even stop on the plane. Even with my father's death, for a year after I had breaks in between cries, but along with *their* death, this was the death of the live theatre that they created. We talked on the phone often, Lynn and I.

George Burns was a great support to her. He had lost Gracie not long before. When he did, Charles and I flew to his Beverly Hills home the second day off from the *Dolly* opening on Broadway. George wasn't stoic like Lynn because he was like we are . . . American. Lynn's British backbone would not allow her to give in to what might embarrass others. I asked George to please call Lynn and tell her what he told me to tell her. He did. He advised, "Don't leave where you and Alfred spent most of your time together. During the day, when it gets too difficult without Gracie, I crawl in on her side of the bed and stay there until I've been very close to her and feel good. Then I get up and can go on with my day. I sit at her vanity to put on my toupee. You must sit in Alfred's favorite chair and let it hold you. This will help. Don't let anyone tell you to leave home." It sustained Lynn. She said, "And these wisdoms from this little man who has given his audiences exclusively comedy."

Everyone asks of a long and blessed marriage, "Why couldn't they have gone together?" It was indeed cruel what happened to Lynnie. After a longer while, in her mind, there was no Alfred. She never met him. She remembered only some young man in London who fell in love with her in her teens. She remembered nothing that happened after meeting Alfred. That was all, especially Alfred, a blank.

Mrs. Nixon

Two days after Watergate broke wide open and we all realized presidential impeachment was unavoidable, the time for an annual Washington tradition rolled around. The tradition was that the congressmen's wives hold a luncheon in honor of the First Lady. My impression was that this has been ever since Martha Washington, so I was honored when months before I was asked to bestow my diamond award on Mrs. Nixon. I was playing the National Theatre for the fourth time. I think one is always surrounded by Washington history when playing the National. Every president as far back as when this perfect monument was erected knew where the star's dressing room was and visited, so it gave me a worthwhile feeling about myself to get up early every morning to go on TV and talk about saving the National from becoming a parking lot. It still stands today, like the Curran in San Francisco, the Orpheum in Minneapolis, the Colonial in Boston, and the Drury Lane in London. So it was simple to go straight to the luncheon preparations, where Julie Nixon Eisenhower was doing a very professional job of sound testing with the microphone man, standing in for the light man, et cetera.

Charles wrote a speech for me to give my diamond award for something good the recipient did. When you're touring, it's difficult to be au courant, so I didn't know if there were something special Mrs. Nixon did for which I could give her the award. Julie Eisenhower suggested "for making friends all the way from Africa to China." Perfect! I wish all benefits had a Julie Eisenhower.

When the time came for Mrs. Nixon to enter, she walked down a runway with her head held high, her back proudly straight, and looking more beautiful than any pictures or TV images I ever saw of her. She exuded a silent presence of "In spite of the impeachment I will do all I can to serve the United States for as long as they need me. I will uphold its dignity and pride the very best I can until that moment that I can no longer be of service." I cried. You cannot cry, you know, just before you go onstage yourself. It causes makeup, wardrobe, and vocal problems, but I realized the entire audience was in the same emotional state. It was Mrs. Nixon's total lack of self-pity, her unwavering bravery.

When she received her diamond from me, she exclaimed, "Oh, how sweet! I can keep this? I won't have to contribute this to the presidential museum or put it on exhibit?"

Me: Well, Mrs. Nixon, I must remind you that the quality that gives a diamond its value is the amount of sentiment attached to it, and this diamond is filled with respect and affection, so it's absolutely priceless.

Mrs. Nixon: Oh, well then, I can keep it after all.

Me: Yes. Today, *you* are our diamond, and we are all your best friends.

She put it on her finger, smiled at the audience, then smiled at me, then walked gracefully and regally offstage. Our hearts went with her.

Me and the Queen and the Queen Mum

*M*y first royal command performance was for the Queen Mum. She was sitting in the royal box on stage right. This was for Bernard Delfont's presentation of *Carol Channing and Her Ten Stout-Hearted Men,* my first performance in London. Bernie Delfont was so wise, he put it in the oldest and grandest and largest theatre . . . the Drury Lane. The British had never seen any show there except the most classic. Many Britishers told me those Drury Lane surroundings for my show and for me made it all the funnier and made me more ridiculous. It was, thank God, a smash hit. When it came time for me to do "Diamonds Are a Girl's Best Friend," I threw diamonds out. The Queen Mum reached and reached until she almost fell out of the box, so I threw directly to her to save a catastrophic death. She grabbed. I yelled over the music, "Are there more people at the palace?"

Queen Mum: The chimney sweep.

I threw her more.

Me: More?

Queen Mum: Yes!

Well, I had to stop, she was so greedy. Then I looked at her and pantomimed: straighten your tiara. It had worked itself to over one ear and not the other from her reaching for diamonds. She straightened it. No wonder everyone there loves her so dearly.

While we're on this subject, her daughter Elizabeth made me cry when they sang "God Save the Queen." Her roses were leaning to her left, her head was turned slightly to her right so that she faced the entire audience. The expression on her face was beautiful: This is not for me personally. I'm only a symbol of England.

It was so selfless, so egoless, and yet her head was held high. I was deeply touched by her obvious dedication of her life to her country. There had to be trying times, especially during the war, when every member of the family spent every waking moment in hospitals standing and sitting by all the soldiers' beds, talking at length with them. Eleanor Roosevelt, Lady Bird Johnson, and the Royal Family did it under the threat of annihilation, I know, but they never, ever let up. I'm sure few actors can fake that expression on Elizabeth's face. Charles kept saying to me, "But it's like Betty Grable's four steps. She does the same ones always. The Queen has her whole life to perfect that look and those thoughts that make it."

"Oh, Charles!" I suppose he was trying to keep me from making an exhibition of myself, but a good cry is a good cry, and I didn't want it spoiled or interrupted.

Touring

Because I've spent as much time touring theatres, concert halls, grand ballrooms, nightclubs, and symphony halls as on Broadway, I am able to know that the presenter in each city is the secret to a completely successful show. The greatest theatre ones were a man named Ariel Reubstein in Portland, Oregon; Hope Quackenbush in Baltimore and Washington, D.C.; and Vinita Cravens in Oklahoma City. They handle everything—their own publicity and advertising for the oncoming show, their subscription audience, the upkeep of their theatres, their strongest contacts for TV, radio, newspapers, and magazines—and they sit in their own box offices and count their own money. Their unrelenting drive gave all three of them superhuman auras. They were my favorite people, I could trust them as true friends because we depended on one another for existence. Ariel Reubstein toured with Chaliapin as his manager and accompanied him on piano for decades, all over the world, before he owned the biggest legit house in Portland.

Vinita Cravens looked arrestingly like a full-blooded Cherokee because she was. All that was missing was a feather up the back of her head. I had four Oklahoma theatre bookings with her. After the opening night party, at dawn, with no sleep, she'd be sitting in her box office with her evening glitter still pasted to her eyelids and her wig slightly askew. She explained to me that it itched. When she scratched her head it moved back and forth as she was talking to the press or on TV. They seemed to be used to her. Her theatre seated 7,500! Mr. Merrick wanted to break the world's indoor theatre record, and he did with her. He added two more matinee days in one week and got headlines in *Variety*, *The New York Times*, and worldwide newspapers. One show was equal to four in energy and projection for me. I did live through that week, which amazed me. It was the prospect of ultra-achievement that held me together. Vinita's theatre—actually it was an auditorium—was right next to Oklahoma City's City Hall. My father lectured in her auditorium there several times, too, to a capacity audience. I looked at the size of it in rehearsal and thought, Daddy, if you could reach this audience and they got your message clearly, I must have many of your genes, so it's likely that I can do it, too.

They named the entire block around the city hall Channing Square in honor of both of us, I've decided. It's still there. What bliss! We made it! They heard and saw us and told us it lifted their lives . . . our goal, of course. Oh yes, I am still an honorary Oto Indian; Vinita arranged that. My entire tribe comes opening nights every time we play Oklahoma. I have this regal Oto father who named me Princess Bakahni Dahkun, which means Princess Blazing Star. I am proud they never forget. They don't laugh though. They sit there stoic and majestic with arms folded. I own their huge feather headgear and a handwoven blanket and a turquoise and silver ring my Oto father wore. Massive!

In Baltimore, Hope Quackenbush told me Deborah Kerr was coming in *Tea and Sympathy* to her Morris A. Mechanic Theatre.

Me: Oh, it'll go through the roof!

Hope: Yes, but I can't pedal her around like I can you.

To me that was a tremendous compliment. She booked Rex Harrison in *The Kingfisher*. He was willing to be "peddled," but he owned a vineyard on Napoleon's isle of Elba and felt obligated to sample his own wine on his day off. He went with Hope to one of her Baltimore society gatherings of theatre sponsors and backers. Hope introduced Rex so he could speak to the matrons. He got as far as "Thank you, uh, Mrs. Mrs. Mrs. uh, Fuckaduck," and never did make his speech, so it doesn't work with everyone, Hope told me.

Charles had the impresario put me on every weather report in every city we played. It was on the news at prime time, and nobody had to pay for it. I knew every weatherperson across the country from 1956 to 1997. After their regular report, they'd introduce me.

I'd say, "Good morning (or evening). My name is Carol Channing. I am from Central Weather Service. We taught so-and-so everything he knows about the weather and we're very proud of him. But I am here to report a climatic phenomenon that's going to take place right here in (say) Chicago (point to map with stick). Here is our state of Illinois. Here is Chicago. Here is, more specifically, the Shubert Theatre. Now you've all heard so-and-so's report. There's rain here, a windstorm there (whatever he just said). Well, it's just a general mess is what it is. But right here on the map at the Shubert Theatre, promptly at 8:00 P.M., a meteorological happenstance takes place. The weather will be ideal. The only rain will be a reign of diamonds, the only gusts will be gusts of laughter. It's a once in a lifetime experience, like a total eclipse. You must bring the children."

The news was always live, so the three of us—the impresario, Charles, and I—would rush to the nearest phone, dial the box office, and ask, "What happened?"

"Oh, we just sold out the mezzanine, half the third balcony, et cetera. All the phones are lit up."

Then we'd rush to another channel for an interview. Then a picture with the mayor or the governor, then a speech with a luncheon for some convention in some hotel's grand ballroom. Usually I'd give my diamond award to the president or grand marshall. If possible, do a fashion show by coming out on the runway as the last model.

Dragging a fur coat, I'd say: "Like many little girls growing up, I dreamt of being a clothes model. When I was trying to get a theatre job, I spent most of my allowance on top balcony seats, and the usherettes would kindly move me down if there were empty seats in the mezzanine. Anyway, I was hungry most of the time and therefore, for the only time in my life, thin enough to apply for a job modeling. They told me a good model can turn into the kind of woman who would wear that outfit. I thought, Oh fine, that's acting; I can do that.

"They tried me out on the runway first with a Traina-Norell. Black jersey from earlobe to earlobe and to the floor. Slinky and tight except for huge dolman sleeves . . . evil! Yes, a totally evil dress! I thought, I'm Mother Goddam coming through the beaded curtains in *The Shanghai Gesture* to put a knife into Mr. Moto's heart. I charged down the runway, pantomiming a knife murder, hacking him to death into the floor.

"I realized I had got carried away when the fashion audience was awestruck. Next I wore a Tina Lazer with jingling gold bells here and there on a paisley print. I did my Uday Shan Kar neck wiggle, which you have to start doing when you're little. I was an expert at it by now. Then they put on me a Philip Mangone riding habit . . . black silk top hat, black riding jacket, white jodhpurs, shiny black boots, and a whip. One of the customers asked how much it was. I answered in a clipped British accent, veddy correct, and a slash through the air of my whip. Finally, I wore a white voile wedding gown and said to myself, 'I'm the virgin of all time . . . I'm June Allyson.'

"All I can say is I got more laughs then than I ever got in the theatre since. So I was, so to speak, as you might say, fired. Well, fired is what it was that I was. Therefore, today marks the healing of a deep wound. Here I am modeling for the most chic audience west of the Mississippi [assume a bored, superior expression and drag that fur coat all the way down, then up the runway and back]. I finally made it just now. Today marks the healing of a deep wound, and I thank you all." (End of fashion show.)

In some cities, like Cleveland, the weatherman would take me up with him and a pilot in a helicopter (because we'd known each other for so many years, so I think he just wanted to give me an extra thrill and that it was). We'd go first to an empty lot in the center of downtown, go straight up, and then weave through the skyscrapers, waving to office workers as they rushed to their windows and then to apartment owners. I couldn't hear what they were yelling at us because of the noise of the motor, but I hoped they knew it was us. Yes, they did, because we were live and they had their sets on. Some of the Cleveland streets are narrow, so we just missed them. I was never sorry when the flight was over, but I wouldn't ever admit I'm not a daredevil because they apparently filled up the theatre we were playing in, no matter how big it was.

Speaking of Cleveland, they have an outdoor Blossom Music Center outside the city. The audience must be used to those midwestern storms, typhoons, and disturbances that blow entire theatre tents away. Lightning struck the center microphone where I was holding it. I swear, I don't remember anything after that, but somehow I was still standing when I came to. I heard the audience laughing joyously. I asked what happened and what was so funny to those thousands of people. They shouted, "You! You looked so funny." I was simply thankful I didn't stop the show or ruin their fun. Machiavellian, weren't they? But they were on my side and were an eager audience and they stayed till the end, through the storm, typhoon, and inverted umbrellas. They were valiant. Every time we played Cleveland I feel we've many of us been through something together, bonding us for life.

Then I'd get on the noon news, then help a local charity, then do the 6:00 P.M. news weather report, and that's how I spent my days off. See what Deborah Kerr has been missing? This is show business! No matter how much pre-advertising they did, we had to let them know we were here *now*, ready to entertain them. The orchestra usually sells out first. I had to let them know the director most always sits in one of the balconies, because that is the complete view of the stage . . . no feet or legs missing. Also, sound always goes up, so the first balcony is the best for hearing. This is true. I've never lied to them. If the mezzanine and first balcony protrude over one-half the orchestra floor—like in the Shubert Theatre in Chicago—the sound gets muffled under it. I know this because one critic (William Hawkins of the *New York Post*) said, after sitting there for a show, "Carol, you must work on your diction." He was sitting under the first balcony. In most all theatres sound makes an arc, and it lands in the balconies, not *under* them. Most everyone I've asked about it is sick unto death of my overenunciated diction . . . unless I should learn the new American language that stems from the Marlon Brando School of Realism. They may be more correct now, though, than I am.

I asked an operator for Mary Mar-tin. "Who? Oh, you mean Mar-umnn" (with the glottis on the *nn*). But I wonder if they'd get laughs onstage with an unintelligible feed line. Time will tell.

I have three good friends (brothers). When I met them, Seth was four years old, Ezra six, and Abraham eight. They're four years older now, but when Seth (the littlest) was four and teaching me how to use the computer, he declared me "hopeless." By the same token, I can understand only a few words any one of them says. Abraham is twelve now, and I understand him less every year. Yet they understand each other and their friends. So you see I have some catching up with the world to do. Diction sloops and slurs aren't easy to learn. They're trying hard to help me. I'm fortunate to have such friends. I don't want to be left out in the future.

Clint Eastwood

*M*y first movie, back in 1956 or so, was called *The First Traveling Saleslady*, which we all referred to immediately after the first reading as *Death of a Saleslady*. Clint Eastwood and I were the cliché stock subplot to the pretty girl–macho leading man syndrome, played by Ginger Rogers and Jim Arness. Sometimes, as you know, this subplot couple is a comic team, but Clint and I had no comedy lines or situations. Sometimes they are eccentric dancers, but the main function of these two is to make the leads look sexier, prettier, and more vibrant. Can you imagine their being that immune to Clint Eastwood?

Ginger's mother, Lela, finally walked in and instructed: "Carol, why don't you say this? Clint, you say that, and, Ginger, you say that."

And do you know that's exactly what we said? No one stopped her. As I say, anything was better than the script.

One day, I said to Clint Eastwood, "Clint, I never get parts like these where I have to go into a clinch. We've got a big one coming up in this script, and I've never done that before. What should we do?"

This smooth-skinned, tall, slight, young boy said, "I've never been in a movie before, either. I haven't the slightest."

So we rehearsed and rehearsed. "Do my arms go over yours or under?" "Do we bend our necks to get both our faces visible?"

Of course, the clinch was cut first thing, but then you guessed that.

To make things worse I got the Harvard Hasty Pudding prize of the year for singing the worst song of *any* year, "A Corset Can Do a Lot for a Lady."

Oh, I forgot to tell you, our little movie rocked Wall Street. They were reviving the halcyon movie days of RKO studios, and someone decided that this opus was to launch the entire enterprise. Millions were invested. We closed RKO in only a few days, and they never re-opened it that I know of to this day. The way I understand it, we reconstructed the economics of the entire United States of America. You didn't know that four little human beings could be all that powerful, did you? But we closed it. All by our own selves. It gives one pause, doesn't it?

I did want you to learn something while reading this book. One thing I want you to learn is never to let busy, brilliant businessmen select your next script. This is not their racket. Businessmen's brains work differently from ours. They are brilliant in an entirely opposite direction. All right? Now that you've learned that, I do want credit though. The moment I read the script, I tried to get out of it. I'm sure we all did. But the producer, Bill Dozier, was adamant. "You'll never work in movies again if you go against your verbal commitment."

And I must say, once people saw it, I never did work in movies again. Not till a decade later in *Thoroughly Modern Millie*, only because Ross Hunter, the producer, fought the entire tide of Hollywood and insisted on putting me in his "Millie" movie. But he proudly pointed out to people that I was nominated for an Oscar and won the Golden Globe award on his good judgment. It fazed no one.

But do you know, I can't get rid of this movie *The First Traveling Saleslady?* In many cities as we tour, the little local movie house digs it out and plays it right across the street from where our tour is playing in some huge auditorium. I can't shake it, I'm sure Clint Eastwood can't shake it, Jim Arness couldn't shake it, and I do hope poor Ginger has been able to shake it *now*, wherever she is.

Anyway, several Christmases ago I was at Doug Cramer's house for a party, talking with a circle of people. I felt a presence behind me for quite a while. Finally, I turned around, and there stood Clint, all craggy and character-lined, like the Grand Canyon. With that "make my day" half grin he said, "Don't you remember me? I was your first kiss."

Bea Lillie

here were three big and thrilling musicals running simultaneously on Broadway beginning in the year 1964. They were Noël Coward's *High Spirits* (a musical of his fabulous play *Blithe Spirit*), *Dolly*, and *Funny Girl*. Noël came over to my table in a restaurant and said, "You see, I said to our choreographer, 'Don't complicate it so much. Get a clear vision of where you're going with your production numbers and keep them as simple as you can, as Gower Champion did with the *Hello, Dolly!* number." Like Richard Rodgers, he never bothered with "How are you?" or any greeting at all. I could see

Noël's misery. People have helped me when I'm miserable. I wanted to help him.

For those of you too young to know, Bea Lillie was the reigning queen of elegant musical comedy both in London's West End and on Broadway.

Noël thought Bea, his star in *High Spirits*, was deliberately ad-libbing to get laughs from the audience . . . messing up the plot. He knew her nature better than I did I'm sure, but to watch your creation get messed up is enough to make you suicidal. However, she *had* to ad-lib. She truly couldn't retain her lines or know that she was ruining Noël's show. Also, Bea couldn't remember one line in *Thoroughly Modern Millie*. Julie Andrews had to feed her each next line, and then they cut Julie's voice off giving her each line. Julie was being truly Julie, and it worked! We all nursed Bea through that movie. Mary Tyler Moore and I followed Julie's example and hugged her a lot. And Bea came shining hilariously through. Bea didn't know she was any problem at all. She was warm and happy with the three of us, with a glimmer of gratitude, but for what she did not know. I rode to and from the Universal lot with her in our limo. She was so very friendly to me, chattering constantly.

By the way, when I arrived on the West Coast to film *Thoroughly Modern Millie*, Ross Hunter put me to work for the entire first month with a group of acrobats. I learned to climb to be the fourth man on top of three of them. One afternoon they told me Ross was on his way to see our progress, so I put on my eyeglasses in order to know when Ross arrived. We were all standing on each other's shoulders. My head was spectacularly almost touching the high ceiling when I looked down and discovered for the first time how very far I was from the floor. Panic! Up till now they all thought I was remarkably brave. We all disintegrated into a heap on the floor in front of Ross, because each acrobat succeeded in catching me enough to break my fall. Never put on your glasses when demonstrating acrobatic work.

Back to Bea. She wanted to write her autobiography, Lady Peel did (she had been married to Lord Peel), and wanted to call it *Every Other Inch a Lady*.

Bea had an accompanist. He became a Franciscan monk and wore those robes. He came in to visit her on the lot for lunch. Bea must have forgotten again, so she looked at him, recognized him, and said, "Oh! And what are you as?"

One night when I was at Sardi's for dinner with Bea before our Broadway shows she told me Fanny Brice had started taking her naps on matinee days with her feet up higher than her head. Six months later she died. "So, Carol, never nap with your feet above your head." She thought for a moment and then laughed at herself with me. I told her my father said, "That's called in Latin *Post hoc, ergo propter hoc,* meaning, 'After this, therefore because of it.' We mustn't think that way, Bea, must we?" "Oh no," she said. "Your father was right. I never put my feet over my head anymore."

Bea had a constant companion . . . a man named John Phillip. He was nearer her son's age. Her son, by Lord Peel, was killed in World War II. I never met John Phillip, but Dick Coe (critic emeritus on *The Washington Post*) said he never left her side. Dick said, "Well, we have to put up with him. Someone has to look after Bea," and John did. Most people couldn't understand the relationship. They thought he was just an ardent fan. However, Bea seemed to be at peace with him wherever they went, the *QE II*, plane trips, everywhere. Finally, she was in a sanitarium outside London. When I asked for the address, my godson Hugo Moreley and his father, Sheridan, told me not to try to visit her, that she won't know I was a friend of hers and it would upset her. John Phillip visited her all day every day until the day she died. John Phillip died the very next day.

I often followed Jimmy Durante at the Empire Room at the Palmer House in Chicago. He'd be closing a six-week engagement with two shows a night, and I'd be opening the next night with my six weeks. Cabaret engagements aren't that long now. They're only for four nights. So I say this proudly, Jimmy and I could fill the joint. Not easy.

Anyway, Jimmy was walking along Wabash Avenue when he got held up. He gave the thief his money and said, "Here you are" or something. The burglar said, "Jimmy! Here, take back your money. I didn't know it was you." That's legend in Chicago now, but I was there when it happened. He burst into the lower lobby on the street floor and excitedly told me. I spread it all over.

And do let me tell you another thing. That stuff about "never follow a smash hit act" is totally an old wives' tale. Just after *Blondes* opened I was booked on a benefit. I had no idea how to do one. I never saw one.

Jimmy's was a dynamite act, and I mean that literally. Clayton, Jackson, and Durante did everything but explode a keg of dynamite! They chopped up breakaway furniture, kept the brasses going at top pitch; the drums and cymbals crashed incessantly. Lou Clayton, who had the loudest singing voice, until Patrick Quinn sang, "Waitin' for the Robert E. Lee" to an overenergized dance and Jimmy was busy with his strut-away. It was funny how you couldn't take your eyes off Jimmy, though, even with all that din and clatter. You couldn't stop laughing because the effect on the audience was much like sugar shock. Jackson's tap dance was so loud it hurt your eardrums. He did it on top of a grand piano that surely had a microphone under the top and, all the time, that Sunny Italy smile of Jimmy's was the centrifugal force of the entire act. The house applause came thundering over the standing ovation. Oh, it was mayhem! Complete chaotic mayhem!

At this benefit, when Jimmy sensed the crux of his applause, he went over to the piano, picked up my sheet music, and yelled, "What the heck is this? Somebody cluttered up my piano. 'Little Girl from Little Rock.' " Then threw it way over onto the floor. "More mess," he said. " 'Bye, Bye, Baby.' " He threw it into the audience. (More applause.) " 'Diamonds Are a Girl's . . . ' " (Bigger applause.) I crawled out, not because we rehearsed it, we didn't, but because I had to get my sheet music back in order to do my little act.

Jimmy: And who's this on her hands and knees, the cleaning lady?

(I was in my "Diamonds" dress and the whole regalia.)

Jimmy: Everybody wants to get into the act!

I was now in the audience, begging people to give me my music back. They let me have it through their tears of laughter. I ran back to get onstage again, overwhelmed with the thought to myself, This is razzmatazz show business, and I'm right in the middle of it . . . my fondest dream. I was now madly in love with Jimmy and never wanted to be anywhere else in the world except right next to him on this very spot . . . center stage. I know. I realize now I'm not monogamous, since this book has forced me to look back over my life. Not my sex life. Nobody ever seemed to come on to me that I can remember. I mean, I fell helplessly and eternally in love with so very many dear, unique men, but look at the men I met and worked with. Wouldn't you?

Jimmy exited with the audience already embracing me because of his attitude toward me, and after "Diamonds" he came back on and we shuffled off to Buffalo together to his strut-away. I was able to do it exactly like him, even to his face, because I loved him. We could tell it was funny. Can you imagine one great entertainer giving a comparative newcomer so much? That's our Jimmy.

Another adorable habit of his was after each show, the dinner and the late shows, I visited him in his dressing room. He'd laugh and say things like "Wasn't that a great ad-lib I thought of? It was funny, wasn't it? Haha. They laughed, didn't they? How did I ever think of that? Huh?" Then he'd savor the line he thought of. That was the bubbling, irresistible childlikeness in him.

At about my seventh engagement at the Palmer House, Jimmy was wheelchaired onto the stage shaking from head to toe with whatever his illness was called. I never could understand why anyone connected with Jimmy allowed this. I got down into the audience so no one could see me and cried from watching him and couldn't possibly stop. I never thought Jimmy Durante would ever get sick or old. He kept smiling, but I know he didn't know where he was. They had put him on exhibit! I'm grateful we were in Chicago for only a couple of thousand people and not on TV or something. I'll bet I know just what happened. Jimmy said, "Oh, I can do this show. I'll be okay once I'm out there. I've felt worse than this before and done terrific shows." But he couldn't move or speak this time.

I have a deal with my fitness trainer. He'll know my mental and physical condition. He's thirty years younger than I am. I made him promise if I pull that speech and he knows better, he'll shoot me first. He will, he says, but so offhandedly I have to be sure it registered. I don't want anyone shooting me that doesn't care for me like I hope he does. Dr. Kevorkian won't do.

Jolson and Burns

I never met Al Jolson. But George Burns, up until he married Gracie, spent a lot of his life with him. George said Jolson was, without a doubt, the greatest entertainer he ever, ever witnessed. Now George was not given to superlatives, but Jolson he worshiped.

There was a group of vaudevillians who shared one dressing room in whatever town and theatre they were playing. It consisted of

George, Jolson, Billy Lorraine (who stammered and finally had to sing it), and Dave Chasen, who could only cook great chili, and Dave couldn't time a vaudeville laugh to save his life. He finally opened a chili stand at the corner of Beverly Boulevard and Doheny Drive in L.A., sponsored by the same theatre dressing room vaudevillians. It grew into the fabulous Chasen's Restaurant that stands there today.

But did you know that Al Jolson always had to turn on the water faucet when he could hear other vaudevillians' applause? Al couldn't take it. Their applause took his own confidence away . . . the incomparable Jolson! He obviously didn't know who or what he was. But neither did the Lunts, or Einstein, or many more.

I'm sure many of you have heard about Jolson, once he went onstage, singing until 1:00 or 1:30 A.M. and announcing between songs, "You ain't heard nothin' yet!" Not one audience member ever left that George knew of.

George told me he'd be waiting in the wings for Jolson's last song. As the sides of the curtain came together at center stage, Jolson would hang on to both sides, backstage of them, head bowed. George always knew at the end of the show Al was crying. He said he'd go to him and whisper, "Come on now, fella, I've ordered whitefish from Lindy's New York. Dave Chasen has made chili again. We're waiting for you up in the dressing room. Here's your towel." George said he'd walk him to the dressing room. Jolson got all straightened out by the time he got there.

Some people have told me Jolson was the meanest man in show business. Not to George! If you were that great onstage, what else mattered? George answered my question "Did anyone else see him cry?" "No, no one I know of ever knew how hard it was for him to leave the audience. Just me. He was the greatest."

When an audience is not a benefit audience, and gives of itself back to the performers, we (the actors) can't clear the stage quickly either after the bows, and once the curtain is down, we yell, "We love you, we love you," and I get the last word again: "Lock all the doors and windows and don't let them out!" The audience can't hear us. It's a shame, because everyone should know when he's loved. That good audience just got the ultimate best out of us. We would break our necks for them and have.

George judged performers only by their work. I remember one

night I was sitting with George in the lounge at Caesars Palace when Alan King came bursting in.

"Oh, my God, George, a terrible thing has just happened. Connie Francis was raped on her tour in her hotel room."

George: "Wait a minute, wait a minute. Did they steal her orchestrations?"

Alan: "No."

George: "Well then, she's still in show business."

But I have to tell you about George's genius, and genius it certainly was, and where it comes from. You see, the least of George's talents was performing. He knew that and said so. He told me he often wondered what he would have become if he hadn't fallen in love with Gracie. He said he would have been like Florenz Ziegfeld, planning shows and overseeing them. That's why he was never annoyed at my bothering him about my act. When we worked together in theatres across the country for two years, he constantly gave me advice, and he was uncannily right.

Now, do you want to know where George's genius came from? Dyslexia! He couldn't read. So he was totally dependent on animal instinct. I watched him working. He didn't know it was his dyslexia that forced him into genius territory, or maybe he did and just never mentioned it to me or anyone I knew who was around him. His secretary, Jack Langdon, read everything to him. Jack just said to me on the phone, "I think George would think that's a hoot that you feel it's his dyslexia that gave him his phenomenal knowledge of show business." I wanted to know from Jack if George would have minded my telling you about it. Jack said, "George would think it was very funny."

Well then. In the second grade, George was sent home from school as hopelessly retarded because they didn't know what dyslexia was in those days. That's how come he never learned to read. He also came home willingly, because he had eleven brothers and sisters in one bed and they were hungry. As I've already told you, he was always the breadwinner, bringing his mother pennies he got for dancing on street corners and singing at churches and gatherings. He developed his animal instincts to such a height that he was walking on eggshells without breaking them, feeling his way lightly. Actually, I suspect it's the only way in show business . . . or any creative business.

If you have a job ahead of you that you've got to accomplish, you're forced to hook on to some creative force that straightens your thought out and heals you and makes you strong enough to get the job done. George could do that. He never missed a single show in his entire one-hundred-year life.

The best comedy work I've ever done was in a tape with George that Debbie Reynolds and Ruta Lee dug up for a Thalians benefit. George when he saw it said, "Save that tape." Neither George nor I knew it was that good when we did it, but it's obvious I was completely responding to George and his divine hookup. It benefited everyone around him. He always told his writers exactly what subject matter to write about and gave them a taste of what made the idea funny. I watched him with them. He gave them the matrix of his plot, the set design to the set designer, the style of music to Morty Jacobs, and so on. That was his talent—directing, writing, producing, and overseeing everything, including finances.

Some of the proceeds of this weekly TV show went to old vaudevillians who were "waiting for this television scare to blow over." There was a fellow in the St. Moritz Hotel who lived in the suite that George kept for him and whose job it was to sort the Burnses' New York mail. Everyone knew George and Gracie came out of L.A., so there was no New York mail, but this fellow was supported for the rest of his life in this vitally important occupation.

One night there was a "family gathering" at Jack and Mary Benny's house. It consisted of the cast and writers on both their TV shows. George was trying out new monologue material for size, with everybody fixing it and suggesting things. George had a brother Willie, who served on their TV show in some capacity. He looked a lot like George. They were awfully cute together. Suddenly Gracie burst out with "Nattie (George), why don't you and Willie let Carol stand between you, and you three do your 'Sunny Side of the Street'?" I said, "Oh, Gracie. How did you know how badly I wanted to be just there?" She said, "It's so obvious, Carol. You've been eating them up alive all evening. Go on. Get up there."

I did. George seemed all for it. I stood about a head taller than each of them, and my dream had already come true. I was Louella Geer between Eugene and Willie Howard in *George White's Scandals*, the second musical show I ever saw in San Francisco, and from that time on I dreamed of being Louella Geer, standing with two great vaudevillians.

Gracie said she could see she had put me in orbit. George said, "Look, Carol, Willie and I will sing the song and do the dance, and all you do is sing the title whenever we point to you." Fine. We danced. It was simple.

I picked it up quickly in my euphoria. George would say, "Hug that floor," and we three slowly hugged that floor. Morty Jacobs would play the chorus on the piano. Then, just before they pointed to me, George said something like "Carol, where do you want to be kissed?" Me (singing): "On the sunny side of the street." Well, it was shocking. They had worked those lyrics so that simply singing the innocent title became the biggest off-color joke in the song, and the most surprised of all was me. I can't remember any more of their lyrics, darn it, but it built and it was funny. That is, Gracie was always such a terrible giggler she could make everything funny. Her health was failing even then, but none of us could bear to believe her or her doctor. George especially.

I can thank Charles that, because of his beautiful relationship with Gracie, I was invited to those gatherings along with him before we were married. Gracie liked him. I knew I'd already been given star billing in four shows *Gentlemen Prefer Blondes*, *Pygmalion*, *The Millionairess*, and *Wonderful Town*, but I also knew Gracie wouldn't have invited me just because of that. She truly liked Charles.

The first dinner I was invited to was a farewell party for Gerry Boggio, who did everything for all the Burnses. She was one of those. She was leaving to marry and live in Italy. I was meeting "the family" for the first time. The Burnses were always happy for new stars and their success in the theatre. I was used to New York resentment at that time. These Burnses welcomed me, and I, like anyone, was thrilled with them. Charles, as I say, represented their sponsor—Carnation milk.

George asked me, "How do you remember the name of each and every one here tonight, including the script man?" I explained to him that Charles had got the order of the dinner place cards from Gracie. For the entire week before, he'd rehearsed their names with me. I had no idea that would send George into changing all the place cards around, of course. So, to this day I think Harvey Helms's wife, Ruth, was married to Bea Benaderet's husband, and that Gerry Boggio was married to Harvey (who wrote the important convolutions into Gracie's lines). I thought Norman Paul (writer) was an ex-alcoholic, so

I kept helping him not to have another beer—"you don't really want that" I said to him after we got friendly that night. I took his beer away and put it in front of Harvey, who *was* an ex-alcoholic. I don't remember all my wrongs that evening, but George always remembered them, and very fondly. He said he enjoyed watching every minute.

Well, the Burns children were crying over Gerry's leaving. Everyone made touching speeches in honor of Gerry's kindnesses until finally George got up and said, "Gerry hadn't realized you cared for her so much, so she has just decided not to go and will continue working with all of us." Everyone stopped crying and yelled, "Oh, Gerry, go already," which tickled George no end since at some weak moment he'd given Gerry 5 percent of their TV residuals. He told me about it that night before making that speech. Well, he had to let off steam to somebody he was so mad at himself. *That* I enjoyed. You see, George had a creative genius, but he was also a businessman, otherwise how could their show have become the great Burns and Allen sitcom and pioneer of many other sitcoms?

At one of those gatherings in Las Vegas, "the family" had arrived to see our new hit act at the Tropicana. I say "our act" because it was really Charlie Gaynor's, George's, Gracie's (she supervised Orry-Kelly's costumes on me), and Charles's (he produced it) and mine. Charles and I gave a "family" dinner in Vegas that we asked my mother to attend. She sat on George's left, and I'll never forget how she loved it. George said to her, feeling her arm, "Mrs. Channing, that's very firm flesh you have there. Your husband was always in religious work, so you're well broken in. I know a very nice rabbi who would love that pretty arm. I know he'd like to marry you." She really enjoyed that and laughed a lot. Then later, when everyone at the table could hear him, he said to her, "The way you're stroking my leg under the table I find most enjoyable, Mrs. Channing." Out of reflex action she swung her right hand immediately onto the top of the table. Everyone laughed, including George. She looked surprised, and then she laughed, too. "Oh, please don't stop," George said and went on teasing her for the rest of the dinner.

When she was ninety-nine years old and living in a Christian Science home, I was able to visit my mother for the first time in many years. There was one long minute when our faces were close. She said relaxedly, almost to herself, "You're so pretty." She never said anything like that before. I kept my face close to hers, looking head-on into her eyes. At that moment we knew we both always loved one another, as parent and offspring do no matter what the past. She remembered every word George teased her with that night and repeated a lot of it to me then. I told George. I could see that it didn't surprise him. He knew he had captured her and remembered a great deal about her. I love you, George. You were the only memory she spoke of.

The Kennedys

The then Jacqueline Kennedy said to me, "I would have gone to that party last night if the Russians had given it." I laughed my head off because it was a dangerous statement to make, since the Russians and Americans were all mad at each other at the time and it came from our newly anointed president's wife, but I couldn't stop laughing at it because it made her nature come cleanly across to me. She enjoyed making me laugh; she had no intention of standing in a line of First Ladies saying the proper expected thing; she trusted me. There she sat, rocking back and forth in the president's rocker, which was there expressly to relieve his back. We were in the second-floor parlor of the family living quarters of the White House. She was like a little girl playing with her father's forbidden belongings. I suspected from her enjoyment and vigor in rocking that it wasn't a good idea to do this when the president was in that room.

George Burns and I had proven ourselves the night before by do-
nating our act and ourselves to the presidential gala to raise money to
pay the president's campaign debts. What she had just done by making
that dangerous statement was that instead of the usual "thank you for
helping to pay campaign debts" cliché she knew she had said it all already (in that shocking crack about the Russians) and she knew I
would know it. What a compliment! She considered me as intelligent
as she was.

That party the night before was given by the vice president and
Mrs. Lyndon Johnson in their home outside Washington, D.C., to be
attended by all the performers in the show that night: Carol Burnett,
Rudolf Nureyev, Gene Kelly, Kirk Douglas, I wish I could remember
some more. Anyway, we were all sitting on the floor and around, when
Gene Kelly announced that the president of the United States would
now join him in singing "The Wearin' of the Green."

Jack Kennedy stood slowly up and said, "Lyndon! Come here and
help me out. Come on. Sing it with us."

Lyndon: Not me!

JFK: Aw, Lyn*donnnn*. (I thought I saw a stamp of his right foot.)

Lyndon (loud and shrill): I ain't gonna make a ass out o' *my*self.

And the piano started. Gene Kelly sang his heart out with the president, who obviously didn't know the lyrics at all. He was watching
Gene's lips and trying to come in a tad later after each word, then getting very loud after he found out what the word was. It was much more
fun than if he had memorized it. Jackie was laughing up a storm, and
you could see all the Kennedys would have gone to that party even if
the Russians *had* given it. It was one magic party.

The next night in George's, Charles's, and my hotel suite the phone
rang. Charles answered. The lady on the phone said she was calling
from the White House. Charles told us she said that the president and
First Lady's plane taking them to Camp David had been grounded.
"We realize that your plane has been fogged in, too, so they would like
for Mr. Burns and Miss Channing and her husband to join them in the
breakfast room of the White House for dinner tonight."

Charles: Thank you. And what is *your* name, madam?

Lady: My name is Mrs. Lincoln.

Charles: Oh, come now, Carol Burnett. I'd know your voice anywhere. (Then he was silent a minute.) Oh! I beg your pardon. May I have your number please? I'll call you right back. George! Baby Lowe! The president and Mrs. Kennedy want just the three of us for dinner tonight in the breakfast nook.

George: No! I can't go. My toupee is packed. You two go.

I realized with the trouble we had getting George there that he was really frightened. Smooth, cool George, with his understated, quiet sex appeal! I couldn't believe it.

Charles: I'll get Gracie on the phone. She'll make you go.

He got Gracie at home in Beverly Hills and explained the situation to her. He put George on the phone with her.

George: Happy birthday, Googie.

George told us she said to please forget her birthday, that there may never be another Irish Catholic family in the White House. George told us, "Gracie says, 'Go and kiss the Kennedys for me Nattie.' (George's real name when they met was Nathan Birnbaum.) She says I should go for her. When she says she loves me, then I have to go."

He called for Charlie, his dresser. George was forever giving entertainers from the then-deceased vaudeville jobs. All Charlie ever did was tap dance with George in front of a mirror, so they'd be exactly together on the choreography. "Open my H & M trunk, Charlie, and take out my toupee." Of course Charlie had no idea where it was in the trunk, so George did it. I was busy getting *my* wig out. Not that I was bald. It's just that my hair was (as Charles referred to it) that shit-brindle ash mouse, and I was allergic to hair bleach.

We got our hair on. I got my dress on. George got out a little ironing board and iron that was a part of his H & M. He was so proud of his H & M trunk with drawers. Only well-paid vaudevillians could afford an H & M. It was his status symbol. He was pressing his when he looked at me and said, "Better take that dress off," and ironed it across the lap. We paid no attention to Charles. He was one of those people who never seemed to need anything. Leastwise from us.

A White House car was waiting for us downstairs, so we had no time to care that George was in his knee-length undershorts and I was in my slip. George and I had been traveling together with Charles and Charlie by now for two whole years anyway, and we were both nervous and rushed, so we jammed on our clothes, hooked each other up, and ran down into the car.

When one arrives at the White House, you know, as one walks between the two white entrance columns, one is overwhelmed by the feeling of: how did I stay out of jail this long, not even knowing this moment was coming?

We came upstairs, and there was Jacqueline Kennedy, giggly with delight that we could come. By the way, she called herself "Jacq*leen,*" not "Jacque*lyn.*" We're now back up to her rocking in the chair. I could see she adored George, and George responded to it. I don't know what she said to him, because just then the president came in and I was bedazzled. By the way, I was right. She shot up out of that rocker the moment he entered and never went back. We all met. George was charming. He said, "Mr. President, let me look at you standing there. You're just beautiful. So strong and young. How did we get such a dream of a president! I'm proud. Just look at you." He looked way up to JFK with a vulnerable child's face.

JFK was much bigger than anyone would think, and his Irish strawberry blond coloring was vivid. He stood still obediently the way George want him to . . . a tender, relaxed smile on his face as long as George chose to worship him. Kennedy was totally unself-conscious. I could see he was receiving the rarest quality on earth . . . love. And he knew it. He was fulfilling little Nattie Birnbaum's furthest vision of an American son. It fulfilled the president, too. But to George's generation people were purely one race, and this was certainly JFK and his singular Celtic heritage.

George was right. The dictionary says a generation is those born within a period of twenty-five years. I was exactly one generation later than George, and during my time Americans went to school with every nationality and race on the face of the globe, so an American family descended from purely one country, as the Kennedy's were, was almost obsolete.

After talking with each of us, the president wanted to get into the breakfast nook; he seemed to be excited about something. I got to sit on his left. He turned to me and said, "Carol, do you realize that in a short time we're going to be able to go to the moon? Yes! Just today in London they knighted the man who contributed the most to inventing the missile to the moon. He's an Englishman. He's now Sir Isaac Mandelbaum. Imagine! We'll have men walking on the moon, and we can look at movies of them taken there! Look at this chart. This is the missile." I couldn't make it out. It was all mathematics and hieroglyphics, but JFK was undaunted. He was going to make me understand it all. He tried several times. He was so enthusiastic I didn't want to wear our president out, so I finally said, "Oh yes. I see." However, he looked dubious.

For sake of accuracy, there were three other people at the table . . . Lee Radziwill, sitting next to Charles, and a Lord and Lady on JFK's right. I knew their name at the time. They had brought this news and chart to the president during that day. JFK was so thrilled he even wasted his attention on me, and I got thrilled by osmosis for him. So I turned to George, who was on the First Lady's right, to explain it all to him, with the chart. I remember Kennedy saying, "No, no, Carol. You have it just backwards. *First* we land on the moon, put the flag in, than take movies, come back, and *then* circle the earth."

I don't remember what I said that was so far wrong, but Jacqueline and the Lord and Lady thought it very funny how I could get it so exactly backwards. And why did JFK care that much about getting through to me? I was flattered he felt one little American citizen was that important. I only wish I could tell you what was so darned funny. I still don't know. George always said when he saw that chart in the newspapers later he'd never understand it once I'd screwed it up like that. Jacqueline loved the screwup. As the evening went on I realized she was also a screwer-upper. For instance, I was trying to thank the president for renewing the patent that year on *Science and Health* with *Key to the Scriptures* by Mary Baker Eddy. I told him that prior to that the Christian Scientists I knew felt there *was* no Democratic party, only Republican. "Now my father tells me they're so grateful to you, Mr. President, that you're their hero. You should know that."

"What's that, Mr. President?" asked Jackie. "What did you do?"

JFK: Well, I renewed the patent on their Christian Science book. Most books have a copyright, but this came under presidential jurisdiction as a patent."

"Oh," said Jackie, "I couldn't hear. I thought I heard you sold patent medicines to Christian Scientists."

He gave her a disapproving look like Charles often gave me in company. But it didn't bother her in the least. I couldn't stop laughing. Sometime after dinner Princess Radziwill and the Lord and Lady disappeared. Jacqueline whispered to me, "Would you like to go to the

bathroom with me? I have some rarest old brandy in there. It's delicious." Why did I say, "Oh thank you, no?" I should have gone. What did it taste like? What else was in there? Maybe books she read or paintings she liked. Oh, Carol. You should have gone. Jacqueline kept talking to me in her trademark Marilyn Monroe whisper, which on her sounded more like "This delicious secret is just between us two chickens." No matter what she said, I would never have had the forwardness myself to keep opening new subjects with her because of Yul's training about the Queen, and Jacqueline Bouvier Kennedy was indeed a queen.

She suddenly said, "If I were a Christian Scientist I'd be as strong as a Kennedy."

Me: But aren't you?

Jacqueline: Oh no. No one is as strong as a Kennedy.

I've thought about that sentence for years. As I say, Catholics and I attract each other, but they mostly feel *I'd* be better off if I were a Catholic. To them their way is not necessarily the only way. Also, the in-laws' respect for the strength genes of the Kennedys was very apparent. At another family dinner I remember Bobby saying to me, "We're planning a raft trip down the Colorado River." I said, "Oh? Where does it end?" Bobby said, "We all slide directly into Cedars-Sinai Hospital."

At one point the president asked George if he'd like to see Lincoln's bed. "Sure," said George. We all went down the long hall to the door on our right. Kennedy opened the door a crack and shut it fast. "Oh! Mother's asleep in Lincoln's bed."

Jackie said, "I knew that all the time. But he's the president."

She took George's arm and led him into the main living room, where the little elevator could arrive and where there was a grand piano. The president led me into this room because he'd been talking with George and Charles, and I with Jackie. Then the tiny elevator door opened, and out spilled this avalanche of Kennedy energy. I'll never forget it. The room was ignited with it. It was like that miniature circus automobile that dozens of people emerge from. First was Bobby, then Ted, then Joan, then, was it Sarge? And then Ethel, who was great with child, which was her chronic condition in those days. Every time I was with Ethel she was in the same shape, yet when we went to Bedford-Stuyvesant, the poorest section of New York, to sing

Christmas carols, all of us who went, including Bobby and Art Buchwald and Rosie Greer, dumped our heavy winter coats on her to hold
and cases of music and handbags, and she didn't let go of anything. Just
stood there smiling, extremely happy, enjoying our singing, uniquely a
Kennedy, which is extremely alive.

Back to this animal energy that suddenly permeated the living
room. The president appointed Jackie master of ceremonies for that
night. She went right over to a wall, took a sword off the wall that she
said was President Lincoln's from the Battle of Gettysburg (what was
Lincoln doing with a sword? Didn't you think he only made an address there?), announced, referring to Bobby, that the secretary of
state? or the interior? or postmaster general? of the United States of
America would now sing "Mack the Knife." Jacqueline knew his title,
I just can't think of it at this moment.

The president said to Jackie, "You will march yourself over to that
wall, put that valuable sword back where you found it, and come and
sit here next to me." We were all on the floor with pillows. She did
what the president said, but none of his orders to her could dent her
fun that night.

Bobby decided to sing instead his summer camp song from when he
was growing up. It was "Camp Wyonagonic." He never could understand years later how I could remember its name, but names like that
always stick with me. Never Camp Silver Lake or dull titles. He pantomimed paddling a canoe. The song was something to the effect of:

> Root tee toot, root tee toot
> We are the boys of the institute
> Peaches and cream, peaches and cream
> The team, the team, the team.

We all applauded. Then Jackie announced that the President of the
United States would sing "The Wearin' of the Green."

"Oh, no." I said, "I can't go through that again. Mr. President, I
didn't get the impression you knew your lyrics."

JFK: Miss Channing, I'll have you know I do know the title of the
song, and I expected you and everyone else to fill in the rest for me.

Me: But I never knew those lyrics, sir. Why should I?

JFK: Oh, well, then, I just won't sing at all with no cooperation.

Jackie: Now, now. Let's not fight. The United States senator for the state of Massachusetts will do his impression of the Kennedy family retainer.

Ted came forward. He imitated a very old man saying something about "little Jack Kennedy is now so tall, his head is in the Stars and Stripes." For some strange reason, this was excruciatingly funny. However, only to the Kennedys. They could hardly live through it. They all grew up with this old gent apparently. Jackie at this point came over to me and whispered, "Could you sing, 'It's Delightful Down in Chile' later? I love that number."

Me: Oh yes. Did you like it, really?

Jackie: I love it.

Me: So do I. Yes, I want to do it for you.

Then she whispered to George, "Would you sing 'La Vie en Rose?' " How sophisticated of her . . . to give us a chance to recollect before doing it.

Then Ted, who was still on, wanted to sing songs taught to him by the Italians of Boston. He was accompanied on the piano by his then wife, Joan, who seemed well rehearsed with him. He was truly quite marvelous and could have been a huge success in vaudeville, George announced. Ted was so encouraged by that he sang some more songs.

Jackie introduced Ethel next to recite "There Are Fairies at the Bottom of Our Garden." Ethel came forward and stood. She had many pretty colored, ruffled petticoats on that shot straight out in front of her because of her condition. Also, because we were all sitting on the floor, we saw very little of Ethel during her recitation. Just the petticoats.

But Joan was awfully good at accompanying people. She had the sheet music for "La Vie en Rose" on the piano. George was irresistible doing it. It was all in his own Houston (pronounced in New York "Howstn") Street French. When he finished, Jackie, still giggling, said, "Isn't that funny? I've been speaking French all my life and never knew I had it all wrong." They all applauded George like crazy.

I could see that when they had show business guests they were eager to enjoy, they made the whole family entertain first so the entertainers weren't treated like court jesters. It made it easy for us. It was very informal this way. I actually enjoyed doing "Chile" for Jackie, and they all responded as if George and I were what they really came for.

George was in bliss, I could tell. Whoever planned this evening was highly experienced and knowledgeable about asking professionals to entertain. They ate George up. I had the happiest of times. Such appreciation!

Exactly one year after the assassination of President Kennedy, Jacqueline, little John, and Caroline came to a Wednesday matinee to see *Hello, Dolly!* It was the first time in that year that they had been out anywhere in public like that. The Wednesday matinee is always mostly women. I was so proud of that audience. Not one person asked for an autograph or even tried to talk to the children. They just seemed to want them to enjoy the show.

You know, whenever a First Lady is in the audience, all heads are turned toward her. For instance, when Lady Bird came, she must have known this because she wore long white gloves and, after the first song, both of her arms shot straight up, clapping as high as she could. To us onstage it looked like a grand gesture of "I approve of this show." She threw the attention off her and onto the stage. We treasured her for it. It worked! She let them know where they should be looking.

But with Jacqueline, Caroline, and John Kennedy that day, it wasn't necessary. People seemed to be making a concerted effort to protect them, even from themselves, the audience, and their own curiosity.

At intermission, the ushers told me John had to be taken to the ladies' room, he was so little. People smiled, at the most, to the three of them, they handed a paper towel to John, but no one intruded on their conversation.

After the show, there was a knock on my dressing room door. I opened it to find Caroline still trying to knock. "Why, Caroline Kennedy," I said. "I'm so happy to see you." She turned up to her mother and said, "She knew my name. Dolly Gallagher Levi knew my name!" Now how did Jackie keep them from knowing the whole *world* knew their names?

Me: Dear Jacqueline, please come in.

Jackie: Well, we wanted to see your great big purple bag. I think it's extremely chic.

Caroline held it admiringly. "Oh yes." Artie Sicardi knocked on the door and said the stage crew wanted to know if John would like to ride on the train. "Yes!" chirped John.

Now I must explain to you that IATSE's rules are rigid, so without reporting it they brought the 8:40 down on ropes and chains from three stories high, John jumped onboard when it landed, and they rode him back and forth for as long as he wanted. The crew was missing its dinner, but I never saw them so unrushed and contented.

Naturally, we had the big purple bag copied by the costumer. I wore the rehearsal bag for two shows. We shot it right over to Jackie's apartment. A week later a handwritten letter from Jacqueline came telling me that Caroline put on her mother's shoes, which extended behind her heels like Minnie Mouse's, put cards in the bag, and went from door to door in their apartment building explaining to people she was Dolly Levi and offering her services of "old corsets re-boned, ears pierced, pierced ears replugged," et cetera. The letter was very funny, and when I read it I knew how much they must have enjoyed the show. Again, Jackie didn't have to say it. It was already said.

One day I went sailing in Eunice Shriver's little boat with the Kennedy clan. I asked where she got such a lovely boat. Ted answered, "She saved her coupons at the supermarket." The family tolerance was Eunice's penuriousness.

At this time, Halston's only custom-made ensembles were for the likes of Babe Paley, Slim Keith, Elizabeth Taylor, and all that crowd. I was wearing then whatever Halston put on me, so Eunice said to me, "Would you ask Halston if he ever has a sale?" I said, "Yes." It was easier than trying to explain it to her, don't you think?

Whenever Eunice traveled by plane she went tourist class. Tourist class in those days exited from the back of the plane, and therefore without planning it she avoided all that mess with the press. She owned one evening gown for formal occasions. For all else she wore a sweatshirt. She told me the evening gown was stolen and that it hurt her to pay again for something she had already paid for. So I suppose she wore a sweatshirt everywhere. It was becoming to her, though.

I used to see the same cook in all different Kennedys' houses in the Hyannis compound. I understood Eunice thought of that. They'd all eat dinner together in one of the houses whenever we were there. Why get several cooks? It was exciting for me because each Kennedy, even in-laws, had the responsibility for five states designated by the president. They'd discuss their states' activities vehemently at dinner. In

Wisconsin, one of Sargent Shriver's assigned states, there was a bridge cracked somewhere in the middle. "Sarge," Eunice said, "are you going to sit there and eat your dinner just because it's hot now or are you going to phone and tell them to fix it immediately?" Sarge phoned. I never heard her order him any other time. She ate a cold dinner, too, for fear there'd be a terrible Wisconsin accident any second.

That's the same spirit Bobby had. When lots of Kennedys and I were driving over Brooklyn Bridge, at the end of it was an unattended baby carriage slowly drifting into traffic from a supermarket on the other side of the street. We were in a snowstorm, but Bobby opened the back car door. We all yelled for the driver to stop, Bobby seemed to leap over the oncoming traffic (with no coat on), grabbed the carriage, wheeled it to safety, and came back to tell us there was no baby in it. But the Kennedy spirit was unflagged. We went right on rehearsing our Christmas carols at top pitch all the way to Bedford-Stuyvesant.

And that's another lesson I learned. When we went to Harlem, to the very poorest sections, they told me to wear my most expensive, spectacular clothes. They were right. I wore the Bob Mackie diamond dress, the Halston fur coat to the floor that they give you for "What Becomes a Legend Most" (it was white mink), and everyone there in Harlem seemed so happy for me that I had such a getup that no one grabbed any jewelry or wanted to do anything to spoil the outfit. They simply celebrated it with me. Isn't that a lesson? Never dress down, as I said before. Especially if flamboyant overboard is your honest, secret taste. They know it's true to you. The uncanny X-ray machine that an audience really is never ceases to amaze me.

Back to Eunice. She explained to me how wrong a particular cartel was. At the time there were five ruling airlines. If the fifth airline voted yes or no on anything, right or wrong, that's what prevailed. She fought it hard. She had the same deep sense of principle they all had concerning civic issues. The others' private moral codes I knew nothing about, but you don't suppose they were right about that code too, do you?

I have never known myself such happiness between two people as I saw one rainy night when the family asked us to drop in after my show to the Fifth Avenue apartment for another gathering. Jacqueline was sitting inside the apartment hall door on Bobby's lap. She was sitting on him as if he were an upright chair. You know, both her knees were directly over both of Bobby's knees, the two of them facing forward like stacked up dining table chairs. I think the incongruity of it appealed to Jackie. The family was all around them, chattering away.

I was trying to unzip my new spiral-zippered raincoat. I finally tried to pull it off over my head. It dripped all over the rug and me. This appealed to Jackie who went into hysterics. Bobby was laughing, too. I finally stepped out of it and witnessed the harmony and dear love they had for each other through their laughter. I felt suddenly it was so beautiful that, of course, to me it was a gift from above. Vicariously they taught me what love is. Are we all wrong to turn our backs on that? So far, what makes my life worth living is, as I say, uplifting people's lives. Is that enough? Not when I saw those two together. You could see it all began with Bobby's feeling of responsibility about his brother's widow.

Now, though, I'll never forget a few years ago (Bobby was assassinated long before) in her home outside Washington, Ethel rushing to me in anguish, holding my hands too tightly, and crying, "Oh, Carol. Will it ever end?" This was during William Kennedy Smith's court trial. Then Ethel leaned on me so hard, she must have thought I was as strong as a Kennedy. She needed Bobby. I towered way over her, so I was glad to be as strong as I am for her and glad that she wanted to lean on me. She could have torn my fingers off. If it might have helped her, I wouldn't have minded at all at that moment.

One day I remember in Hyannis, Rose invited me to walk along the beach with her. I had just finished four shows back to back in New York, two Saturday and two Sunday. This was a Monday morning, and I must have looked it, because we wound up sitting by the grand piano with Rose telling me who everyone was in the crowded silver-framed pictures on the piano. Those Kennedys! Once they take you in, they trust you all the way. What an offer that was from Rose to want me as her friend. One picture was of her son Joseph, who was killed in the war. Another was of three people—Joe the father, Rose, a big steamer trunk, and Gloria Swanson—all on an ocean liner on the deck. Rose said, "You know, Gloria has written a book. I begged her, I said, 'Gloria, why don't you tell the truth? You were always our family friend. Must you say it was your love affair with Joe? It's not true, you know. Please!' But Gloria wouldn't change it."

My own experience from doing several one-hour TV interviews with Gloria Swanson when I was on tour was that I couldn't say anything that didn't anger her . . . right on camera. I can't help it, I don't believe anything Gloria Swanson ever said. I believe Rose Kennedy. She had a severe sense of honesty, which affected all her children. Based on my experience with her, I'd say Eunice is the supreme example of Rose's candor. Bobby, too.

There was a bill that had to be voted on by the Senate and the House. It concerned big corporations buying blocks of tickets to Broadway shows, then doling them out to employees as a bonus. Naturally Broadway producers, from Harvey Sabinson (the then president of the Broadway Producers' League) on down, wanted this bill to go through.

Again I was selected as spokesperson, with Harvey Sabinson right on my ear. Eunice went out of her way in Washington to sit Charles and me down with her while she earnestly repeated, "It's not faaaa [fair], this bill. What about little old ladies who want so much to see a Broadway show but can't afford it? It's not faaaa." Somehow this bill, to Eunice, robbed little old ladies, and many other people, of their chances. I couldn't answer her. I was unaware of that. So, since I was the only one really listening, I got the full scolding.

It was the first time I was scolded by a Kennedy. One night at a family dinner Bobby stood up and said, "I know it's terribly funny about Carol bringing her own food and so much of it, but there's something wrong with that. No one should eat that much food at one sitting. Carol, you should find out what's wrong with you. There is something wrong with you. Shut up, everybody. It's not funny."

So I found out, and it was from eating all those potato puffs in *Dolly*'s eating scene, they were made of pure spun sugar. At the same time, Mr. Merrick had a doctor come and investigate it. Merrick said, "Somebody's poisoning her." I must have looked it. The doctor asked what all those big sugar bags were for. Artie Sicardi said, "Because in a scene, she eats from seven to nine pounds a week, depending on how long the audience laughs." That much sugar gives one some terrible disease I forget the name of at this moment.

After that we made them of baked Kleenex, with instant coffee powder to brown them. I felt much better. But when I go, the coroner is going to find all my lower insides lined with Kleenex. I didn't exactly eat the Kleenex, but after five thousand shows I'm sure bits of it are still with me. It turned into spitballs in my mouth and I got them out with a napkin while Gower had the judge bang his gavel on the other side of the stage to distract the audience. So Bobby was right. The truth doesn't hurt anybody, according to Rose's children.

Well, remember JFK and the Bay of Pigs? Same darned thing. He didn't care about the embarrassment of being wrong. He said, "I was wrong."

When I played Shaw's *The Millionairess* for the Theatre Guild, all the Kennedy offspring came. Eunice carried on about "this is the story of our lives . . . a father who was superhumanly artful and we all were obligated to come up to it. Carol is playing us." I knew that too, all by myself. When *Dolly* came to Chicago at the Shubert Theatre, Charles and I invited Joe Sr. to the show. He was bedridden in the hospital with a severe stroke, so they put him in an ambulance in the bed, and then the family arranged for him to be wheeled into the theatre in the bed and put in the stage left box with a dark curtain all around him except on the stage side. He had a full view of the stage with his head propped up on a pillow. The moment the curtain went down I was next to him. He tried and tried to speak. It's an emotional blow to watch a concentrated force like Joe Kennedy finally succumb to crying frustration. His face was wet with tears. He was looking at me helplessly. How I wished someone could have said one word for him.

I *did* my term thesis on George Bernard Shaw at Bennington and discovered again all by myself that his heroines are all the same woman—Eliza Doolittle, the Aviatrix, Major Barbara, the Millionairess, and Saint Joan. However, Shaw's focus was always on his own political views, like how wry it was that they canonized Joan *after* they burned her at the stake. However, I feel she was naïve about human nature. She thought everyone would be glad to see her. But why should all those VIPs of France move over for a sixteen-year-old girl when she wasn't offering anything to them in return? Naturally they couldn't wait for her to be captured by the British and burned to death, even though she won the war with her French army, and drove the British out of France right up to now and maybe forever. Of course this is only my opinion of Shaw's revelation. The British owned the profits from French labor.

Most men find these women to be holy terrors on wheels. Shaw just dandied them on his knee and seemed to think they were his own baby Aphrodites. To Shaw, Joan and the Duke of Orléans, sitting on the banks of the Loire River waiting for the wind to change so they could sail and go into battle, is a most provocative scene glandularly. Their metabolisms are in an uproar. They are and have been dependent on one another to survive in battle. In a short time they will be either annihilated together or self-sacrificingly victorious. Nothing in the world could bring them closer together. They have to believe in one another.

My first professional experience with Shaw was in *Pygmalion*, just one month after I gave birth to Chan. The prestigious Theatre Guild, headed by Lawrence Langner and Armina Marshall, said to me, "Carol, you should play a Shavian heroine."

Charles, Chan, and I were all living in New York when I began rehearsing Shaw's *The Millionairess*. At that time the Shaw estate would not allow one word to be cut.

You know it has always been said that art should never be didactic, that then it isn't art anymore. But Shaw argued constantly that art should *always* be didactic. The result in any Shaw play is that Epifania (my part) would say to her suitor, excellently played by John McMartin, lines to the effect of "I love you," and McMartin would say, "I love you, too. Will you marry me?" Epifania would say, "Yes. But first let me discuss income tax." The monologues go on for three pages. Or "I'm leaving you." "Oh please, don't go." "I won't go until I tell you how I feel about organized religion." This one goes on for *four* pages.

Now the Shaw estate allows you to cut all you want for a musical. This is why Shaw's plays make much better musicals, like *Pygmalion* into *My Fair Lady*, or *Arms and the Man* into *The Chocolate Soldier*.

There's a big sink in the middle of the second act of *St. Joan* that no Joan could possibly overcome. I don't think she's even in it, while everyone else analyzes something like the stupidity of social classes, or the economic structure of France and England. You see, the problem with Shaw is he doesn't follow an emotion that could lead the actor into his next line. But once the lines are learned solidly enough, Epifania, for instance, could be one of those British eccentrics much like Lady Astor or Margaret Ramsay (London's foremost literary agent), who get wound up like a buzz saw.

After we opened, I could hear the audience laughing and, in some cities, applauding in the middle of a speech because they agreed with its content. Oh, Shaw is something. As I say, he treated these female tornadoes as if they were adorable romantic leads. So he dandied them on his knee and lovingly sent them spinning to frighten the rest of the world, but they never frightened Shaw. He kissed them with his vocabulary and hugged them with his political views.

Oh, yes, Shaw had Epifania perform Jujitsu on the man who asked her to marry him, so we got a trainer and I threw big, tall John McMartin all over the stage. John got the worst of it. Later he was so divine with Gwen Verdon in *Sweet Charity*. I always wanted to ask him about his back and spine when I went to see him perform, but I never got backstage before he left the theatre. Wasn't he great in *Charity?* The way he did Neil Simon's stuck elevator scene made it a poem. I'll tell you later about Neil's claustrophobia. It gave him the ability to write that hysterical scene.

efore I started the run of *The Millionairess*, David Merrick (for those still in their bassinets, he was the most prolific of Broadway producers; his backers used to fight over putting money into his shows) flew to Minneapolis to see my show *Carol Channing and Her Ten Stout-Hearted Men*. Mr. Merrick (I could never call him David because of my respect for his showmanship) came backstage, and I had to ask him, because he didn't mention it. "How did you like the show?"

Merrick: I didn't look at the show, I was counting the house. I'm going to organize a Broadway musical for you. I'll call you the moment it's ready for you to look at.

I told him right then and there I needed Gower Champion. We didn't have him in *The Vamp*. We actually had no one at the head of *The Vamp*. I explained to you before how disastrous I knew that can be for a show.

So, while I was touring *The Millionairess*, Mr. Merrick decided he would produce a musical based on Thornton Wilder's *The Match-maker*. The title of the musical would be "A Damned Exasperating Woman," and he offered me the part of Dolly Levi. Gower Champion would be the choreographer and director. However, Gower told Mr. Merrick he would absolutely not have me as Dolly Levi. Now I must tell you the history of *that*.

Oliver Smith (coproducer of *Gentlemen Prefer Blondes* with Herman Levin) had asked Gower and his first mate, Marge (as Marge was proud to call herself), to choreograph *Blondes*. The Champions were all ready to start when Agnes de Mille came to Oliver and said, "Oliver, I need and want to choreograph *Blondes*."

Oliver told me he said to her, "But it's all set. We have Gower."

Agnes: Oliver, you owe me this! I worked with you all during your central position as cofounder and producer with Lucia Chase (money) of the New York City Ballet. You owe me this!

Oliver told this to me to explain why I had to stop looking forward to the Champions joining us. When the Champions were let go and Agnes came in, Gower hated me! Is it possible he honestly thought that in my first starring part *I* had anything at all to do with making decisions? He *must* have known better. Marge told me after Gower died that it turned out to be the best thing that ever happened to them. They were asked to do important movies instead, and President Truman publicly stated that they were the great, typically-young-American-looking dance team and everybody loved them.

But at the time Gower did not want me as Dolly. Merrick insisted the two of them drive out to Matunuck, Long Island, to see me in the Theatre Guild's *The Millionairess*. Merrick saw it in Westport and was seeing it again. Gower hated it. He thought, What has that horsey British woman she's playing got to do with Dolly? He told me he hated my broad grin and the way I rocked my head (I never heard that one before, not even from Gower).

I said, "Gower, let me audition Dolly for you. You owe me this!" Agnes de Mille couldn't have put it more succinctly. I don't know what I thought he owed me, but that line worked for Agnes, so I used it. Mr. Merrick stood by me and set up an audition, to take place across the street from his office in the theatre where the set for *Oliver!* was all around me. Mr. Merrick came to the audition. He acted as if he were sauntering past to go somewhere beyond me and just as he passed me he whispered, "This is ridiculous. Totally unnecessary."

Mr. Merrick could be extremely attractive, I want you to know. He could give you a sudden, sophisticated, confidential warmth. Provocative! Its power over the recipient comes from the shock of sensing his easy respect . . . his temporary fifty-fifty relationship with you. I was his teammate for that moment, his oldest friend, and with a mental elbow nudge in my ribs of camaraderie from Mr. Merrick, we were putting this deal over together. He was backing me secretly with all his quiet energy. He was a cagey, clever animal who, when he wanted to make a deal with you, rendered you helpless against the deal. He simply sensed who had the same goal he had and thus knew you were with him so he didn't have to work on you.

He let me go ahead and do this manipulation of Gower my way.

Not that I knew how. He gave me not a word of advice. I was never so respected in my life. To me, a man who is stronger and more experienced than I am, and who trusts his future in a woman's hands (mine) without guiding her, has more sex appeal than any macho movie star. He must have been desperate to reach Gower, and I was his last resort. He wasn't nervous or frightened about leaving Gower to me. He was just a sly fox hidden in the empty seats of the unlit theatre watching every move and sound. What a brilliant man! He surely knew when to shut up. It worked! Well, I guess you knew that.

I read from *The Matchmaker* with our stage manager, Lucia Victor, playing Vandergelder. By the time I got to Wilder's "manure" money speech, Gower had been moving up and down the orchestra aisles to view from all sides. He was leaning on that bar between the orchestra pit and first row when it was time for the money speech. I had it memorized. Thornton Wilder almost always wrote the important things to be delivered straight out front, for only the audience, not the onstage characters, to hear. It's called breaking the fourth wall. Wilder believed in it for all his plays. He said that's why musicals are so much more popular than plays. The audience is not ignored in musicals. Who enjoys being ignored? It's rude, Thornton felt.

I delivered Dolly's longest speech, well known to every businessman or mogul that I ever knew, from Ted Mann to Walter Shorenstein. (Mann is the owner of a chain of movie houses including Mann's Chinese in Los Angeles. Shorenstein changed San Francisco's skyline, including erecting sixty-five-story buildings that he made the safest places to be in an earthquake.) They both know this speech and treasure it. It starts with "Money, you should pardon the expression, is like manure. It's not worth a thing unless it's spread around." My cousin Dickie knows that part of the play. That sentence alone has carried him a long way. I knew all this when I delivered the speech to Gower. Those men gave me an authority I didn't even know I had. Well, I didn't have it. I simply stepped into their natures and mentalities like actors are supposed to be able to do.

The moment it was finished, Gower put one arm and finger straight up and said, "I buy that."

That was it. We never, ever disagreed on anything from then on. When he said fourth position (ballet), he got fourth from me . . . not fifth, not third. I haven't wavered to this day. I am right on the spot where Gower told me to go, and no force on earth can make me change it.

Mr. Merrick made an appointment for Jerry Herman to play his score for me. I went down to a ground-floor apartment on Ninth Street just east of Fifth Avenue. The rough-hewn, brown wooden front door opened to reveal an extremely good-looking young man standing in the midst of all-white, bare stucco walls that enhanced his rich coloring. It was a monastery overseen by this movie version of a monk (Jerry). The movies would have cast, at the time, Tyrone Power or some such beauty as Jerry when Jerry himself would have done handsomely. He was smiling at me and for me. It was love at first sight. Jerry insists it was mutual. I could never believe that. He was conventionally gorgeous! But we hugged and cuddled an awful lot from then on, or at least until we got used to doing it. That was for about a month. Then we went on to more important things, like deciding on Dolly's voice to go with the music. He played the perfect score and lyrics for her character, I thought. He asked me to sing some songs with him to find Dolly's key.

"Speaking of China," there was a girl who dogged Jerry's footsteps. I warned him she said she wanted to marry him. I got rid of her fast. Jerry said that's what cemented our friendship: "I knew then Carol really cared about me." It wasn't noble friendship, Jerry. I was spitting jealous. I was married to Charles Lowe at the time, but Charles always knew Jerry's and my love would remain unconsummated. Charles was all for our "affair." How did he know? By then I was in love not only with Jerry but with his music. It turned out to be true love right up to this very minute. Just eternal, spiritual, true love.

ack to the first day of rehearsal in New York for "Damned Exasperating Woman." Gower told me this show was going to be an intimate musical with a small cast, small orchestra, et cetera. He told the company, "If I were Josh Logan, we'd first be on the script. In two weeks it would be memorized and we'd all be on our feet. But I am a dancer. I think in terms of movement. Therefore we will spend the first two weeks on the 'Hello, Dolly!' number. That will give me the level of the entire show." So with poise and ease, Gower coveted the territory in which he was the shining, supreme master. To watch his sure decisions was exalting. He would stand quietly, demanding total silence and stillness from the company. Then he'd tell us what to do. Then he'd run up an aisle to the back of the theatre and shout, "Now do it!" We'd do what he just asked for, all of us being trained dancers.

The first direction he gave us was to have the dancers pick me up and hold me horizontally over their heads, with me leaning on one elbow. "Stop! Put her down." Down the aisle he'd come. He always spoke separately to each member of the company so no one else could hear or no one could be embarrassed. I never knew what he said to each one. They never knew what he said to me. He whispered to me, "I'll never take Dolly off her feet again. Her feet should be firmly on the floor so she goes where *she* wants to go."

Me: I'm with you, Gower.

Gower: Instead, let's go back to the opening of the number.

Gower already had wooden rehearsal steps built that were placed center stage. I ran up them to the top and waited. Phil Lang, the music arranger, was sitting in the orchestra pit waiting, too. I could see Gower had already told Phil he wanted a traditional burlesque-music introduction for Dolly to descend the steps. Somebody was say-

With President and Mrs. Lyndon Johnson. Note Barbra Streisand in the background, cleaning her fingernails. (White House Photo)

With the wonderful Louis Armstrong. (Sammy Siegel)

Meeting the Queen. (Author's collection)

Backstage with Al Pacino after his performance in American Buffalo. (Sammy Siegel)

With the Chief of the Oto Indian tribe in Oklahoma at my adoption ceremony.
(Author's collection)

With Elizabeth Taylor in my dressing room during intermission of
Lorelei *and Richard Burton's* Hamlet. *(Sammy Siegel)*

With Princess Grace. We're waiting to go onstage at a benefit. (Sammy Siegel)

Lady Beekman is trying to sell her family tiara to Lorelei. Lorelei never saw one before. It raised her up out of her chair. Lorelei gets Lord Beekman to give it to her. (Author's collection)

Lorelei holding her diary and singing "Looking Back." (Author's collection)

Dancing to "Tea for Two" for Sir John Gielgud. It only took John four months to learn that. But then, I can't do Hamlet. *(MPTV)*

Lots of admiration and gratitude and love to CAROL from the ship's cook Old Thornton

With Thornton Wilder on the Bremen. *(Author's collection)*

*With President and Nancy Reagan and Mr. and Mrs. Nelson Rockefeller.
(White House Photo)*

*This is the most Nordic German and gentile-looking picture I could find. Just so
the reader doesn't imagine I look like Sammy Davis, Jr. (Author's collection)*

Meeting President Bill Clinton. (White House Photo)

ing, "But there was no burlesque music at the turn of the century." Gower was answering: "I don't care. It's what Dolly and these waiters hear."

Gower showed me precisely where my hands were to go on the banister and where the waiters went. He ran off the stage again to halfway up the aisle. "Now do it!" We did.

Gower: I'm going to need more cooks. I'm going to need more waiters. The steps have to be higher and wider. I'm going to need more voices singing. I need a deeper and slower beat from you, Phil."

Can you see how Gower and Bob Mackie took what they had, knew how to frame it, enhance it, and bring it into a close-up? Do you wonder if I'm willing to die for these people? Well, I am.

Jerry Herman (telling the rehearsal pianist): Start it in the key of C.

Phil Lang: But my flutes won't go down that far.

Jerry: Then just use tubas and basses for her singing chorus.

Phil: Do you really want it that way?

Jerry: I conceived it that way. I never wanted it any other way.

Jerry was lying and standing by me, I was sure now. I know no composer wants his music sung in a low key, but Jerry insisted he did. As he told me later, "What else could I do? Mother Earth is what I was forced to want." I've always suspected Jerry subconsciously wrote his songs for his mother's clear soprano, but he was smart enough to see I wasn't his mother and about-faced his concepts. That is a talent in itself. He, like Gower did, sees the particular performer he's dealing with.

Gower: We'll modge up later, Phil. (modulate)

We learned what Gower gave us in a flash, as all performers do when they can't wait to do it perfectly. Gower went on to the musical bridge. The bridge was in a tinkling music-box style that Gower called the Flora-Dora dance section. Its style was deliberately music-box and dainty, which always sounded like the way Marguerita Merrick played the whole thing, charming, but it was meant to be a contrast to what was coming. She wasn't old enough yet to conceive of driving sex. Then Gower slowed it to just that . . . driving sex. He had it sink into half time around the runway and modulate up. I got to lead "Well / well / Hel / *lo.*" The next time around the runway was half-half time, with an even deeper drum and "modged up" another note. This time around the runway, we must have used a tympani drum. Gower let me lead this stomping herd of animals behind me again. "Well /// Well ///

Hel /// *lo*." That same heavy beat that I first heard with Ethel Waters came crashing down. After Gower gave us *that*, and we did it for him, we had to stop rehearsal and scream, all of us in ecstatic appreciation.

Later, one critic described this number as an orgy. Another critic said, "Every single waiter in it stands out as a leading man, and Miss Channing treats each one as such." I'm convinced that if I could have done what I wanted, which is crawl into bed with every one of them, it would not have saved that beat that makes the world go round strictly for the performance. It would have been pregratified, therefore dissipated, but I'll never know.

Gower never complicated the steps, so that they came purely out of the strong, uncluttered emotions of Dolly and the boys. Gower built that Dolly music right up to the orchestra tacit (silence) for me to sing, "Wow, wow, wow, fellas, Look at the old girl now, fellas." Music, cymbals, and drums together crashed straight into the final "Dolly'll never go away" three times, with the boys kicking and singing at top pitch.

Gower: Carol, cover as much ground as you can and stretch your legs down that runway to center. Joel, follow her, and all of you follow her onto the runway.

I gave one quick look to Joel; his look back to me was filled with unabashed love. In fact, his look at me should have been censored.

Gower approved. "Phil, ride them home, but loud, then ignite."

I always had to pull with all George Channing's powerful body bone structure to be stronger than, or at least *as strong as* the boys because *they were very strong!* For me, it was newly convenient to be tall.

In performance, weeks later, the sudden, deafening crash of the audience reaction and applause walloped straight through us to the center of our solar plexuses. It nearly knocked us over. I could feel the weight of the audience reaction pounding on us. For me it landed right where I carried Chan. We learned to withstand it.

Oh, Gower, what you gave us, you uncluttered, clear-cut, shining showman, you low, lusty, down and dirty, beautiful bastard you, and all cloaked in what's labeled great theatre. I know from watching you perform *that* would have been a star's turn to remember. But your great performances were outshone only by your showmanship. And you gave your showmanship to us. Every one of those gifted, handsome young men except Joel Craig was dead within the first two years. For the next years of playing *Dolly*, the company and I did AIDS benefits every Thursday night after the show for the memory of those glorious men.

Back to Gower's staging. He knew he had to do an encore or the audience would be left unsatisfied. How did Gower know that in rehearsal, without an audience to tell him? There would have been many a quivering clitoris left unloved. Gower knew!

Gower gave me the responsibility of timing the applause. I held third arabesque like he wanted. All of us held until my right arm swiftly gestured in pantomime (come on, dear gang). Orchestrally Gower had us go back to three strong chords before this first half time. Gower yelled from the last row, "Okay, now you've learned the steps. *Now! Think* them." Of course it made all the difference in the world.

The following are the thoughts going through my head on Gower's "Hello, Dolly!" number and his encore in order to "think it."

Pick up your long train on first chord, Dolly. Heave it mightily to your side and throw it down on the second chord. Give your train a violent kick. Don't take any nonsense from that train. Make it land straight behind you, clearing the way ahead for yourself. This is *YOUR BATTLE CRY*, Dolly, into rejoining the human race. That ain't easy! So pull your torso up to its most regal stance. Enjoy the length of yourself and charge! With every man charging *behind* you and *with* you. Use long, sure, elastic strides. All those men's legs are exactly as long as yours, so feel it. Know it. Your quadriceps are moving with their quadriceps. The second half time is even slower. Turn Dolly into an arrived woman, smiling insurmountably at being on her own, but as femininely strong and proudly a female as you can conjure up. The final stretch down the runway is victorious, only slower, with an even deeper drumbeat. This time never take your eyes off Joel Craig. He and the boys are kicking as high as humans can possibly kick. Joel's eyes are reignited. You know it, Dolly. You know he's yours. All the boys are yours. Not a thing they can do to fight it, you are on the runway now, Dolly, center stage flanked by the boys. Camel your spine from the base of it on up through your waist, shoulders, neck, and head, like no white woman ever could, and throw yourself into that final third arabesque. Let the last musical note explode again. Everyone hold.

In rehearsal:

Gower: Don't anyone dare move until Carol does. Not you, Phil, or your conductor.

No one ever did. Not for five thousand subsequent performances.

The third day of rehearsal Gower announced to all of us that Mr. M was on his way to see our progress. I was busy onstage trying to cement what Gower had given us only the night before. Charles told me my feet were dancing in bed all night long in my sleep. It was the fastest I can remember amalgamating direction.

As the company arrived, some warming up, some giggling, most still getting acquainted, Gower correcting some, Mr. M walked in. He sat down ready to observe. It was too soon to be seen, but we did it anyway. I grabbed Dolly's character, including her New York accent, together in my mind, and somehow remembered all the moves. After we got up to the 2:40 and the 8:40 (as the crew called the train that crossed the stage with most of us aboard), Gower stopped us.

Mr. M stood up and said, "That's the most disheveled, disorganized, sloppy third morning of rehearsal I have ever seen. These comments I am making apply to everyone but Miss Channing. She was ready and superbly so."

He went into great detail on how little ready everyone else was to tackle such a tremendous project. This didn't make me any friends, but then that wasn't what we were there to do. Then he walked all the way up an aisle, opened a door onto the street, and stepped out into his spotlight of sudden sunshine, knowing he left utter silence behind him. He turned toward his office and disappeared. My first thought was Mr. Merrick might be proving his own ego by showing he was right about insisting on wanting me—but my experience with him is devoid of his ego—or he was angry at Gower for something. Gower certainly knew himself, without Merrick, how to ignite a company into action. That was part of his talent.

I've heard always how impossible Mr. M was. He was never impossible with me. Why wasn't he? The New York critic Howard Kissel wrote a book on him called *The Abominable Showman*, and everyone in show business knew who the book was about just by the title. Merrick swore he reveled in the title, but if someone called me that title I'd say I reveled in it too, wouldn't you? It remained a gross untruth about him, however.

Mr. Merrick died as I was writing this paragraph, immediately after I phoned him in New York. I left a message on his machine. The Merrick Production Company told me they're saving my love message for his memorial service. This message was left before I knew he died. Now nobody says he was insane or even difficult. It shows it was only petty jealousy . . . one tiny human about another tremendous human. They don't remember it now.

Well, as he hoped, Gower found the level of the show that he was after by getting to the kernel of the "Hello Dolly!" number. Of course, it took every minute of the first two weeks of rehearsal, and the level turned out to be far from intimate or delicate or small. Gower never complicated the steps, so they came purely out of the strong, single emotions of Dolly and the boys. He never was tempted to show off how tricky and difficult a choreographer can get unless there's a reason.

Gower knew we were building to a point where Mr. Merrick would have to go into overcall from the backers. Merrick never questioned it. That great man! He knew Gower was right.

Equity allows only seven weeks' rehearsal, so we had just five weeks left before opening in Detroit. Not even one finger was ever changed on the "Hello, Dolly!" number from those first two weeks on . . . ever.

Most every worthwhile project as far as I have seen goes through a period of "It's not going to work, why did we ever start this?" The storm has to come, I find, when creating *good* work, not just work. The ship you're on in the middle of this storm usually almost capsizes, but Gower and I stood together. Just hold on and keep going through the storm and finally the essence of the problem shines out like a neon sign. I guess nothing good comes easy, true in childbirth or true in anyone's occupation. What is it about entering untraveled paths in rehearsal? Your hair grows faster, your nails are stronger, your energy is sustained, and all five physical senses are at top pitch. It always seems to be the healthiest time there is.

Principals are allowed by Equity to work longer each day than the ensemble (chorus), and we did indeed. Gower came to me and whispered, "If you ever get tired, tell me. I'll let you lie down on the Equity cot. Don't take anything to keep you going. I can, but you can't. You have to hold this show together after we open. You cannot fall apart."

Me: Gower, I don't fall apart.

Gower: You will. You'll crash if you take anything.

Me: I don't take anything but coffee, Gower.

He stared at me firmly: Good!

Then he went on to "Put on Your Sunday Clothes" (the next song he continued to choreograph). He pinned on each of us a swatch of the color we were wearing for this song so he could weave us in and out from hot to cool colors and cool to hot.

A s far as I know our *Hello, Dolly!* was the first big musical to go to Detroit for its pre-Broadway run, not to the usual New Haven or Boston, or Philadelphia or even Washington, D.C., for a tryout. We opened at the Fisher Theatre, as in the automobiles with "Body By?" That Fisher. I met several Fisher spawns. It was interesting that many of them had intermarried. Something like Essex once married Buick, Lincoln married the old air-cooled Franklin, and their children and grandchildren had intermarried again. They had to have had hemophiliac reactions and more.

At the time, I couldn't think about these unfortunate people, though. Of course we were all completely consumed with getting the show on, learning new lines every night as Gower and Mike Stewart drastically changed the script.

On opening night, the Michigan critics royally panned us, seeing absolutely no hope for the show. Only Shirley Eder on the *Free Press* and Fred Tew on *Variety* said things like "But that's the way big musical shows look on a pre-Broadway opening. This is not the ten-year touring company of *Oklahoma!* or *Carousel*."

Shirley said this show had the ingredients of a smash hit. So did Fred. They saved us. None of us has ever failed to see or call Shirley or her dear husband, Edward. We don't know how to reach Fred Tew now, but we would if we could.

On the second-year run of *Hello, Dolly!* in New York, one of the Detroit critics came to my dressing room after seeing a matinee and said, "Is this dud still running? Why?"

Back to *Dolly* preopening Broadway tryout. Mr. Merrick made his way to Detroit from New York. I knew nothing of his plan to close the show, but others did.

As you probably know, *The Matchmaker* always was a deliberately complicated ensemble piece. Thornton Wilder adapted it from the Viennese style of its time, "*Un Tag Ist Ein,* whatever," in which closet doors were opening and closing just in time and everybody was tear-assing all over the stage. But Gower and Mike were simplifying the plot and cutting fabulous Jerry Herman songs because entire scenes had been substituted and these great songs no longer made sense in their new, scaled-down plot.

Opening night at the Fisher Theatre was the first time Charles was allowed to see the show. He saw it every matinee and evening for four days. After the fourth night's performance, he handed me a big yellow pad with lines—they're called legal pads—and started dictating to me. It was entitled "Notes for Gower." Charles wanted them in my handwriting, signed by me. I realize now that he knew they'd never accept them from him, because he had no official capacity on the show. I did as I was told by Charles every night after the show until 3:00 or 4:00 A.M. and slipped them myself under Gower and Marge's door in the same hotel. Charles often had me use the phrasing "I, Carol, feel I am losing the audience when I say . . ." or "I feel I could gain them back if I were to make it clear that . . ." et cetera.

I asked Charles how he knew what the changes should be. He said, "I'm sitting in the audience. It's obvious. You're too busy trying to remember new lines every night. Also, I have a fresh eye and ear, seeing it for the first time." Charles took courses at universities from playwrights. One of his one-act plays was produced in Czechoslovakia, where it won that year's medal. He always wanted to be a playwright.

Gower put every one of these changes in and never took them out. They were only for the first scene and a few others as I remember.

Before Gower died on opening night of his *42nd Street*, he returned to me all of my yellow lined pages with a note saying, "You should have these and know how much you contributed to the show." "*I*?!?"

As we put these changes into the show, we had to stuff our stage manager, David Hartman, in a barrel that was onstage for the hay and feed store scene, keep pushing him in (Hartman is six feet, five inches tall), put a flashlight in his hand with the new script for that night, and a lid on top of him so the mezzanine and balconies couldn't see him. There were smaller people who could have done it more comfortably, but Hartman (*Good Morning America* host on TV after all this) had good diction, and we could understand him through the lid. He was an actor. Dancers, singers, and crewmen were often difficult for us to decipher. We had pregnant pauses so we could hear Hartman give us the next new line, and then Davey Burns or I would repeat it. The scenes always went slowly the first night, but that gave Gower, Mike, and Jerry Herman the chance to find out if these changes were for the good. They were.

I hope to find these notes in Charles's files when I have access to all the memorabilia from our forty-two-year marriage. I must add here that Charles never told anyone (I know of) he had anything to do with these changes. It was big of Gower to send them back to me, but Gower never told anyone either he didn't suggest them himself. Well, why should he? He was the Benevolent Despot. I didn't tell anyone, either, until now.

Since the show was no longer an ensemble piece, "Damned Exasperating Woman" was retitled *Hello, Dolly!* and now we needed new songs for Dolly. Jerry figured them out. (By the way, I mentioned that some of Jerry Herman's marvelous music and lyrics had to be taken out because the plot was being so very much simplified, but Lee Roy Reams built an entire nightclub act on only the songs that were cut from *Hello, Dolly!* It was one terrific act.

What was Thornton Wilder saying essentially? My surmise is that the spine of his *Our Town* was Don't go to the grave with your lovely young bride, stay with us, the living. The spine of *The Skin of Our Teeth* was Mankind can survive the ice age, the stone age, the dinosaur age, if we just hold fast to one another. And the spine of *The Matchmaker* was Dolly Gallagher Levi, stop talking to your dead husband and rejoin the human race.

These are only my surmises, but they did lead to Jerry's phoning Charles at 3:00 A.M. in Detroit and asking him to wake me and send me right down to his room. I arrived in my long, white flannel nightgown. Jerry was openly ecstatic. He sat down at his upright piano to play and sing "So Long, Dearie" for the first time, for only me. *I* was ecstatic. How good of him to play it for me alone first. We called Gower, and he came tearing down the hall in his unclosed hotel bathrobe. When Jerry calls, I can't remember to put on a robe, I just run to him. Gower tied his robe together after he got in Jerry's door. Lucky he didn't meet anyone in the elevator or hall, or he would have been arrested for streaking. Gower and I both listened, and he and Jerry jumped up and yelled, and both agreed, "That's the greatest fuck-you song Dolly could ever have!"

I just jumped up and down and started learning it then and there. Christian Scientists don't generally say "fuck you," but I've learned to since.

General MacArthur

hen Gwen Verdon opened in *Sweet Charity*, you surely know or have heard, she was spectacular! However, a person like a past United States president, or Cardinal Spellman or some such, died on the same night Gwen opened, so *Life* magazine had to put him on the cover for that week and devote most of the magazine to the story of his life. It was truly unfair to Gwen, but, as they say, that's show business.

Now! It's January 12, 1964, and we're on previews till January 16 at the St. James Theatre for the Broadway opening of *Hello, Dolly!* General Douglas MacArthur is suddenly very sick and feared to be on his deathbed that entire week. Can you imagine the frantic state Mr. Merrick was in? He took Jerry Herman to Temple Emanuel with him to light candles, with Biff Liff to back them up. Harvey Sabinson, our press department, had a private line to the hospital for days. Gower was sent to the Episcopal church, then left Marge there so he could go on rehearsing. I was sent to the Christian Science church, my Tiv (the world's greatest dresser) to the Reading Room of my church with orders not to stop reading till he heard from our front office.

The entire company had to keep praying for MacArthur's life, or at least for him to hold out long enough to make sure we had the *Life* cover sewn up. They wouldn't have time to change the cover after 2:00 P.M. on Friday. At 2:05 Mr. Merrick walked into the St. James and announced, "Stop praying! Let the sonovabitch drop dead."

I suppose there are reasons why a tough cookie like Mr. Merrick is labeled abominable, but when he was on your side he looked like the Mother Teresa.

Opening Night

or me, every opening night is sheer, agonizing panic. The problem is that in the theatre we are all dealing with intangibles and ephemerals—moods, auras, emotions. Anything can blow them away.

The question is not how to keep a show as alive as it is on opening night. The question is how to get the opening to be as good as all the following shows will be if they will allow us to run. There is no true emotion unless it flows through relaxation. Even if you're playing nervous tension, onstage it doesn't come out as nervous tension if you are really nervous and tense. I learned in Detroit to embrace fright. I found that with fright a wonderful thing called adrenaline shoots through your body and enables you to be brighter, clearer, or more lithe than at any other time. An actor must tell the story with his body, face, and voice, and that's all at top pitch with adrenaline. At least it was getting to be for me. I was learning that stress is God-given.

By January 16, 1964, our Broadway opening, I sensed, at the times I was alone onstage with the audience, that there was a solid block of people in the center section from about the third row to nearly one-third of the way back: the first-night critics. There was absolutely no honeying up to this block. There was no enjoying life together with, no falling in love with, no laughter or tears with this block. Beyond this solid block, everyone seemed to be having a fine time. But I realized that this block of people was in exactly the same fix we actors were in. They had to call the cards right. They were as stage-frightened as we were. This was their opening night too, and I couldn't stop feeling like Julie's Florence Nightingale: *These people need help! Just like I do!* Way in the back of my mind, I couldn't keep from nursing them all through opening night—kindred souls going together through the same hell.

Charles told me after our New York opening that one man seated in the last row, near the lobby bar, died on the final "Dolly'll never go away again," and the bartenders covered him up with an overcoat so as not to ruin the ending. Another time a man had a heart attack during intermission and was carried by the ushers to the floor of the men's room. As they and his wife fanned him, she asked loudly: "Has the 'Hello, Dolly!' number begun yet?"

Even Irving Berlin was helped up to standing room by his two young male nurses at least once a week, and usually three times a week, just long enough for that one number. He was over seventy-five years old at the time and no one had seen him for years, or was allowed to. Only our usherettes saw him and held space for him. They never told anyone who he was. I find the usherettes' natures are like the stage crew's. Their mission in life is to protect the show, especially if they respect the show. To this day most of them are the same ones in any Broadway house when I go to see a show. We catch up quickly on things while programming and going down the aisle. After all, we were once all on the same mission—to love, honor, and respect the show.

The album recording of Jerry Herman's music and lyrics of *Hello, Dolly!* knocked the Beatles to second place on the charts, and we solidly took over first place. *We* did. Our original cast did. There were cartoons of Venetian gondoliers paddling through the waterways of Venice, singing "Hello, Dolly!" There was one in *The New Yorker* of an old, sick man propped up in bed saying, "And I do bequeath my two tickets to *Hello, Dolly!* to . . ."

Louie Armstrong's smash demo of the song didn't hurt us either. His happy recording focused people on the show, and I got to ride on a float with him on the worldwide television Super Bowl game in New Orleans. We were both thrilled about that.

We are all asked what it feels like to read good reviews about oneself. My overwhelming feeling is, Thank you. Now all the wonderful dreams we dreamed about this show—the dreams I had about this monumental character—now, I will have the time to perfect her. You have given us the chance to bring the performance all the way up to all of our highest vision. What a privilege you have given me! That is exactly how I feel about every good review in any show. "Thank you for letting us run. That's all we ever wanted or needed."

Gower, after reading the reviews on *Dolly* opening night, added, to me, "Boy! Success is better than sex, eh, Carol?"

Me: If you say so, Gower. So far it's better than anything *I've* ever known.

Right after Thornton Wilder saw *Hello, Dolly!* for the first time, he said to me, "Why didn't I realize it was Dolly's story and eliminate all those subplots?" He thought it was because of the songs and dances that we didn't have time for extensive subplots.

No. It was because once Dolly says to her dead husband, Ephraim, almost in the beginning of the show, "Ephraim, I'm gonna marry Horace Vandergelder for his money," the audience gives its anticipation and approval that it is going to witness this campaign. But instead what we had originally here was a brilliantly funny song to be sung by Vandergelder with the entire ensemble. Gower, Mike, and Jerry in desperation decided to watch one matinee audience, rather than watch the show. Most of the audience went to the ladies' room or read programs whenever we got off Dolly's main action, which was, I had decided, "to rejoin the human race." Their confusion about anything *outside* of Dolly was not because of me or my performance. It was because Thornton Wilder created the character of Dolly and added her to the translation of the English and Viennese versions.

In London I saw *On the Razzle*. It was the original *Matchmaker* without Dolly or Thornton. Whenever any of us creates something, we unknowingly re-create ourselves, that is if it's truly honest work. How can we create anything or anybody outside of our own experience or understanding? If it's outside of *my* comprehension, for instance, I don't even know it's there. Therefore, after knowing Thornton Wilder better all the time, I suddenly realized in the middle of the stage one night, "Oh, I *am* Thornton Wilder," and, by the self-hypnosis that I'll bet most actors also use, "I'm not acting Thornton, I *am* Thornton!"

Right there that makes Dolly the centrifugal force of his play, and she is the funniest character only because Thornton was so very funny in his eccentricities and delights. He must have known that he himself was deliciously comic, but he couldn't stop it or forget it.

In the photo insert, there is a picture of Thornton being bon-voyaged by me for his trip on the *Bremen*, a ship left over from World War I and therefore the slowest vehicle on the high seas. He wanted to be on the slowest so he could get his *The Skin of Our Teeth* rewritten for one actress to play both Mrs. Antrobus (the eternal mother and home-maker) and Sabina (the eternal "other" woman or mistress). Thornton told me Sabina and Mrs. Antrobus are the opposite sides of the same woman, and therefore, in order to make the play clearer, he felt they should be played by the same actress. When I saw it and read it, I never suspected this. I'll tell you later what actress he wanted to do it. Well, I'll tell you now . . . me. But one never knows. The producer or director or now the almighty casting director might have had someone else in mind so, Carol, don't cry over Thornton's death, which terminated his rewrite. Cry over the real issue . . . that the warmth, affection, stimulation, and laughter caused by simply being with him has left your life.

Before the *Bremen* set sail, Thornton took me by the hand and led me into the main lounge and bar. Passengers were sitting at tables for drinks. He brought me up to each table and said, "Look who I've got. his This is Dolly!" (his voice rising steadily higher with excitement). "Dolly, say hello to the people at this table. People, say hello to Dolly!"

He forgot to tell them who *he* was. Some just stared at this almost apoplectic, childlike leprechaun. He kept kissing my hand like a knight in shining armor, then almost skipped to the next table. I had played the essence of him for almost a year now, so it wasn't at all difficult to go along with him enthusiastically. There were probably two of us Thorntons skipping around that ship, I don't know. I was in friendly bliss with him, but his fellow passengers weren't used to being as friendly as we were. Then he took me over to a corner to discuss our secret plot. Nose to nose with him, I listened. "When the bell rings for the visitors to leave, you go down the kitchen gangplank so no one will see you. We'll go up now to my stateroom so they see us go. I'll have all my meals there. When no one is looking, I'll sneak you out, and they'll all think you're in there with me for the entire trip. If we do it right, they'll think we're having a wild affair."

I used to get worried when his face got that red. I wanted to calm him down. It was red when he came backstage after a Broadway preview of *Hello, Dolly!* The company was lined up onstage to meet him. He kissed each one near him and squeezed their cheeks together, mine too. He told them how delighted he was. Solidly heterosexual David Burns was happy that Thornton was so happy. I loved Davey for liking Thornton so much. But of course, he *would*. He was the great Thornton Wilder and Davey was the great David Burns, with Thornton telling him he was a great Vandergelder. All of the letters Thornton sent me had little flowers he drew with crayons around the typing. Tiny roses in pink with green stems, purple violets, and little butterflies with birds flying. He was an enchanted man.

Barbra Streisand

When Barbra Streisand opened *Funny Girl* on Broadway, we opened *Hello, Dolly!* She came backstage after the Actors' Fund performance of *Dolly*, and it began a beautiful friendship. When she got the movie of *Dolly*, that was the end of that.

Back to the beautiful friendship. Barbra and Elliott Gould visited me after shows two or three times in our apartment. One time Charles combined them with Lynn Fontanne and Alfred Lunt. I was happy they were impressed by them. Another time, Barbra asked if I had ever seen Fanny Brice perform.

Me: Yes.

Barbra: You saw Fanny Brice?

Me: In person. She was doing a personal appearance at the Paramount Movie Theatre in San Francisco to promote *The Great Ziegfeld*, a tremendous movie in which Fanny had a large part.

I didn't tell Barbra this next bit. I went so crazy about Fanny that I had to *be* her for weeks, so I finally sang and danced "I'm an Indian, Too" for a show on the Lowell High School auditorium stage. My fellow students loved her, too, so I must have been pretty accurate.

Barbra: What was she like?

Me: Chic, like you, but she was tall, had what's labeled "a suit figure," so she wore one immaculately tailored and looked terrific, quite the opposite of the hilarious characters she played onstage, except for "My Man" in a black evening gown.

Barbra was eager to hear more, but I saw *Funny Girl* and realized the title was meant to be ironic. It's essentially about the *un*funny side of Fanny's life and was, as we all know, and as Barbra created it, great! Vocally, sometimes reedlike and delicate . . . altogether a work of art. Irene Sharaff's costumes on her were works of art. Barbra was even greater in the movie, which was another work of art. So much for art.

As I told you before, the year 1964 was the birth on Broadway of *Funny Girl, Hello, Dolly!* and Noël Coward's *High Spirits,* starring Bea Lillie. At Sardi's restaurant, everyone seemed to be talking about who was going to win Best Musical Star—Barbra, Bea, or me.

Bea said to me: I think you're going to win it, Carol.

Me: No, I'm not, you're going to. I lost it on my first starring part in *Gentlemen Prefer Blondes* to a lady named Patricia Neway, who learned her opera singing well but pioneered no new trails herself. I've learned to lose the Tony.

Bea: It might be Barbra.

Me: Yes, it might, but I don't know. And on it went.

Another time:

Barbra asked me: Did you feel you were losing the audience just before the first act finale last night?

Me: Yes, I did. It doesn't often happen, but it did last night. Why?

Barbra: The same thing happened to our show. There was nothing I could do to make them respond.

Me: It lasted till the middle of the second act. I couldn't make the show build.

I went to the phone and asked for Bea. "Yes," she said, "around 9:45." So I suggested I get a *Farmer's Almanac* to see if it was something beyond our faults. Now, I can't read the almanac, but there was a boy in our ensemble who was raised on a farm and he said it told about the moon and the ocean tides and the soil and all. We looked up the night before in the almanac and, sure enough, there was a big sink in lots of things. We all felt better about ourselves, at least I did.

Of course, everyone, not just actors dealing with live audiences, knows that a full moon affects animals and people and whatever's left on earth. Sometimes I didn't notice we had a full moon, but I knew there *was* one by the way the audience responded. I honestly did. They laughed at the Ephraim speeches (Dolly talking to her dead husband) and cried at the eating scene (Dolly consuming potato puffs while refusing to marry Horace). At one show in the Shubert Theatre in Chicago, there were two men in the mezzanine who answered me during the Ephraim speeches. There's a sting in the music, and the lights change to convey that Dolly is in another world mentally, and suddenly show the frightened side of Dolly.

I began the speech: Ephraim?

Two men: Yeah?

I waited, hoping I didn't really hear them.

Dolly (me): I'm gonna get married again.

Them: Awww!

Me: I'm gonna marry Horace Vandergelder for his money.

Them (petulantly): No . . . oh . . . no no!

Yes, it was a full moon all right. But then I suppose they could have been drunk, too. So you must take my discoveries for what they're worth.

Well, the night of the Tonys, *Hello, Dolly!* was winning with a clean sweep. I came in feeling healthy enough, but by the time *Dolly* had won in every single category (but they save Best Actress in a Musical till last), I got sicker and more miserable because if I didn't win, it meant *Dolly* was a hit in spite of me, and if I did win, it would be our tenth award that night, which was more than any other show in the history of Broadway or the theatre or anywhere in the whole world. I couldn't stand the suspense. The only way to sit there with poise was to decide if I lost I'd simply jump out the window of my fortieth-floor hotel suite and thereby end the anguish.

Are you still curious about who won the Tony? Or have you finally lost interest because I can't seem to come to my point? Well I won it, which prompted Barbra, according to Harvey Sabinson, our publicist, to get up and walk out saying, "They're all anti-Semitic." Only she said, "Simetic." I wanted to shout "It's Se*mit*ic not Si*met*ic. You're not a Se*mete*; you're a Se*mite*," but I didn't.

Dear, if you take all the Semites out of show business, there'll be very little left, including the Tony award committee.

But we know Barbra is perhaps our greatest creative force musically. Jerry Herman tells me she plans to do *Mame* next for TV, that fabulous comedy that will be as hilarious as her *Dolly*. Of course we're all very happy to settle for her great artistry. A barrel of laughs she ain't.

If you're still reading this book, you've decided long ago not to trust any of my opinions anyway. You're so right. My opinion of Streisand is completely warped. What opinion would you have if someone got together with the agent Sue Mengers and kidnapped *your* baby? My baby was *Hello, Dolly!* She and Sue went after it hard for Barbra. Mike Nichols told me he helped them and suggested her. Her movie of *Dolly* was the biggest financial flop Twentieth Century–Fox ever had. *There!* I said it. I've never said it to anyone until right here. I've been so noble. It's off my chest forever, and I've promised myself I'll never mention it again. The *Dolly* set of the Harmonia Gardens is still there on the Fox lot. Every time I went by it to do an episode of *Love Boat*, I did a Dance of Death, enjoying it abandonedly.

In hindsight again, who could do *Dolly* without Gower? He choreographed the scenery, the lights, the costumes, even the flowers in the hat shop scene. In the movie there was none of what Thornton Wilder had approved of so heartily.* Not so long ago, Barbra was asked in an interview one question about *Dolly*. She said, "Oh well, that was a mistake." We've all, including certainly me, made many more colossal ones than she, but, like the phoenix, Barbra rises above everything. She should. She can't help it. She's unique. I can't stop admiring her.

Duchess of Windsor

harles, Chan, and I lived in the Waldorf Towers while I was doing *Hello, Dolly!* There was a telephone operator who had been there ever since President Herbert Hoover had been a permanent resident. Well, that's what Charles decided. When Hoover finally was carried out from there, she was the one who called the coroner. That was her claim to fame.

* Poor Thornton Wilder. He thought he wrote a comedy. (I, too, have a bitch side like all of us.)

Then, in the sixties, there was a Mr. Lawrence of Revlon, who made eyelashes for the Duchess of Windsor and me, his only two clients in the Towers. Mr. Lawrence told me the Duchess said on the phone to this operator, "I wish to place a long-distance call. Yes. It's from the Duchess of Windsor to—"

Operator: Is that Mr. or Mrs. Duchessofwindsor?

Mr. Lawrence told us about this after Charles placed a call for me through this same Waldorf Towers operator. Charles had lost patience long before with her. "I wish to place a call from Carol Channing," he said.

Operator: Who?

Charles: Now look, we've been here for two years, you know by now I said from Carol Channing!

Chan, who was about eight then, came in to get me. He said, "I don't think you want to miss this, Mom. Hurry up." We listened.

Charles: She's on Broadway right now in *Hello, Dolly!* . . . *Hello, Dolly!* Certainly, I'd be glad to. *C* as in *cunt*, *h* as in *hell*, *a* as in *ass* . . . Hello? Where'd you go, you bitch?

He bang, bang, banged the phone rapidly.

Chan: I didn't think you wanted to miss the floor show. Right?

Me: Right. But it would have been funnier if I thought she passed away right then.

Chan: No. She always leaves him hanging like that, because he always yells at her.

Okay. Now we're attending a large dinner at a restaurant. The Duke and Duchess of Windsor were paid guests, as was their wont. Charles was seated next to her. The wine may have been quite strong, and the Duchess was known to tipple just a bit. She said to Charles, "Oh, look there's Hello Dolly down at that end of the table."

Charles said, "Yes. Carol Channing."

"No. The one down there. That's Hello Dolly."

She must have thought my first name was Hello. Charles was adamant. "Yes. Her name is Carol Channing."

"No it's not. It's Hello Dolly."

"I ought to know, I'm her husband."

And you know what she said? She said, "Well, you're wrong!"

Lately I've been thinking back to my final visit to my love-aunt,

Mrs. Charles Bedeaux of the Château de Candé outside Lyons, where the monks first invented gunpowder. The Duke and Duchess were married there. My dear aunt Fern Bedeaux was their hostess. Aunt Fern and I were trying to figure the Duchess out.

She told me the Duchess was as rough as a cob. The only way she could account for Edward giving up his empire for her and being so wildly in love with her was, she said, "I'm sure he never met anyone as street-tough as Wallis or who sassed him around the way she did. He found that constantly funny." Those of us who have gone to public school with accomplished street-fight people don't think they're all that funny. But apparently she was a novelty to Edward.

"I myself," Aunt Fern said, "never want to get into a fight with her because I'd lose."

By the day of the wedding, Wallis had already had the royal crest embroidered into all her linens, and Edward had already abdicated. Right there, Aunt Fern said, much of the wind was siphoned out of her sails. However, she would not allow herself to gain an ounce. She would push herself away from the plethora of lavish French food at each grand dining room meal and watch everyone else eat. You could tell she wanted the food, all right, Fern said.

Well, the day of the wedding, nobody could find Edward. Everyone thought he was dressing for it. He wasn't. They searched and searched. Aunt Fern told me the Duchess was standing on the very stone entrance steps that she and I were sitting on. Finally, she said, the Duchess exasperatedly sat down in her wedding suit on those same steps, spread her knees apart, leaned her right elbow on her right knee supporting her face, and said, "Oh, the hell with him. I've had it. This is too much." And seemed suddenly to drop her entire facade. I never saw Aunt Fern so confused or searching my face so hard for some explanation.

Eventually Edward was found on the golf course in his golf knickerbockers. I don't know if he forgot the time, but Wallis was furious at him, Aunt Fern said, all during the wedding. Fern was one to abide by the etiquette rules of once you open your home to someone or once you are a houseguest you do not reveal intimacies or criticize one another. But Aunt Fern is gone now, so I don't have these tender feelings about the rules, and I'm relating to you her exact words. The reason I have this memory for the precise words is because I love to savor them and see if they lead me into understanding the character of the Duchess. That's my fun time.

This is now December of the year 2000. Lately there has been a vicious and hilarious floating rumor that the Duchess was really a man! Yes, I know. If this is the first time you've heard it, you may be laughing as much as I did.

And when the royal couple was on Rex Harrison's yacht, he wrote in his book that she was the ugliest woman he ever saw in his whole life. Well, there's nothing wrong with that. Some men don't make pretty women, if that's the case, but it certainly would have answered Aunt Fern's confusion, wouldn't it? And her knees falling apart, which is not easy for us girls to do, unless, of course, we're madly in love with someone, and even then some of us have to be married to him, depending on the generation of which we are members.

No wonder Edward laughed at her so much. What a joke on the British Empire! What a joke on the entire world! And only Edward and Wallis were sharing it. How provocative for them! This must be what's called bitch humor.

Lady Bird and Lyndon Johnson

*A*s I say, *Hello, Dolly!* opened January 16, 1964, the year of the presidential campaign. The song "Hello, Dolly!" was also the perfect campaign theme song. Barry Goldwater thought so, too, so he used it and somehow forgot to ask Jerry Herman for permission. Mr. Merrick was a Democrat, Jerry was, and everyone in the show that I talked to was. Jerry is so unabrasive, he can hardly say no to anyone. So Mr. Merrick charged in and got the song back for us. That's how come *I* got to sing "Hello, Lyndon" to open the Democratic presidential campaign and be televised in that huge arena, the Atlantic City Convention Hall. Jerry wrote special lyrics for "Hello, Lyndon" ending with:

> Be our guide, Lyndon,
> Lady Bird at your side, Lyndon.
> Promise you'll stay with us in '64.

I was as thrilled as the audience, which seldom makes for the best performance, but this isn't art we're dealing with at a presidential rally. I sang up the biggest storm I ever sang. A recording was made of it so that Lyndon, before each campaign speech from then on to his elected presidency, shouted out, "Where's mah girl? Put her on!" And my recording was played until, Liz Carpenter told me, as much as she likes me, my voice, overly loud in her ear, sometimes five times a day, got quite palling. But Lyndon refused to say a word of his speech without it.

On election day he and Lady Bird called to the phone in my dressing room in our St. James Theatre in New York. The company and I were all onstage re-rehearsing. (Gower kept changing the show for months after we opened.) Our Benevolent Despot had such a whammy on me that I refused the call. Charles called back from our hotel to the theatre and asked Lucia Victor (stage manager) to tell Gower to tell me to answer Lyndon Johnson on my phone. Gower told me, "Go!" The whole company, including Gower, came to listen.

Lady Bird: Hello, Carol. We have just finished voting, and we're recounting our blessings. We're calling only three people. Henry Ford, you, and (there was someone else, but I was so transported by this call, I don't remember who it was).

Lyndon: We want to thank you for singing that great song, Carol.

Me: Oh, Mrs. Johnson and—

Lady Bird (interrupting): I called you Carol.

Lyndon: So did I.

Me: Oh, dear little Lady Bird and Mr. President Lyndon. I love you both.

Both: We love you.

I told the company what they said. I told all of national television what they said. I told Jerry Herman he had a "great song." I never got over it, but it was only the beginning. The entire Johnson family kept coming to see *Hello, Dolly!* making themselves noticeable by cheering and standing and carrying on. Onstage we were overjoyed with the honor of it. Charles from then on would call to my dressing room phone and ask, "Is this the hot line to the White House?"

Then Mr. Merrick did an unprecedented thing. At the end of the second year on Broadway, he sent much of the New York company, including me, on the grand national tour, while the enormous hit was still news and the box office was sold out into the next two years. I hear he also didn't change the names on the marquee out front in New York. It was the first time any producer ever did this, so there was no rule against it, because nobody had ever thought of doing such a dastardly thing. Also, Merrick explained, the theatres on the road were all at least twice the size of the St. James. We opened in a blaze of excitement at the brand-new Dorothy Chandler Pavilion in Los Angeles, with pictures in the papers of people sleeping on mattresses in the line to the box office.

Our opening night party after the show was hosted by Elizabeth Taylor and George Burns, no less. Elizabeth sent me humongous lavender flowers that I had to put on exhibit for the rest of the company as they sent anyone who saw them into orbit just because they came from lavender-eyed Elizabeth, with love. We were already good friends, and I was crazy about her, as every friend of hers is. Most of her fun, by the way, is ridiculing her own attraction to diamonds and champagne and love. We already know George Burns's fun was connected to whatever makes the world go round.

Well, it seems Elizabeth sent word backstage to me during that opening night show that one of her bra straps broke, and could I help? You know, every opening night on tour is total hell to pull off. The critics are redeciding about all of us, and every new theatre is a tremendous adjustment. With this mishap, that night I also had Elizabeth to worry about. You know that one of her blessings is being beautifully endowed, so I imagined her having to sit in the audience with her arms folded over her endowment until I could send someone to even them up in some way. Tiv, who never left my side or took his eyes off me once the curtain was up, grabbed a safety pin and a roll of gaffer's tape and ran to her seat. I don't know what she thought of a very good looking male dresser fixing her bra, but somehow he did it. He was once a photographic model for men's fashion. I was so used to Tiv after all these years that I didn't notice him, but I could tell she must have noticed him when I saw her at the after-show party. She looked at me with delighted surprise. I'm sorry I missed all the fun she may have thought I was having.

The next day was a matinee. I also remember the fire alarm going off during "Before the Parade Passes By"—the Dorothy Chandler Pavilion was that new. I thought quickly: I will direct separate sections of the audience out first while I remain center stage and do a Joan of Arc at the stake until they're all safe. I didn't know where the fire was, but it did cross my mind that this part of *Hello, Dolly!* is leading to the end of the first act, and at least the burning at the stake scene with screeching alarms going on over it won't be a first act finale letdown.

For some strange reason, actors onstage are electrified into heroic deeds. I am. Offstage, I'm overemotional and only cause more trouble around me. Onstage, I was telling the audience where the centers of their rows were. They have continental seating in the Dorothy Chandler, so I ordered different rows to go out to their right and their left. Oh, I was magnificent, until Mrs. Chandler herself appeared and told everyone it was a false alarm. Then there was nothing to be magnificent about. She told a crewman exactly where to go to turn the alarm off. Our conductor and musicians had decided to remain in the pit and fry with me, out of chivalry I guess, or else there was no way out except the basement elevator, which is dangerous in a fire. So they gave us a big long A-flat chord. I took a bow with Mrs. Chandler, and we received applause from what was left of the audience.

Johnsons! They turned up in all forms on the tour, here, there, and everywhere. Then the Johnsons decided to open the fall social season in Washington with a special performance of *Dolly* in the White House for the Senate, the House, the Supreme Court, the whole works! Oh, it was gala. At the end of the show, the president, onstage, handed me a glass of champagne. He made such a grand gesture out of it, I guess I was supposed to propose a toast. But instead I said what was really on my mind, "Oh, thank you, Mr. President. I'd love to drink that, but we open in Dayton, Ohio, tomorrow night, and I have to face a battery of critics again. You wouldn't understand."

"Where's zis girl been, ah wouldn't understand facin' a battery a critics? Did you hear what she just said? I wouldn't understand facin' . . ." and he repeated and repeated it. "Betty Beale, did you hear what she said? Helen Thomas?" He called to every member of the press, well, everybody he could see.

Everybody tried to calm the president down, but there was never any point in trying to get Lyndon to do anything he didn't want to do. So I got my cue and changed the subject by saying to him, "I'd like to tell the United States Marine Band they were excellent as a Broadway show orchestra."

Lyndon: Okay. May I have this dance?

Me: Now, Mr. President, what do *you* think? Please. I'd love to dance with you.

He just wanted to dance with me to hear on our way what I wanted to say to them.

He danced me over to the marine band and said to them, "She wants to tell you that you are every bit as good as a Broadway orchestra, the brass section was jes' as loud, the drums and bass were energetic with their ber-la-cue beat." He said everything I told him. And then said to me, "Now, tell 'em." So I looked at the conductor and all the different sections, spread my arms with palms forward, shrugged my shoulders, and all they could do was laugh.

He was a lovable man . . . to me. I know. My dentist disagrees, and I can't answer while he's drilling on me. But he's wrong! I'm judging him as my friend. He was a great, unwavering friend. When he and Bird drove from Austin to Dallas to be in my opening night audience at the Fairmont Hotel, he sat stoically while they "booed" him, in his own home state! This was toward the end of the Vietnam War. Then, he stood up with Lady Bird, straight and strong, applauding his friend (me). I had to hold back the tears.

Lyndon didn't have the gifts of a fine ballroom dancer, but he *was* fine. Lady Bird or someone must have impressed on him that he had to focus on that and get good at it if he was going to be president. He surely knew how to lead, though. If you danced anywhere that he didn't plan, he simply put you where he *did* plan. If it required picking you up for one step, he could do that, too, all in good nature.

It was so easy to talk with Lyndon onstage in front of an audience. He let you know immediately where you fit with him. He put his big, protective arm around you with an attitude of "I jes' love women," so I knew immediately to play the most feminine, sweetest, even adoring Texas girl-girl. If you're a girl, don't you appreciate it when a man lets you know . . . bam! . . . this is what I like from you? It's no effort at all to fit into it. Of course, I don't know if Janet Reno or Madeleine Albright would have trouble with that, but for most girls it's a favor he's doing us, right? He lets us know clearly where *he's* comfortable and, of course, whether you're a man or a woman, we all want the other person to be comfortable, especially if he's the president of the United States.

Lady Bird has always been my role model. You'd think it would show more on me, wouldn't you? I try, but I'll never make it. I can only appreciate her sensitive aristocracy. Before the final *Dolly* performance in Austin, she came in with her own hand-picked wildflowers to give me and to chat because we do that from time to time, I'm proud to tell you. This time she said, "May I ask, do you have grandchildren?"

"No, dear Lady Bird, I don't want to push and aggravate either of them."

She said, "Push! I would say poo oosh! Do that, please." She said it so intimately, slowly, and sweetly that I knew she simply wanted me to be happy and have a full life.

Another time we were having an ice cream party at Luci and her husband Ian Turpin's house in Austin. A young man attempting to make a name for himself as a member of the press decided to try to anger me into a fight. "You Christian Scientists know you're crazy eccentrics, don't you?" Et cetera. You know. *That* one. I told him I'm not a practitioner, I'm an actor and entertainer. No, he wanted a fight out of me. Lady Bird said to him, "I think if you were a Christian Scientist, for instance, you would be a far better and more intelligent member of the press. The rest of us will go over and have some ice cream, and you may leave the premises now." Wow! That is my otherwise always gentle friend. I want so much to be like her.

When Mary Martin and I opened *Legends!* for Bobby Fryer (the then head of the Ahmanson Theatre in Los Angeles), my telephone rang before the show started. It was Lady Bird. Of course, I was nervous. Just what I needed! She is a tranquilizer for me. "Oh, you dear friend, Lady Bird," I said.

Mary came flying in in that stocking cap she wore under the wigs just for this show. "Did you say Lady Bird?" She grabbed the phone and let out one of those Texas screams that they've all had to develop because the distances are so far from rai-ench to rai-ench. "Ohoho-hooooooo, Lady Bird!"

I could hear Lady Bird muted through the phone from across the room but very lengthy on "Ohohohohohohhhhhhh-ohhhhhhhhhhhh, Mary!"

"Mary!" I said. "This is *my* call, Mary. She called *me*. I want my phone back and my Lady Bird." Mary was a lot littler than I am, so I just took it. Bird (as Lyndon called her) was full of support and affection. This sounds as if Mary and I weren't devoted to one another. We were. Mary never had any sense of competition. She had a drop-dead presence on the stage. I could feel it, but we never competed with each other. Mary and I held hands all the way through this one year and one month tour, and we sustained each other.

Off my subject again. Back to the Johnsons.

On one of our weekends at the ranch, Lady Bird offered to drive Charles and me around it in her golf cart. She said, "Now these are the *barbe*dose sheep."

Me: Oh? How do you spell it?

Bird: Like Barbados.

I told Liz Carpenter about it. She said, "But that's the way they're pronounced here." I said, "Well, cela va sans dire." (Translation: "That goes without saying.") Liz yelled, "Honey, you are in Texas now." Charles so often heard Chan and me say that, he finally announced at a formal dinner at a neighboring ranch, "Well, saliva la guerre."

One of Lyndon's dying wishes was that the recording of "Hello, Lyndon" be put on automatic repeat in the Lyndon Baines Johnson Museum in Austin, like that eternal flame in Arlington, Virginia. That one. So when Lady Bird took me to the museum she said, "I know you'll understand. I want you to enjoy the museum. I'll wait for you outside here. It's not easy for me to hear the record once more. You do understand?"

I certainly did understand. But it's harder for me to hear the sound of my own voice than for anyone else to hear it. Even Barbra Streisand whispered to me at Marvin Davis's Christmas party, "Did you ever go to a party and they played only your records? As if they were doing you a favor?"

"Yes," I said. "That makes the party so that I can't hear a word anyone says to me. I just agonize, wanting to redo that note I just heard again."

Barbra: Exactly!

Well, Barbra, if *you* feel that way, then there can't be anything the matter with all the rest of us who can't stand to hear our own voices. Apparently, we weren't meant to.

So you see, Barbra, it's no surprise that you are a perfectionist. The whole of show business operates on that premise. Even the Rockettes are all perfectionists. One-sixteenth of a beat off from one of them and the entire effect is destroyed. Without the rest of the Rockettes, the slightest wrong move from any actor stands out onstage or on camera like a neon sign. If show business didn't require perfection, wouldn't everybody be in show business? Oh, I'm sure you never said you were a perfectionist. Some press agent who never set foot onstage thought he discovered something unusual about you. Because you're far from dumb, you couldn't have said that.

Back to the Johnsons. Liz Carpenter told me Lyndon would say to her (Liz was always gloriously plump), "Liz! I want you to pull hard and tighten the laces on your corset, go and tell that senator I want this bill passed; put on your best whore perfume, and don't come back without everybody there signs it."

Me: Oh, Liz, isn't that dramatic? Is it exciting being the president's right arm? What's it like?

"It's very character building," Liz yelled.

Was it Jack Valenti who told me Lyndon was in his office at the ranch with the radio going. It was playing "Hello, Dolly!" and Lyndon blasted out with "Somebody stole mah song!"

Now I understand a man like that. In an exacting and exhausting trek like a presidential campaign, how would he ever hear of *Hello, Dolly!*? Either you want to be president or you don't. Eunice Kennedy Shriver told me in a campaign everyone gets tired except the one running for office. With a Broadway musical, we're all running for office. We rehearse day and night. Once as we (our company) were all walking home together, the lit-up headlines were revolving around the *New York Times* building. We all asked each other, "Did O. J. Simpson do something?" None of us could answer. I suppose that's obsessive compulsive whatnot, but either you want a hit show or forget it. Yes?

*D*uring the *Dolly* run, Mr. M descended the stairs to the basement dressing rooms shouting: "Where is she? Wonderful woman!" (Vandergelder's last line to Dolly in the show.) I quickly put my head in the script (I was memorizing up to the fifth year of touring whenever he arrived). That could be another way of accounting for Merrick's and my smooth relationship.

Merrick dearly loved to negotiate. He called my then agent, Lee Stevens, often and said, "Let's negotiate Carol's contract some more." The result was I never signed one. Not in all the *Dolly* years. Everyone else was signed.

Mr. M arranged with his own PR department to escort me to the world premiere opening of the movie *Thoroughly Modern Millie*. Halfway through the movie I was so shocked and despondent over not looking as cute as the character I had in mind that I was playing, I couldn't hold back my tears. Mr. M gave me his handkerchief. I blurted out, "Oh, thank you, I still have you." He put his arm around me and patted me on the shoulder. "You *always* have me." He had tears in his eyes, maybe to convince me how terrible this movie was and that I need never leave *Dolly*.

Actors can be wrong about judging themselves. For *Thoroughly Modern Millie* I got an Oscar nomination and won the Golden Globe award, which Julie Andrews wanted for me, and the movie was the biggest box office bonanza for Universal since *To Kill a Mockingbird*.

Different producers produced *Dolly* on tour. Mr. M was the first tour, Jimmy Nederlander was the second, and Manny Kladitis with PACE was the third.

Mr. Merrick came to Providence on my last tour of *Dolly* and begged Charles and Manny to let him (Merrick) open it and play it just on Broadway. He described the marquee: HELLO DAVID. HELLO

CAROL. *HELLO DOLLY!* He reflashed that old friendship warmth and said to me, "Wouldn't you like that?"

Me: Yes!

Charles and Manny: No!

Merrick was right. Manny and PACE prematurely closed *Dolly* on Broadway because road tours, not Broadway, were PACE's native habitat. Also, as I told you, there are bigger houses on tour, therefore more money.

Mr. Merrick wouldn't speak to me after that . . . made terrible growling noises and turned the back of his chair to me. Natalie Merrick, who, I think, got her surname legally changed to his, was good to me. She said, "He's hurt. You're like an old love gone wrong." She made me proud saying that. In Providence she interpreted his stroke-constricted speech in my dressing room into what sounded like Chinese to me, but her heart was right. Maybe it *was* Chinese, since she'd arrived in New York City straight from Shanghai a short time before meeting Mr. M. I felt she loved him though; I could swear she did.

Many people liked to laugh about Mr. M's "insanity." Not because he was ever diagnosed as insane but because he had to spend months in a hospital. He somehow got out of it in his wheelchair (according to the headlines in the New York papers) and, working the wheels with his hands, raced down Third Avenue, hospital gown flying in the wind, automobile brakes screeching at the cross streets, and made it back to his home. After so many months in a hospital room, wouldn't you? I certainly would. If you've never spent time in a hospital, then you wouldn't believe he's sane from this story.

Sometime in 1964, the year *Dolly* opened, Merrick and his then wife, Etan, my elegant, tender, and helpful friend, invited us to dinner at their apartment. Their daughter, named Rosebud, but given the privilege of changing it to her own choice of name whenever she wanted, decided on Marguerita. So, Marguerita Merrick—rhythmic name, don't you think?—answered the door. She was about eight years old then, I'd say, and European-lovely. Well, her mother is lovely. She couldn't miss. She asked us to please sit down around the piano. "Us" was Jerry Herman, Mike Stewart, Charles, and me. She played "Hello, Dolly!" with no burlesque beat, no half time, and then no half half time, no funk. It was a minuet . . . charming. Then she explained it was the first piece she'd learned at her own request from her new piano teacher. She spent most of the rest of the evening standing behind wherever her father was sitting, with her arms gently around his neck or shoulders. This position was home to her. Near him she was happy and secure. Mr. M was too.

On our second tour of *Dolly*, produced by Jimmy Nederlander, when we got to Los Angeles again, Mr. Merrick called to say that he was coming to see the show. Everyone said he couldn't possibly like it because it wasn't his production. Charles had me make a speech at the end of the show that wound up with "I give you our guiding force . . . our creative father, David Merrick." I asked Mr. M to stand. Charles and I had rehearsed the spotlight man before the show so he knew Merrick's seat. He stood, and of course the house came down with applause forever. Mr. M took out his white handkerchief and blew his nose standing in the spotlight. The audience was eager to show him its profound gratitude and cherished him.

After that speech at the Dorothy Chandler Pavilion, Mr. M came backstage to see me. He asked me, "Could you please make that speech again at tomorrow's matinee? I want to bring my daughter to hear it." I said I'd love to.

At the matinee we arranged for the usherettes to give Marguerita an old program saying on the cover, "David Merrick Presents *Hello, Dolly!*" I understand she never knew the difference. When I pointed to him to stand for his bow, he tried not to need it again, but the big white handkerchief had to be pulled out. There were two or three times I've seen him very emotional about *Hello, Dolly!* I remember him as an easily touched and vulnerable man. *Dolly* was his treasured show, and the creative forces, including me, were his own family. I was proud of that. Michael Stewart, the writer, felt the same about him that I did. Michael planned anniversary dinners with the same group every January 16 until he died as a young man. A doctor told Michael after an X ray that there was a little tiny polyp on his intestines . . . Nothing really, but "Why don't you let me take it out now so it's sure not to cause any trouble later on?" So he did . . . right there in his office. Mike's intestines leaked for three days, and then that was the end of him.

I have found that within a hit show everybody loves everybody. Not so with a flop. So that's why the *Dolly* decades are sounding saccharine sweet, you see. From my experience alone with Mike, I can say that we deeply appreciated one another's work. I loved Michael. He loved me. That will be forever.

Jean Kerr

y beautiful and elegantly comedic friend Jean Kerr was trying out her play *Mary, Mary* on its pre-Broadway run. It was her opening night in Washington, D.C. "Speaking of China," you may not have realized Washington, D.C., audiences are exemplary. Well they are and always were since 1952, that I know of. I once asked President Johnson (to drop a name), "Lyndon, why is Washington, D.C., two or three beats quicker to react as an audience than other cities? Is it because the nucleus of the audience is brighter and smarter and it affects the rest of the audience?" "Nope," he said. "I haven't seen anybody particularly bright or smart here." So that explodes that theory. Anyway, Jean's play was to open in one of Washington's theatres, and she was late. Finally, she arrived and started down the unlit aisle when a young schoolgirl usherette stopped her and said, "I'm sorry, madam, but no seating is allowed after the show begins." Jean brushed her aside quickly, saying, "It's all right, dear, I'm the author." She found a seat, looked up at the stage, and there performing was the distinguished pantomimist Marcel Marceau.

Now to me, the most interesting part of this story is that Jean, an imposing but lovely creature, is over six feet tall in her tennis shoes, which she wears with all ensembles. I know she wears them because she broke her ankle, but that was many years ago. I think she's gotten so used to them that she thinks everyone else is. However, it still takes nerve to wear them along with your chiffon evening gown with no explanation.

Anyway, back to the interesting part of this evening. Jean was so embarrassed to face this high school age ingenue usherette that she slid down in her seat, watched Marcel Marceau for his entire show because he had no intermission, and missed her opening of *Mary, Mary.* It must have been agony, because your opening night is nerve-racking enough without wondering what's going on where it's taking place. When I think of it, though, if her audience, with the critics and TV cameras there, had called, "Author, author," which she deserved, she would have appeared onstage in that chiffon gown with those tennis shoes. Given that possibility, I'm glad she missed the whole thing.

Betsy and Walter Cronkite

etsy Cronkite is a very funny but dreadful girl. I have kept telling her how dreadful she is, but she's incurable. For instance, her husband, Walter Cronkite, could be getting slightly hard of hearing. Every time he says, "What?" to Betsy, she mouths silently what she just said, which, of course, frightens Walter momentarily—he thinks he's gone stone-deaf. But someone who loves him, which is everybody, including me, always jumps in and tells him, "You're fine, Walter. Betsy is just a dreadful, dreadful girl." Betsy has totally adored him since their first term together in high school and couldn't stop it if she tried, but she remains dreadful.

Which leads me to Leona Helmsley. Leona used to give "I'm Just Wild About Harry" parties, at which Harry looked as if he wished he were at home in bed. Well, he was obviously a very brilliant business-man whose energies went into being only that. I met the Helmsleys through Bennett Cerf, who was a regular on *What's My Line?*, the long-running TV celebrity game show, put me on more than a dozen times as a disappointment act since I was available on my way to the theatre anyway whenever somebody didn't show up. I was made up for my show already, so it was no bother.

Bennett was a magical, bubbling child. He used to walk from his home in the Sixties off Fifth Avenue to Random House on Madison, which he founded and from which he published all those books. I walked to my theatre from the Waldorf on Park, so we'd often meet with noisy, joyful greetings, as was his wont—mine too.

One matinee day, there was a St. Patrick's Day parade up Fifth Av-enue. Several marchers in their enthusiasm, and perhaps Irish Mist, picked us both up and pushed us onto a float. There was nothing to do but wave back to the people. We must have passed for Irish. I don't know about Bennett's next appointment, but my Tiv was fit to be tied when I was late. Being with Bennett was so exhilarating, I simply lost my head, and also the float wouldn't stop.

Bennett and Phyllis Cerf invited me to many dinners at their home, where I got to know some of their fancy friends, like Frank and Bar-bara Sinatra, the Helmsleys, and Irving Lazar. Irving and I always got to sit next to one another at the table. We wondered how people could tell us apart, since we wore the same self-designed eyeglasses. Irving said he copied his from the legendary comic Bobby Clark, who painted his on. Also, Irving told me how he bred horses and that peo-ple should be bred exactly the same way. I told him I never met a Jew-ish Nazi before, and he said, "Nevertheless, it's true." He said it like the principal of the school who announced, "Agnes Schwartz will now sing 'Trees.'" You surely know it.

Some student shouted, "Oh, Agnes is an old whore."

Principal (very slowly): Ne-ver-the-less, Agnes Schwartz will now sing "Trees."

The reason that was a favorite of people like Jule Styne and Bennett Cerf is, I think, because it depended solely on the timing, at which they were experts.

Well, Harry Helmsley was at the other of two dinner tables at the Cerfs'. At my table sat Mayor John Lindsay. On the chair next to him were Leona's famous cleavage and Leona. Leona never looked at anyone else at our table or at her dinner plate. She was riveted on the mayor. You see, there was an article that week in *Life* magazine with pictures of Bess Myerson (the former Miss America, she was Lindsay's head of Consumer Affairs) and the mayor laughing together, romping around Gracie Mansion's lawns. Leona hadn't realized, apparently, until that article that the mayor was up for grabs. We got Mary Lindsay down at our end of the table. She was a pillar of poise and to-the-manor-born-ness. We had a good time at our end.

After Bennett died (too young), Phyllis married the former mayor of New York Robert Wagner.

The way I understand it, Random House's edifice was declared a New York Landmark, so the Helmsleys had to build their biggest hotel on top of Random House because it was illegal to tear it down or touch it—not that anyone wanted to except the Helmsleys. This cemented a beautiful family relationship. Well, a family relationship anyway between the Cerfs, the Wagners, and the Helmsleys. It meant I saw quite a bit of Leona for dinners. So Leona, who could cry publicly at will over her son contracting some terrible disease, asked me to do a benefit for free on my night off in honor of her son and this disease. I'm sorry. I can't remember the name of it or her son because Leona cried so much all during her opening speech at the benefit I never did get the name of either.

Shortly after, Mayor Bob (Wagner) kept phoning to ask me to please call Leona—that she wanted to offer Charles and me a suite in her Helmsley Hotel. I told him, "Mayor Bob, she scares me. I can't seem to get up the nerve to do it."

He kept calling me saying she was insisting I call her. Finally I did it. She got on: Yes?

Me: Leona, Mayor Bob told me you wanted me to call you.

Leona: About what?

Me: He said you wanted to offer us something.

Leona: What?

Me: He said it was about a suite in your hotel.

Leona: Not a chaaaance. (It rings in my ear to this day, that flattened out Brooklyn shrill *aaaaa* sound.) You show people come around wanting haaandouts. Not a chaaaance. (Brooklyn people don't even have it. She exaggerates it to a snide repulsion and revels in it.)

Mayor Bob was flabbergasted when I told him. He was a protective, affectionate man, and it hurt him. He said it was all her idea and she kept complaining that I didn't call. He heard I did a very good show, too. She's lucky I didn't hand her Lyndon's famous quote, so sensitively put, "Never get into a pissing fight with a skunk." So I didn't.

Telling you all this is by way of getting back to Betsy Cronkite. My point is, prior to this we were invited for dinner to the Helmsleys' triplex on top of their hotel with the winding marble stairs between floors and the little elevator for Harry.

I used to have to bring my own uncomplicated food with me to people's dinners because, with eight shows a week, many ingredients can fog up your voice. So Charles bought silver containers from Tiffany's to put my own food in. At the end of the dinner I was putting my empty silver things back in their case when Betsy said to Leona that I had just included her silver salt and pepper shakers. Then she said, "She took your sugar bowl, too, Leona, and some silverware. Did you have more candlestick holders before Carol arrived?" This finally stopped people's conversations, since not everyone is acquainted with Betsy's sense of humor, leastwise Leona, who has nobody's sense of humor.

Years later, while Leona was sitting in the slammer, I said to Betsy, "I just want you to know, Betsy Cronkite, that I was never invited back to the Helmsleys after your little joke."

"Of course not," she said. "They caught *her*. It's only a matter of time for you."

n the closing night of the road tour of *Blondes*, I was sitting with Oliver Smith and Dick Maney at the farewell party and got to know Dick for the first time, even though he had been our fantastic publicist all during the New York run. Oliver Smith, one of our two producers, was a very long, lean glamour boy. A beautiful, brilliant man with manly grace. Dick was the overweight but distinguished newspaper crony, dressed like an unmade bed, perfect casting for something like the editor in chief of that newspaper the cast of *The Front Page* was on. Oliver meant to simply sit with his legs crossed but, as usual, his left leg was wrapped twice around his right and his right arm was over his head and back around under his chin to scratch his right ear. Dick was spouting classic poetry. I was listening. In the middle of Dick's incantations, he swung a big arm up in the air and landed it pointing to Oliver—"and this twisted eglantine is my finest and most respected friend."

Me: What's an eglantine, Dick?

Dick: Don't you know your Milton, Keats, or Shelley?

The Something Something
The clinging Vine
The twisted eglantine (in long, loud, rhythmic George
    Channing tones)

I was in bliss. I never wanted to leave but never saw Maney again because Bobby Fryer asked me to do his production of the musical *Wonderful Town*. I'm very grateful. But it's an unfinished symphony for me concerning Dick Maney.

Those Richard Maneys, Joshua Logans, and George Channings die young. Mostly, I think, because of a new phrase I just learned: obsessive compulsive disorder. I used to believe it's not excessive or compulsive or anything but normal behavior, but I'm wrong. To me it was either you want to do something or you don't. If you want it, then go for it whole hog and sink your soul into it. Well, I'm learning at my late age to get over that. My cousin and cousin-in-law are helping to cure me. Little Missie Sylvanna hauled me to a doctor to find out what was the matter with me. After tests, he told her I had hypoglycemia. Now I get fed small amounts of food every two or three hours. At first it just teased my system into craving like never before. I hired Dickie's exercise trainer, who won't let me exercise more than ten times each one. Instead of starting with an hour on a bicycle I had to start with one minute, then slowly up a minute each three days. Agony!

Some people can leave food on their plate, or a few drops in their cup. That requires more restraint than I've got. My stomach is a bottomless pit. I used to say to my father, "I think I'll pop some popcorn. Are you hungry?"

(Answer) "What's hungry got to do with it? I want my popcorn."

Same with everything. Don't start with a hundred laps in a pool. Start with five. I feel it's not worth the bother of getting in the pool, but soon I'll be up to a hundred and happy again. My trainer's wife told me he (the trainer) used to have obsessive compulsive disorder and is now cured. That's how I got caught by him. It must be that it takes one to know one. I gather it's a disease. I'm recuperating slowly from a lifetime of unrecognized illness. Not easy. Everyone has to really like his trainer or everyone won't do his own exercises. I love my cousins and my trainer so much that I've completely changed my nature for them and hope they like the improvement. Don't write for sixteen hours every day and then nothing for the next two. Give yourself sensible office hours. I'm trying.

To the reader: We must all learn moderation. I don't know yet what the benefits are of that, but apparently you live longer, if that's your only plodding, mundane goal.

My father and I used to get drunk on my mother's chocolate cake and go out to put pennies in people's expired parking meters. He'd say, "Now this poor sonovabitch won't get a ticket," and then go on to fix the next expired meter. This was not so much humanitarianism as it was outwitting those "bulldozing, smart-assed police who love to ruin everybody's day." We knew some policemen were darling. We were just outwitting the smart-assed ones. Once finished we'd sing at the top of our lungs walking all the way home. No more of that. My cousins and trainer tell me I'll be much happier and will see the improvement in my daily living shortly. I'm waiting.

I'm sure most of you have found out that food is an addiction. When I was addicted to birthday cakes, I worked out a method for finding out what flavor an uncut cake is on the inside. You can't always tell by the icing, you know. You take a wire clothes hanger and unwind the neck—it's sometimes not easy, but if you really care what's on the inside of the cake you can do it. Delicately make a hole through the icing so as not to crack it or chip it. Carefully insert the end of the curved part into the inside. The reason you insert the curved part is because it will pull out a piece of strawberry or marshmallow or whatever as you remove it. If you're lucky enough to strike whipped cream, it adheres to the wire.

The first of my shared birthday cakes with Tallulah I'll never forget. It was a three layer. The top filling turned out to be, lo and behold . . . chocolate mousse! The second was orange. Fascinating combination. You keep maneuvering the filling out until it seems almost gone on that side. Now close up the hole in the icing with your fingers very gently. Then turn the cake around and repeat the process on the other side. When you've satisfied your addiction, put the cake back in the cardboard box so no one will notice.

My husband, Charles, who never discussed with me what to do with any of my most treasured possessions, like birthday cakes, gave the cake to Charlie Gaynor, our concert writer, to take to a birthday dinner for the editor in chief of *The New Yorker*. At that time, he was someone named Ross. The next morning Gaynor returned to us in an emotional state saying, "We announced one of Tallulah's and Carol's birthday cakes ceremoniously. It was on a silver platter. We cut it at the table and it collapsed! Completely collapsed! It was a hollow shell of a cake. How did this happen? I was so embarrassed."

I remained quiet, listening intently. Charles slowly turned his gaze, which landed with a penetrating thud on me. I decided to change the subject to . . . "I wonder how many of Tallulah's friends got all that booze she took home with her."

Gaynor, aware of my addiction and sensing my shame, said, "It's all right, Carol. It eventually added to the merriment."

He was a kind man. Charles went about ordering things to prevent this from happening again. He ordered a dog's leash and collar to strap around his leg and mine so that in the middle of the night I could not get to the kitchen and devour half the contents of the refrigerator before I woke up. But he got annoyed with being dragged toward the refrigerator out of a sound sleep so often, so he finally got a chain to put around the fridge and a padlock. I understand this is not all my fault. Hypoglycemics' blood sugar plunges at about 3:00 or 4:00 A.M., and one must get food even when asleep.

All the children in Chan's preschool class at Isabelle Buckley were assigned to write a composition on how they spent their weekend. Chan wrote of us going to Disneyland and said, "We rode home, put the chain around the refrigerator, clamped the padlock, hid the key, and all of us went to bed." The end.

The children were asked to read their compositions to the class. Chan came home that afternoon all upset and angry. "Why didn't you tell me other people don't lock the refrigerator?" And he was right, why didn't we?

In a short time we were on tour in St. Louis taking Chan along. The owner's wife of the then Chase–Park Plaza Hotel, Mrs. Harold Koplar, often visited us when we were there. When she saw the padlock and chain on the fridge, she asked, "Is our help that unreliable? Why this?"

Chan said immediately, "That's where Mother keeps her diamonds."

Neil Simon

Whenever I'm at a gathering with Neil Simon I ask him, "How are you doing with your claustrophobia? Are you improving?"

"Oh yes," he says. "I'm cured."

"You are?"

"Yes. I just stay out of the backseats of Volkswagens or I never sit in the center of a three-seat airplane between two large people. Also, when sitting there, I don't wear a turtleneck sweater under a button-up vest with a jacket with the buttonholes too small to open quickly."

For those of you fortunate enough not to be plagued with this disorder, let me explain what Neil was talking about. If you are like Neil (or me), first it crosses your mind that if you wanted to get out of wherever you are, you couldn't. With this realization a seizure strikes you. You've got to get out . . . now! When you finally get the seat belt undone (it takes a while because you have shaking, frantic fingers), while stifling a scream, you must get to a standing position quickly for breathing space. So you naturally crack your skull into the carry-on luggage shelf above. The huge person next to you, sitting on the aisle does not understand that he must move like lightning into the aisle or there will be dire effects. It's impossible to be calm enough to put into clear words, "Would you be kind enough to step out, sir?" because every time you try, you elicit such a strange, loud growl that passengers put down their newspapers to relax and watch you. This same pachyderm next to you couldn't be pried out of his seat if he wanted to be, so you step over his knees and land facedown with your head on his shoulder. You grope to a standing position and continue to fight with the too-small buttonholes. Sometimes one has to pull the buttons off in desperation. One's strength in pulling is much greater during this crisis than usual. Oh, why do I go on trying to explain? I've never been able to make this misfortune understandable to unafflicted people.

Charles had so often said to me, "When these attacks descend upon you, do you ever consider the people around you?" What am I supposed to do? It's embarrassing for me. "What if we were watching an opening night play sitting among the critics, and you suddenly shot up like that, making those noises, removing your coat, sweater, shoes, and whatever? Don't you have any consideration for other people at all? You could destroy the audience's attention focus. And what do people think of me, putting up with such behavior? Why do you do that?"

Well, a group of Neil Simon onlookers didn't get it either. Neil had a brownstone house in New York with the usual steps up to the front door. He says he got stuck in a turtleneck sweater while inside the house and couldn't get it on or off. He got frantic with no oxygen, so he pulled the front door open from inside the sweater and continued fighting with it outside, at the top of the steps, where there was more air. He could feel two empty sleeves flying around him; he was yanking forward, back, and sideways as if he were fighting a straitjacket. It must have been stuck on a shirt button or something. When he finally got it off, there were four people just standing below on the sidewalk; they were holding shopping bundles but didn't want to miss the outcome or finding out what the problem was that caused such a sight. He told me they could have been there for ten minutes.

Neil's beloved first wife didn't get it either. Her initial encounter with Neil on this subject was shortly after they were married. Again they were on a plane. At the end of the movie, of course, everyone wanted to go to the lavatory. Neil got there first. He told me he kept opening the door of it only one inch and closing it, working his arm around backwards to prove to himself that he could get out. His wife told him the lighted sign kept going from "occupied" to "vacant," and the passengers kept getting up out of their seats when it said "vacant" and sitting down again on "occupied." Up and down they went with each door opening, until the flight attendant held the door closed, which brought Neil out into the aisle with attention-getting velocity almost knocking her over, fighting for his sanity and freedom.

Please do go and see the stalled elevator scene in *Sweet Charity*. To me, it's the height of Neil's playwriting achievements. Or just read it in the library. However, as I looked quickly at the audience, a lot of them were taking this scene as a heavy drama, and far fewer of us who were so afflicted were out of control just wanting to help the actor up there (John McMartin), who made it so hysterically real.

One of McMartin's lines—"Just let me out of here for one minute. I promise I'll come back in and be quiet"—was the most memorable to me. I'm relieved that Neil is cured now. Otherwise, one never knows when this could seize him again. I wish I were cured. My last attack was in the backseat in the Holland Tunnel during rush hour, when traffic came to a standstill with the luggage and coats piled on top of me to the roof of the car, the doors locked, and the windows closed. I was wearing a one-piece, heavy wool bodysuit with the zipper up the back, so it was inaccessible and . . . Oh, sweet Jesus, please, let's think about something else. Immediately! Now!

Hayes and Loos

hen Anita Loos first introduced me to Helen Hayes, I, like every overwhelmed tourist, said, "Miss Hayes, this is a privilege. It's indeed a dream come true for me. Thank you for going to the bother of touring your great performances and thank—"

"Come off it, Carol," she interrupted. "I thought we were going to be friends."

"Oh!" I said, suddenly speechless.

"Yes, now let's the three of us go shopping like we planned." She took my hand affectionately to be sure I wasn't hurt. As I told you,

Anita was four feet, nine inches tall, and Helen was smaller. I was six feet, one inch in four-inch heels, so people walked backward after they walked past us.

The three of us went straight to the children's department, where we bought the only two hats in Saks that fit both of them, then the children's shoes for them, then a middy (her favorite blouse) for Anita. It was actually a whole sailor outfit. I don't know where she was going to wear it, perhaps to church or PTA meetings that she attended in her adopted daughter's interests. The child's name was Miss Moore. She never was given a first name. She was Afro-American. They didn't use that phrase then, so I can only tell you she was all brown sugar and that's what she should have been labeled. Anita promised we'd get me walking shoes later in Paris. It turned out to be years later because *Blondes*, thank God, was a big hit.

So, years later, when Anita and I went to Paris together to see *The King's Mare*, a play for her to translate for me, we decided against it, so we went shopping for my shoes instead. In a shoe store, we talked to a tidy, snappily dressed saleslady. Anita said in French, "My friend here is looking for a walking shoe in size nine." The lady looked alarmed. She said, "Mon Dieu! Oh! I am so sorry for your friend. What misfortune for her! No. I do not know where in Paris you could possibly find such a size." Since then I understood why Jacqueline Kennedy tried so hard to get out of putting her footprints in the Sands of Time in India. The moment she finally did, the press measured her footprints and it was published all over the world that they were size 10½! *Now* the average for our female younger generation is a ten, so the heck with that chic, tidy French broad. Right?

Then we decided to get tickets for that nude sex show written by Ken Tynan, the most prominent and distinguished London theatre critic at that time. Oddly for him, everyone in it was nude. That's when, during intermission, Helen said, "Oh, I don't know. One reason I enjoy going to the theatre is to see the pretty costumes." She was, of course, in her Mrs. Antrobus characterization from *The Skin of Our Teeth*.

When Helen played Mrs. Antrobus, it was as funny as Thornton Wilder meant it to be. She was a satire on everybody's mother. She wore a small straw hat with a brim head-on. She had one daisy shooting straight up from the center front of its eyebrow-leveled brim. And, do you know, when I used to run into her shopping at the A&P in Nyack, she had that very hat on? She liked it. It was so sure of itself, that positive little statement of a hat with the daisy leading her head and the rest of her around.

I'll never forget the tiny bunch of violets in a milk glass vase she sent me when I moved to a house in Nyack near her for Chan's babyhood. It was to welcome me. There were stories from the milkman and other Nyack residents about Ben Hecht and Charles MacArthur, her husband (one of the famous playwriting team of Hecht and MacArthur. You know, *The Front Page* and other classics). It seems they played baseball all night long on the Main Street Square—keeping the town up with cheering each other on.

Much more recently, Rosie O'Donnell bought Helen's house down by the river—rose garden and all. I can see one reason why she bought it; it's a perfect place to raise all those children Rosie keeps adopting. But I remember once asking Helen, "How are you?" And she said, "Oh, you know, I'm like an old house. You brace up the stairway and it makes the veranda slide. You fix that and they run into a pipe, so the plumbing leaks. I'm like my old house." I really should have warned Rosie. Anyway, I had to say, "But, Helen, you look younger and more beautiful than you did ten years ago," which was true. This particular conversation took place on a Greek cruise ship. The trip was sponsored by the Theatre Guild. Helen felt we should help save the Theatre Guild by going on this Mediterranean expedition. Also, she was desperate to get away from the mail and the telephone. So we went.

Back to our conversations. She said, "That's ridiculous. It's impossible for me to look younger, Carol. Tomorrow I'm ninety-three years old." Well tomorrow came and the ship's chef brought her a birthday cake with a big "93" on top. The press came from Port Said, where we were docked, and took pictures. We always ate together, so I was right on her right, just the two of us. You should know, in all Semitic languages they read from right to left, so somehow in the translation her name got under my face and my name was under hers, with the big "93" between the two of us. When we got off the ship to see Port Said, the natives yelled "Happy birthday" to *me*. Charles, who came along, said to them, looking at me fondly, "Oh yes, it's Miss Channing's ninety-third, you know." They smiled back and shouted, "Lookin' good!" Helen loved it. I, of course, didn't. I think I was around seventy at the time.

By the way, on this last cruise Helen and I returned to Istanbul, which now feels completely French. Not one burnoose, or camel driver humming those Andalusian flutelike notes that floated constantly over the city, no full white robes on the men, no minarets with Asia Minor melodies. Just modern Paris. Men in custom-tailored suits.

Helen loved to go to the bow of the ship before dawn to see the rounded white mosques as the sun came up. This was at the time Saddam Hussein was taking hostages. I went up there with her, trying to convince her how easy it would be to take her in the dark. President George Bush would have had to say, "All right, Saddam, what do you want from us to give us Helen back again—the state of Rhode Island? Chicago?" Helen never, of course, thought she was that important. Well, she was.

Back to the point I was trying to make. Wouldn't you know our Rosie would want to live in the home of the family that stood for decades as part of the essence of Broadway aristocracy? Every time I was in Helen's house one could sense the electricity created by dedicated and sophisticated work done here by Hecht, MacArthur, and First Lady Helen. I'm sure what Rosie felt there was what I felt there—the excitement that goes with the great creations done in that home oozes out of the woodwork. I'll bet Rosie said to herself, "The heck with the fact the house is falling apart. Buy it! Live in the middle of it. And teach your children to revel in it and adore its rare and regal theatre lore." Her children will surely sense it, don't you think? They'll get it from Rosie.

Ethel Merman

thel Merman was always friendly enough to me after *Gentlemen Prefer Blondes*, my first starring part, opened. A short time after it opened, she grabbed me at a benefit or something and seemed absolutely giggly, telling me, "You walked like you hadda pee."

That was her complete summary of my portrayal of Anita Loos's monumental character Lorelei Lee. Of course, I adored Ethel, as we all did. Onstage she was magnetic, and the thought of her hasn't ever released me. On screen, though, she was like sun through glass . . . no ultraviolet rays or A or D vitamins. Or else the director and writer didn't understand her and love her like her Broadway audience and we all did. But on screen her shocking vocal cords were still there, which she herself seemed to feel were just like everybody else's. In fact, she seemed to be totally unaware of her entire shocking personality. Well, of course, this made her even more eccentric because it was beyond her own understanding. Later her constant question to me was "What the hell are ya laughin' at?"

Anything she did onstage was riveting and unexpected. Anyway, as I sat in her audience long before ever meeting her, she certainly had the whammy on *me*, to say nothing of the rest of the audience.

But after *Gentlemen Prefer Blondes* and my doing two plays for the Theatre Guild (*Pygmalion, The Millionairess*) and on Broadway a musical, (*The Vamp*), *Hello, Dolly!* came along. Suddenly, to Ethel, I was invisible. At actors' gatherings I would say, "Hello, Ethel." And she would look right and left of me, wondering where my voice came from. Radie Harris (the chronicler of live theatre) would say, "Don't you answer Carol when she says hello?"

Ethel: Carol who?

I thought to myself, Maybe she doesn't like hit shows that she isn't in.

Radie: Did you see *Hello, Dolly!* Ethel?

Ethel: Yeah, I turned that show down.

And I found out years later she did indeed, but I suppose, naturally, nobody ever told me.

One time I was asked to hang somebody's caricature at Sardi's restaurant for pictures for the press. When I got there, I found they had invited Ethel so we could hang the picture together.

Ethel: Nope, no picture. Not wit' Carol.

The Press: Why not? Oh, you mustn't feel badly, Miss Channing.

I didn't. I was already used to her. But it threw the sympathy to me, which I loved.

Another time was when Ethel was the last Dolly on Broadway. I only saw the end because I was playing Abe Burrows's *Four on a Garden* at the Broadhurst across the street and rushed over for the last scenes. Jerry Herman worshiped Ethel. Well, as I say, we all did, so he filled me in on how fabulous she was from the opening up to where I came in and saw her. I'm sure he was right . . . she sang as only she can and two octaves higher than I ever could and therefore sold his score. At least that's how I reasoned it in order to keep myself happy concerning Ethel's greatness in my part. It was her last performance and the original company of *Hello, Dolly!*'s last one on Broadway. Again, Ethel refused pictures with me. "I knew you'd make certain to be here tonight, Carol." And she shut the dressing room door. So *The New York Times* ran one of just me, out of sympathy or necessity, whichever, but I remember everybody was placating me. I wallowed in it.

Now Doug Cramer, the producer of television's *Hotel* and *The Love Boat*, wanted to win the TV sweeps that year. In case you don't know what the sweeps are, all the television programs put on one special show to raise the average of their ratings. He asked me to go to Hollywood and do a two-hour special with Ann Miller, Merman, and Della Reese. I went. The driver of the limousine picked me up where I lived in Los Angeles and started driving up to the Beverly Hills Hotel. He explained, "We're going to pick up Miss Merman on the way to the studio." Profound silence from me. I decided, There's only one way out of this, I'll be diligently learning my lines, squeezed into the back corner.

Well, *out came Ethel!* Into the bright California sunrise. She looked oddly like Harry Langdon, the silent film star. Her famous beaded eyelashes were coagulated after she'd slept on them, so that they made one straight, black, perpendicular spike, like the circus clowns wear from the center of their upper eyelids to the center below the lowers.

She got into the backseat with me and yelled, "Hi, Carol!"

Oh good, she's *talking* to me.

Ethel: I had the strangest airplane trip out here. A passenger was bleeding from the rectum.

Now that's the first thing she'd said to me since 1964. Why was she so chatty when I was invisible for so long? Later, Mary Martin told me Ethel had that tumor in her brain and nobody knew how long it had been growing. I told Mary I thought it must have been ever since *Girl Crazy,* since Ethel was never any different that I knew of.

Anyway, I repeated, "A passenger was bleeding from the rectum?"

Ethel: Yeah.

Naturally, I said what you would have said, "How did you know?"

"Well," she said, "there was no doctor on the plane, but I'm a nurse. What the hell are yuh laughin' at? I'm a *good* nurse. I volunteered to serve at Roosevelt Hospital for every Thursday."

Now I ask you, if you were strung up in Roosevelt Hospital, wouldn't you dread Thursdays? I mean, this woman walks into your room with her little white nurse's band above her forehead and screams, "Ah'm your nurse! Roll over." Wouldn't you? Dread Thursdays?

Back to the plane. Bob Six, a big, dear teddy bear of a man who lived in Denver, owned Continental Airlines. The way I understand it, but then I get most things inaccurately, part of Ethel's alimony from him was that she could fly anywhere free of charge on Continental Airlines. So, of course, she felt she owned the plane. Well, I guess she would have felt she owned it anyway. So Ethel stood in the aisle and announced to all passengers, "I will diagnose this case." She said to the bleeding gentleman, "Take down your pants. What did you have for dinner last night?"

Him: Mexican.

Ethel: I don't think that would cause all of this.

Finally, she told me, she declared to all, "I diagnose this case as di-verticulosis!"

I interrupted her, "Ethel, I know, because Lynn Fontanne had it and she said it was diverticulitis."

Now, you know that beat that Ethel put before her punch lines that made the line even funnier? It went: (Beat) "That's the singular."

Me: You mean this was a multiple case of it?

No answer. She was hurt. I never corrected her again. It might take the wind out of her sails. After her considerable quietude, she returned to her story.

Ethel: By this time we were way off our course. The pilot wanted to save this man's life, so he was trying to land the plane in Denver.

(Now back to her full energy): I swung open the door to the cockpit and told the pilot "Do not land this plane in Denver! They have nothing but inhumanity in Denver! No one will take pity on this poor man in Denver."

Apparently, she saw herself as this sad little waif running from door to door, hoping for freedom from Bob Six in Denver. My advance man on tour once went ahead of me to Denver and called me from there to say, "I don't see any inhumanity here in Denver."

So, it shows you how little perspective Ethel had on herself.

Well, the pilot, who I'm sure never heard or saw anyone like Ethel before in his life, U-turned the plane and landed next to the pre-ordered ambulance in Phoenix. Ethel told me she just got a phone call from her patient, who she thought was "kinda cute. I liked him. He's better and going to get well." She grinned.

By this time, we were the best of friends. My head was in her lap from laughing. Ethel didn't seem to think that was odd of me at all.

Now, the first rushes I saw were of Ann Miller and Ethel and me in-the-middle. The moment a voice-over said, "Action," Ethel and Annie moved diagonally together in front of me so that during every take I was pointing to the floor saying, "*There's* your mark, right there and *there's* yours."

Consternation from them! "What is she talking about?"

Innocence! My voice rose in each take until voice-over said, "Cut."

It took an entire morning to shoot the scene, and then they couldn't use any of it.

Doug Cramer decided a short time later that Ethel and I would ride to the studio together. I found out later it was at Ethel's request. Of course, I was delighted. At 5:30 A.M., when it was still dark, the Ethelladen car would pick me up. Half asleep, I'd stagger through the front gate to the car and say, "Why do they want us so early, Ethel?"

Ethel: (Beat) So's you'll be fresh! Now get in.

Then there was an edict from on high that rubber bands must be placed on Miss Merman's temples to pull her face up. A few days later they wanted two more under her chin, pulled to her ears. This left her with a perpetual smile. Now we were picked up at 5:00 A.M. instead of 5:30. One morning after rubber bands were placed, the hairdresser felt Ethel needed two extra curls. She put Ethel under the dryer. These particular dryers could only be lifted up by the hairdressers. In a few minutes we heard, "Hey, I'm burnin' up. Come here, you bitch. Get me outta here."

We looked at Ethel. She was still smiling, so we didn't pay any attention. I thought she was just rehearsing something, but for a week after that, her ears were red and swollen.

The rushes on her big scene with Van Johnson, who played her high school sweetheart but now they each have children by two other people and must part, went:

Ethel: Well, g'bye, Van. (Continued big rubber-band grin)

Van: Darling, we do still love each other.

Ethel (top of her lungs): Yeah!

Now, glyccrin tears were added to the grin.

Ethel: This breaks my heart.

Voice-Over: Cut.

Ethel, still on camera: What's the mattuh?

I must tell you now in meetings for the script changes Ethel asked me, "What the hell page are they talkin' about?" I knew there was something wrong when her brilliant, electric mind couldn't fathom these corrections. I pointed to page 72 and whispered, "Two more lines to yours." But she asked *me*! She must have trusted me. She did! She also couldn't remember that my character's name was Sylvia. "Hey! Cybill! Sophie! Shirley! Come here, ya dumb cunt!"

And I would come. All I had to do, of course, was say, "I have no idea to whom she is referring," but I always came, just like any of us would once we experienced her onstage.

Every day the rushes were so much better than the TV show that I don't know how we ever won the sweeps for Doug Cramer, but we did.

Several rushes later, the three of us were in line again. Now the moment the man snaps those two wooden sticks together and says "Action," I sweat.

Director: Cut. Powder down, Miss Channing.

While makeup was powdering, I said, "How come you two girls are so dainty and feminine and I have to sweat like a truck driver?"

Annie never wants you to feel badly about yourself, so she consoled, "Don't you worry, honey, everybody sweats, but in a different place. You sweat in the face, some people sweat in the armpits, I sweat in the crotch."

The last sentence received attention from lighting men, cameramen, makeup staff: "I missed that, what did she say?"

Ethel didn't care for the attention Annie was getting, so she pierced the atmosphere with "Sure, everybody sweats in the crotch." (Continued rubber-band smile.) Aha! Attention! Now louder. . . . "Everybody sweats in the—" My hand covered her mouth.

Me: Ethel, we heard you. In the first place, you don't know. You haven't asked anyone. Have you asked anyone? It may not be true.

Ethel (even louder): *Everybody* sweats in—

I had to swing my hand on her mouth again and keep it there. Muffled incoherence.

Annie: Oh yes. In *Sugar Babies*, between scenes, my little blow dryer was just about worn out.

This sort of talk went on for two months, with none of it on the final show. Apparently, according to what I saw in the rushes, the cameraman had lost interest and forgot to turn the camera off till long after "Cut!"

We talked a lot on those limo rides to the studio. I'm sure everyone's life has a flip side, but the flip side of Ethel's life was horrendous. She told me her daughter married when she was way too young and had committed suicide. Ethel was choking with tears. Then her son, Bobby, was married to a girl that Ethel thought was wonderful for him. Bobby's wife went to find her parked car behind Will Wright's Ice Cream Store on Sunset Boulevard and was shot to death right next to the car. No one ever found out who did it or why. I held her hand tightly, vainly trying to give her support.

While she cried, I remembered Anita Loos telling me that Ethel was married to Robert Levitt, a brilliant editor in chief of a magazine. He was the father of her children. She said Ethel always wanted a few drinks after her shows at the Stork Club. Anita thought she fell in love with Sherman Billingsley, but I'd met Billingsley and I didn't think that was possible. I think she just fell in love with those few drinks after her shows. Anyway, she divorced Levitt. Levitt tried for years to get along without her. He married his head model, a lovely, very intelligent woman. Anita said they worked together on his magazine. She was one of its editors. He tried for another year and finally gave up. He committed suicide! Naturally, I didn't know how to help Ethel.

The next morning on our ride together, she told me she had to go to Rio de Janeiro after this *Love Boat.* She said she asked her son, Bobby, if he would like to fly with her. Bobby said, "Sure. I'll meet you there."

Ethel told him the only reason she asked him was so they could visit together on the plane. Then she looked at me and asked, "How do you raise a son so he understands?"

I had to say at the time, "I'm the last person you should ask that question, Ethel. Apparently, I'm the world's worst mother. Mary Martin thinks she is, but she's not. I am."

Today, I have to say I don't know what I ever did to deserve such a great son. I loved him with all my heart. A broken one, admittedly, because I thought he didn't want to be with me. Now I know he must have sensed how I loved him. Today, I could have helped Ethel, *maybe.* I wish so that I could have then. I told her Bobby, her son, often came to visit us at the Waldorf after my two shows nightly in the Empire Room. He reminded me of Chan growing up in the sense that the only people that seemed to frighten him were dear little old ladies. Chan would go trick or treating on Halloween to Judith Anderson's door at Chateau Marmont in L.A. I heard her ominous contralto tones say, "Come in, little boy." And he'd be gone for an hour. Or once he rushed up to Hermione Gingold in the Beverly Hills Hotel lobby at four years old to hug her and tell her how he loved her on TV as Cinderella's wicked stepmother. Hermione looked up at me with her irregular English teeth and whistled, "Sssshweet child." And that Chan always was and is.

Weeks after we finished the *Love Boat* episode, my phone rang in New York; it was Jerry Herman telling me he had just visited Ethel and she wrote on a piece of paper asking for Cybill. Her son explained to Jerry that "Cybill" was Carol Channing. I immediately came to her hotel. As I walked in, Bobby said, "Mom, Carol's here."

Ethel: Who?

Me: It's me, Cybill.

Ethel: Awww.

She was bedridden, couldn't speak, and had no hair from the chemotherapy. She was trying to cover her head with the sheets, like a wounded animal, and looking helplessly, almost sadly, up at me. I asked, "Where is your wig, Ethel?"

She was only able to make noises. She pointed to all the drawers. I set about finding it and did. She pulled on the front of it while I pulled the back. We relaxed. I did the talking, of course.

Me: What are the doctors giving you to help you?

Ethel: Aw-aw-aw cor-cor-cor-corti-corti . . .

Me: Cortisone? Well, Ethel, it swells your face up and you look like you're twelve years old.

She went slowly to a full smile.

Ethel: Yeah?

Then laughter. "Ha! Ha!" With a how-do-you-like-that? sound.

Me: Ethel, who is your doctor?

Ethel: Ah-ee-ee-ah.

And after much trying, she opened her mouth and sang as clearly as she ever did.

Ethel: He was my father's doctor.

She could sing anything. If she sang it, she could enunciate perfectly. We celebrated discovering this miracle. I talked, and she sang around me; we sang separately; we sang together. Then she'd groan or wail loudly, and since her soul was *normally* on the enormous proportions of a Clytemnestra, she now became the most overtly sick, noisiest woman in the world. That was our Ethel. If you're going to be sick, don't mince around about it. Naturally, anyone's heart would go out to her, wanting to help, but she was also, in a sense, letting off steam. She was no ingenue about this illness. She was one of the great Greek goddesses, overwhelming.

I went from Ethel's hotel straight to my lawyer to make out a living will. No one should suffer like Ethel did. But I don't think of all that. The laughter and theatrical excitement she created with her voice and how she generated people's lives, even when she was bored with a quiet audience, actually, particularly when she was bored she was funniest. Sometimes she'd come back onstage, take a deep breath to sing an encore, decide there wasn't enough applause, yell, "Aach," and go on with the dialogue instead. No amount of applause after that could get her to sing that encore. She just waved the audience down.

Shortly after she died, Doug Cramer invited us to fly in his plane with him for a visit to his ranch. A windstorm threw us perilously up, down, and sideways. He acted as if he were putting down a telephone in the plane and said, "Carol, that was Merman. She said she expects to see you shortly for lunch with her today."

Of course, he was joking, but just *think*. Wouldn't *that* be heaven?

Mary Martin

lose to what I didn't know was the end of Mary Martin's life, she said to me, "People say the reason we work well together is because we're so opposite, but I know that way down deep inside we're exactly alike."

Oh, Mary, what a beautiful thing to say about a lifelong friendship. To be like you, with your lack of competition yet healthy ambition, with your unvolatile nature in the face of evil, your vision of everyone through your own clean windows, and your understanding of others.

I just read this paragraph over. Doesn't it sound saccharine-phony, though? But it's all true. All right. She had only one of what most people call faults. It was labeled a fault only because most people didn't have it. Just in order to make her sound like a human being: she had an addictive nature. To what is none of my business, and it's certainly not my business to tell of it to somebody else. Now, of course, you can't stand it until you know. She never tried to hide it from me. I'm into *food* myself, and don't think that's as innocent as it sounds. It can rule your life. Back to the subject.

Mary. She made a deal with her landlord, here in the California desert, to let Charles and his friend Willie and me stay in a house near hers. I bicycled to her house every morning so we could learn our lines for *Legends!* together. We dismissed any help she had so we wouldn't be tempted to talk with them. I dismissed the housekeeper. We even asked her to take Mary's dog home with her so we could concentrate. We decided we were going to be our most disciplined and not give in to our usual gabbing and giggling. After learning about four lines, though, somehow we got off onto the subject of that fire escape that connects the Broadhurst Theatre in New York to her favorite Imperial Theatre. Mary said in the summertime the actresses playing nuns in *The Sound of Music* would sit out on that fire escape to cool off in full view to any passerby. They had their legs spread apart, waving the skirts of their habits up and down to create a breeze, guzzling bottles of Coca-Cola and smoking cigarettes hanging from the sides of their mouths. People complained. Mary said, "Don't laugh. It created a problem that went all the way to the archdiocese of New York. I felt so badly about it. My dear friend is the Mother Teresa and I didn't want her to hear about it either."

The reason I couldn't stop laughing was because this was to Mary a backstage business problem to be conjured with, and apparently it took a great deal of serious straightening out on her part. At first she thought it wasn't true, but when passersby began to gather on the sidewalk below, it required Mary to take time and thought for correcting the girls.

After Mary and I learned two or three more lines, I was somehow surprised to discover she hadn't heard about Tallulah getting arrested and jailed in Boston. It was for drunken driving, which didn't surprise either of us. I heard about this from my dear friend Roger, who lives next door to Talloo's brother in Newport Beach, California, so it's totally reliable.

All right, you perhaps knew of how Talloo organized gin rummy games with the stage crew to take place between the matinees and evening shows of any show in which she was playing.

It seems this jail in Boston was very small, so they had only one cell.

That meant they had to put Talloo in it with hardened criminals, I imagine like various hit men and ax murderers. The brother flew to Boston, paid her bail, and found she had organized another gin game in their one cell. When the guard slid the jail bars open he said, "Miss Bankhead, you may leave now." She answered, "Well, I can't go now, you fool, I'm *winning*," and remained there for I don't know how long, perhaps into the night.

I got myself together, and we learned four more lines. Then we'd get hungry. I'd ask Mary, "Is there any food in the house?"

Mary: I d'know.

Me: We could open a can of soup.

Mary: Yes. But I d'know haow.

Me: Maybe I can try. Where are the cans and can opener?

Mary: I d'know.

Me: How do you eat, Mary?

Mary: The housekeeper.

Me: Oh.

Mary: We could go to the Morningside Country Club.

Me: Oh, let's go there.

Mary: Let's.

So every day we got in her little red convertible with her vermilion-colored hair (she changed the color of it every time she washed it). We had three meals a day at the country club and just signed the check. It was as simple as that.

After we got to the Ahmanson Theatre rehearsal hall in Los Angeles, it occurred to me to ask Mary, "Was that a big bill for all those meals at Morningside?"

Mary: I didn't pay it. Did you?

Me: No. I thought you did. Did you tell them when we were leaving and where they could reach us?

Mary: Didn't you?

Me: No. I don't belong to the Morningside Country Club.

Mary: Neither do I.

Me: Mary! You suggested it.

Mary: Well, you seemed to want to go there.

Me: Then why did they keep feeding us?

Mary: I guess the waiter thought we were members.

Me: Oh, Mary. We could both be arrested.

Just recently my cousins invited me to the Morningside Club for dinner. I told Dickie that Mary is gone now and I'm afraid they're still looking for me. Dickie told me to come along anyway. Nothing happened. I don't want to ask them about the bill. Mary would have thought my not asking them was doing them a favor, not to stir up trouble. Why confuse them?

Then we learned a few more lines, and somehow Mary told me that she and her son, Larry Hagman, were once hailing a cab to go to the Desert Inn show in Las Vegas. The cabs all whizzed right by them, as they do at show time. Finally one jammed on the brakes and yelled to Larry, "J.R.! Get right in." Larry did. The cab started off immediately, before Mary could get in. Larry leaned out the window, tipped his ten-gallon J.R. hat to Mary, and shouted, "That's show business, Mom." When Mary finally got to the Desert Inn show room, she sat down next to Larry as Dean Martin announced, "We have in our audience from the TV show *Dallas* none other than J.R. himself." Everyone applauded wildly while Larry bowed. Then Dean said, "And now the Peter Pan of all time, Mary Martin." Of course the house came down and never seemed to stop, during which, Mary told me, she leaned over to Larry, smiled, and said, "That's show business, son."

Well, of course, all discipline went right out the window as usual with us, and I told her about Zoe Caldwell breaking in "*Mahsteh Clahss*" (*Master Class*) at the Kennedy Center at the same time we broke in the final tour of *Dolly*. I came to her dressing room, and Zoe resounded, "Don't come in! Stay right there in the doorway. I have this fatal cold and you mustn't get it before we both open in New York." I already had it. Her hairdresser, who was busy working on her, said, "You know, I have a sore throat. I think you gave it to me." Zoe turned and stared at him. "But with you it doesn't matter." I could just hear Bob Whitehead, her husband and producer, saying after that, "What happened to your hair, Zoe?" Zoe never thought that was funny. Mary and I did, because we were terrified of closing down the entire show if we lost our voices. Zoe, just like all live theatre stars, was so frightened by the thought that she *couldn't* find it funny.

I used to awaken every morning trying out my voice. Was it there? The high notes? Or the low notes? If there was one section missing, was it something I ate? Something I didn't do? Was I in a gas-heated place? It becomes a phobia. People in the live theatre are laughed at for their beliefs, like dairy products creating mucus. Well, they do.

In rehearsal we had an English director. I can't ever remember the name of anyone of which I think so very little. We would have understood each other better if he were Chinese. But you know who we got later for a director? Mary's son, Larry Hagman, and he was superb. He played no favorites with us. He has a fine divining rod as a director. It comes from being basically an actor. We all know those are the best live theatre directors.

On opening night in Pittsburgh, Larry said to me, "You lost your nerve." He hit it smack on the nose. I knew it wasn't right for this character I was playing. When playing some characters, you have to let the audience know you don't need them. They catch that and come around to reacting to you if they know you just don't give a fig whether they do or not. Larry was right. I lost my nerve and tried to get along with an opening night Pittsburgh audience.

However, sometimes, when the audience catches every nuance and lets the actors know it, we all shout backstage, "Bless you, adorable lovable people! You all must have been sitting on a feather." Nancy Walker, the heaven comedian, used to get down on her hands and knees before the show, lift the curtain slightly, sniff in the air, then tell the company just what the audience was going to be like. She was most always correct, I hear. I tried it. It works, but only sometimes, with me.

A happy attitude doesn't work with a bad audience. In other words, a benefit audience. They almost resent you for being so glad to see them. Their focus isn't even going toward the stage. It's on one another. Who's here? Oh, there's Sarah. Wave to her. With a healthy audience a college professor is sitting next to a truck driver, who's next to a script girl or cameraman, and so on. The professor reacts to one on-stage incident, the truck driver to a different one, and so on, so it's like rubbing sticks together until they ignite, and finally the entire house is warm and cozy. Also, a healthy audience is unself-conscious. They don't know each other. With a benefit, we have all decided, they probably have a pinochle game going on behind the last row of the orchestra that keeps their attention so very far from the stage.

Every actor I know is preoccupied with analyzing a benefit audience. We have to find out why they're so sick. If our job is to uplift people's lives, the way ours are uplifted when we go to the theatre, then we've got to get to the bottom of this. Anyway, this is one of my versions of the benefit problem. So take the above for what it's worth.

Back to Larry Hagman. A few years ago there was a lot of noise about Larry needing a liver transplant and getting it ahead of a whole lot of other waiting people because we all love him so much on TV. At the same time he was lying in bed inside a square of white curtains in the surgery section of L.A.'s Cedars-Sinai Hospital, awaiting his new liver, I was outside his curtains waiting for an operation to remove a cataract that developed strictly from staring into the spotlight all my life. I asked the eye doctor why he didn't tell me before not to do that. He said they didn't know until now. They knew "now" because of me, because no one else that the AMA knew of ever stared into the biggest supertrooper spotlight, without blinking, all her life, every night and all day Saturdays, Sundays, and holidays, so light must be what causes cataracts. Anyway, apparently I did something to uplift the world of ophthalmology at least. I heard Larry's voice, so I got off the gurney and went to his curtains. "Larry, it's me," I whispered. My eye doctor called out, "Come back here, Carol. He'll only want your liver."

"Yes!" said Larry. "*She's* got the liver I want. No cigarettes, no booze, no sugar . . . *I want her liver!*"

So my Dr. Salz wheeled me right into the operating room with Larry still calling after my liver and shut the door. In the operating room assistants were wearing the usual starched white coats, but along with turbans and fezzes and burnooses and all softly singing "Hello, Dolly!" while they antibacteriaed instruments. I read in the paper Larry got his liver, but I want you to know it wasn't the one he wanted. I do like being wanted . . . any part of me, don't you?

With Larry's direction, Mary and I played *Legends!* for over a year. I never knew she had cancer. She never missed a performance.

One morning Charles told me Susan Grushkin (Mary's assistant) had called from the Springs, where Mary lived in the California desert, and said, "Carol should come to Mary as soon as possible." Willie drove me. I walked into Mary's house, and her doctor said, "Mary is in a coma, so she won't hear you, but you can go in and be with her for a short time." She was lying in her bed on coral linens, her favorite color. I hadn't seen her looking so young since I first met her, when she was in *South Pacific* and I was in *Lend an Ear.* Not a line on her face. I took her hand so she'd know 'twas I. I just kept talking about all our old jokes. She couldn't answer, I knew.

Then I told her Helen Hayes sends love, many people send love to you, and I love you, too, Mary. She squeezed my hand! Because I knew then she could hear me, I told her, "You know better than I do, Mary, that nothing can ever stop you from being you, no matter what happens to you. You'll always be safe in warmth and love because that's what you give out . . . affection and happiness and friendship that's constant. It's all around you now, and there's no reason for it to go away."

She slightly smiled and squeezed my hand again, so I looked at our hands, and that's when I first saw a rainbow in Mary Martin colors. Clear Chinese yellow, delicate coral, pale green into aqua (not turquoise, that's too blatant for Mary), ice blue. The rainbow stayed on our holding hands as I kept talking. It slowly moved to where the cancer was. It must have been her pancreas, from what I've learned since from my trainer, Ken, about where a pancreas is, but it focused right there. Then it moved slowly up to her heart and rested on her neck affectionately. Those pale shades made her so softly pretty; they don't become me at all. I need red, white, and blue. I get all washed out and sick looking in those subtle shades. When the rainbow moved up to her forehead, I finally had to say, "There's a rainbow on you, Mary. Mary Martin, there's a rainbow on you." She was serene, as if she knew it.

Susan was sent in by the doctor, who said, "You've been with her three-quarters of an hour. I heard the laughter, so I let you stay much longer than the ten minutes I planned." I told him I'd go.

"I hope you see the beautiful rainbow on you, Mary. Bye-bye, dearest Mary." The moment I got back to the house, the phone rang. I ran to it before anyone else could get it.

Susan said, "Mary's gone. And you know how we knew? The rainbow went away."

I phoned Helen Hayes and told her. There was a cab waiting for Helen in front of her home in Nyack to take her to the airport to fly to Mary. She dismissed the cab, and I told her about the rainbow.

Helen said, "Isn't that strange? I've never told anybody ever—they'd think I was crazy—but when my daughter died there was a light in the upper-left corner of my bedroom that I could only see when the sun went down. It shone all night till dawn for two weeks. Then, when my husband died, the same light appeared for two weeks."

I asked her, "What do you think it is, Helen?"

"I have no idea," she said, choking up. "The rainbow is just as confusing, isn't it?"

I said, "Yes."

On my early morning walks I have asked the heavens, then stayed quiet and still for any kind of understanding. Was it Dick, her husband? I finally asked my Dr. Bill (Cahan) in New York. He said, "Here at Memorial Sloan-Kettering, when patients go, sometimes the entire bed lights up, or it can be a very small light. It's a spirit, Rifkele (me). We don't know yet." Dr. Bill's nature could tranquilize his patients when needed. He had tranquilized me indeed. I told him, "When I go, I'm going to make an American flag."

Liz Smith and John Barrymore

*I*n 1988 or 1989, Rocco Landesman decided to open his newly designed theatre and call it the Walter Kerr, which was as it should be. The night of the dedication, Jerry Herman and I appeared on its stage alone together. There were many other Broadway people. Jerry wrote brilliant lyrics to "Hello, Walter," and I got to sing them, with him playing the piano. On a benefit performance like that, something comes over you that you've got to be the two best on the show or you'll have to live with this failure for the rest of your lives. At the end of the entertainment, Jerry and I were sitting side by side backstage. He said, "The applause for us was very good, wasn't it, Carol?"

"Oh yes. Tremendous. But, then, you never know if the others got more, do you, Jerry?"

"No. Backstage it's difficult to judge."

"And if we didn't get more than the others, Jerry, I'll never stop being miserable."

"Neither will I."

Just then a reassuring, loving arm came around Jerry's shoulder and around mine from behind us with the voice that belonged with them saying, "*May* I go down on both of you?" We turned around and both saw Liz Smith.

"Dearest Liz, it's you!"

Jerry said, "Simultaneously? How are you going to do that?"

Liz said, "Oh, don't you know the famous old John Barrymore greeting after he truly enjoyed someone's performance? It's become a byword now and its meaning isn't as off-color as it sounds anymore. He'd go backstage, overcome with admiration, ask, 'Where is the star's dressing room?' stagger across the stage, arms open, his resonant tones almost singing, '*May* I go down on you?' "

Me: Yes. He wanted to give them something special, you see, Liz.

Liz: That's right, Carol. We know that.

(This was before Clinton. It's not special now, I understand.)

Barrymore would repeat, "Where are you? Ah, here is your door." He'd swing the star's dressing room door open with another slower, more poetic "May I go down on you," so that now it's only a means of saying, "You were superb, the greatest!"

Well, both of us were so relieved that we were up to John Barrymore's standards that we celebrated with Liz with bear hugs. Also, Liz was our oldest and kindest friend, and we adored her. I just want to be sure you know that Liz does not go around saying this to just anyone. Only to those who were the best on the program, which we like to think was only us.

By the way, now that we're on the subject of Barrymore, I'm sure you know about him buying a necktie at Sulka's and telling the clerk to charge it. "Yes sir," said the clerk, "and what is the name?" (Now who else looked like John Barrymore?)

"Barrymore."

"And how do you spell it?"

He spelled it.

"And your first name, sir?"

(Long, unfriendly pause.)

"Ethel."

Carole Shorenstein Hays

arole Shorenstein Hays owns three legit theatres in San Francisco: the Orpheum, the Golden Gate, and the Curran. She's a heaven producer because she's there always during rehearsals in case of emergency. She has three hit plays that she produced on Broadway as I write this. Before these hits she produced Eugène Ionesco's *The Chairs*. She follows her heart. She produces only plays she has fallen in love with. August Wilson's *Fences* tried out for Broadway at her Curran, and when it came to New York it won the Pulitzer Prize. I did *Showgirl* with her, *Dolly* twice, and *Legends!* with Mary in San Francisco.

I told her that when I was in school they put the last row of the last balcony aside at 50 cents a ticket for students. She insisted that now it would have to be $2.50 a ticket. Okay. I asked her to do that for me. She said, "I suppose you want those to be called the Carol Channing seats?"

"Yes!" I said. So for opening night of *Legends!* she went to San Francisco's traditional Podesta and Baldocchi florists and selected opening night flowers to be delivered to my dressing room. What arrived was one wilted poppy, some weeds, leaves that had turned yellow, and a dead rose . . . with a card saying: "You want $2.50 tickets? You get $2.50 opening night flowers."

Patrick Quinn

atrick Quinn is our new Actors' Equity president, elected just this year, 2002. I voted for him. He was good on the Equity Council for twenty-three years and had been our first vice president since 1988. He'll make a fine president.

He had tremendous energy as an actor and singer. In fact, it was overpowering. More like cyclonic. Out of control is what it was. Patrick was our Cornelius in *Dolly* for years. His singing voice was so powerful you could hardly hear the orchestra on "Out there, there's a world outside of Yonkers . . ." from the song, "Put on Your Sunday Clothes." He held the notes so long and unrelentingly that I, sitting nearest him in the scene on his left, am now deaf only in the right ear . . . not the left.

When Rock Hudson was touring with the musical *On the Twentieth Century*, he said to me, "That guy is a menace! He's dangerous!" Rock didn't realize it was only onstage.

I saw Rock and Patrick in *Twentieth Century* in Detroit. In one scene when Rock had a bit of dialogue with another actor, the door swung open and I knew Patrick was on his way through it by the velocity of the opening of the door. It crashed against the wall, pinning the other actor behind it. When Rock, who had been facing the other way, turned around to answer, he couldn't find the other actor, but Patrick stood triumphantly in front of the open door, giving a joyful greeting to Rock. Rock obviously was supposed to have more dialogue with the other actor but instead said to Patrick quietly, threateningly, and with serious concentration, "Where's Ned?"

Patrick strode victoriously across the stage, leaving the door to slowly close, revealing Ned, who was slumped against the wall and holding his nose. Rock was trying to revive Ned, so the dialogue sort of fell apart while Patrick spoke on undauntedly.

I don't know if the Detroit audience could tell what the problem was but, of course, I knew. The problem was that Patrick (an affable enough fellow offstage) has, as he passes the proscenium arch to go on stage, some sort of propeller inside him that charges immediately into high gear and renders him totally unaware of the havoc he creates.

In *Hello, Dolly!* there was a floor trapdoor that Patrick and the actor playing Barnaby entered from. Patrick has lifted and closed that door on Barnaby's head more than once, leaving Barnaby sealed in the basement. When that happened, Patrick had the good sense to begin his song without their dialogue, even though that dialogue explained all the rest of the plot. The pretty hats that were displayed in the hat shop window have gone spinning across the floor as he passed them, and so have the flowers, which were then trampled on by the oncoming dancers.

But to me, Patrick's most memorable achievement was when he hid inside the closet as he was supposed to. I was directed to peek in, opening the door one inch to see him. Patrick was supposed to close the door, but one matinee he swung the door wide open—so as to get better momentum to close it, I imagine—and closed it on my right arm, breaking it. Why actors don't feel pain onstage during a performance I'll never know, but we don't. At least it's not so acute that we can't keep going on.

Before intermission the stage manager, at my dresser Tiv's behest, had already called Dr. Bill in New York, asking him to recommend a doctor in Detroit to set my arm. Dr. Bill must have been arranging with a Detroit bone specialist while I was still onstage to get right over to me, because when I got on the stage manager's phone to Dr. Bill, he said, "Hello, Rifkele? How's the Rif?"

Me: I've got a broken arm.

Dr. Bill: In which scene did you get it?

Me: The hat shop scene.

Dr. Bill: Which part of the stage? I'm writing this all down.

Me: The closet door. What difference does it make?

Dr. Bill (impatiently): Well, we've got to fix the door first, don't we?

Instead of crying I got a fit of the giggles. Dr. Bill did the right thing again. By this time the Detroit bone specialist got there, set my arm, and shot something in it for the pain. I trusted him because Bill told me to. Tiv cut up a big piece of red fabric for the sling and got the red dress and red feathered hat on me, and we were all ready to descend the red velvet stairway into the "Hello, Dolly!" number. Once I was on the red stairway, I didn't feel a thing till the final curtain.

But my friend Patrick, who has always indeed been a friend to me, was solicitous for the next six months, coming and looking at my arm in its sling and saying each time, "What maniac could have done such a thing to you? How could this have happened onstage? Have they checked the door to be sure it won't swing closed again?"

Please, anyone, don't tell Patrick he did it. He would be unbearably chagrined. In fact, he wouldn't believe it, so I'm not going to worry about it.

Now, he's safely off the stage (that's the main reason I voted for him, to get him safely off), and he'll make one of the best presidents Equity ever had.

Children of Helen Hayes,
Zoe Caldwell, and Me

elen Hayes was appearing in Los Angeles in George Kelly's play *The Show-Off*. James MacArthur, Helen's son, was sitting next to me in the audience. It was Helen's opening night, so her lines were not yet subconscious. All right. We heard Helen repeating a sentence she'd said a few speeches back. Then we heard the entire paragraph repeated. I had my hand resting on the arm of my seat. Jim's hand clutched the arm of my chair and squeezed it to the breaking point, but my hand was still under his. Do you know, I can show you to this day where the bone in my fourth finger has this unique deformity. Of course I didn't yell or even move. It was her important speech-build at the end of the first act. Helen somehow wound out of her problem, kept on talking, and got herself back on track.

The moment the houselights went on for intermission, James took out his handkerchief and mopped his brow. Naturally, I didn't tell him he had maimed me for life, but he had. Like with Patrick Quinn, I haven't told him and don't intend to. Jim lives near my little house now. I know the agony he went through that night about his mother. He went through enough, I feel. I know you won't tell him because, for one reason, his house is very difficult to find and he's not in the phone book. You see, if it had happened to Jim, he would never have been so helpless as when he was trying to help his mother. Also, no doubt he cued her on all her lines, because that's what sons are for, aren't they? But he never dreamed she'd go up on this line, so he blamed himself. I know.

Now me. My father was asked by the University of California to deliver the baccalaureate address for the graduating class of 1937. It was excellent training for a growing child (me) to see him give up

Thanksgiving, and all Sundays, holidays, and evenings off, to get it written to his own satisfaction.

My mother and I sat on the grassy campus hills along with hundreds of Cal students to hear his address. It was going unforgettably well when I heard him flounder. He never floundered for words! I leaned back on the grass and passed clean out! My mother must have thought I fell asleep, because when I came to, my father was still standing up there delivering a whale of a lecture. But I knew, years later, what Jim MacArthur went through over his mother's flub. As I say, it's so much more agonizing for the loved ones than for the one in whose hands the performance is. There's nothing one can do to help. Chan told me he went through the same with me once.

Now for Zoe Caldwell, my very most favorite straight legit (nonmusical) actress, now that Lynn Fontanne, Helen Hayes, Katherine Cornell, Alla Nazimova, Tallulah Bankhead, Dame Judith Anderson, and Ethel Barrymore have left us. Ah, but we still have Julie Harris, and the live theatre doesn't intend to let her go. And Broadway people always knew Elaine Stritch was as great as she is now. I wrote her fan letters myself. Anyway, ever since *The Prime of Miss Jean Brodie*, I realized Zoe can slip you from tears to laughter all evening long with the greatest of ease.

Well, Zoe has two sons, Charlie Whitehead and Sam Whitehead. Their father was the distinguished straight play producer Robert Whitehead. When I met their sons, they were both college age. I was around seventy-two so, of course, I fell wildly in love with them equally. Zoe and Bob came shining through both of these perfect boys.

Well, Zoe and Charlie went up to the registration desk in a hotel near the Shubert Theatre in New Haven. That is where most good shows try out and correct themselves before their Broadway opening. Zoe asked for one room for both her and her son. The hotel clerk said, "I can offer you two rooms if you'd like." Zoe snapped, "No. I want one room and one queen-size bed." Zoe told me the man looked from one to the other of them as if he smelled something. You see, it's obvious Charlie looks like his mother. Then the clerk said, "We have one room with twin beds." "No!" said Zoe. "How am I going to learn my lines if he's in the other bed? He'll keep falling asleep. Obviously you don't have any sons." She said she quoted me on "That's what sons are for."

I felt honored when she told me, but that's what they *are* for. Of course, the man was silent. He probably wasn't clear on who I was, even though I'd played that Shubert Theatre a good five times before this incident. It may be though that I never saw this clerk, since I've found it much easier on a pre-Broadway tryout simply to make a tent with sheets and pitch it next to the stage manager's desk until the kinks in the show get straightened out.

Indeed, that's what sons are for! Well, Chan had a best friend in the Allen-Stevenson School, Peter Bregarnick, who stayed overnight with us from time to time. He was there on this particular night. Chan left the bedroom and came back with Peter from his room. They started cuing me, handing the script back and forth whenever they got mad at me or while the other one napped, but they never gave up. We worked till dawn. I was so frightened at the thought of opening so soon, I didn't even know I was tired.

I felt completely defeated by trying to learn lines for the opening of *The Millionairess* in Louisville, Kentucky, in less than a week. In fact, I was panic-stricken. I said, "I'm simply beside myself." Chan said, "Don't worry, *beside herself* is Mom's favorite position." However, Chan had seen theatre shows often enough to know what disgrace and disaster it would be if his mother just stood there like a dumb cluck and not a word came out of her, or if she had to apologize and say she didn't remember what she was talking about.

There's nothing like sheer panic to make the adrenaline jazz up your brain, so I got through it without missing a word, thanks to Chan and Peter. There were the usual pictures, and press and TV interviews immediately after the final curtain. By the time we got back to the hotel, at 1:00 A.M., the desk had several urgent messages from Chan and Peter to call them. They were up so late. How cruel! I had wanted to phone them immediately after the show, but part of an actor's job is publicizing his show, and thank goodness the press and TV wanted me to.

Chan and Peter on the phone: Well, *did* you remember your lines? "Yes!"

But, if I have my way, I'll be with one or the other of you again someday, Chan and Peter, and be able to tell you I don't remember the lines now, but I never, ever will stop remembering each of you and how much you cared.

Hines, Hines, and Channing

G*regory* Hines has a brother, Maurice, and they have a father and mother. They were billed as Hines, Hines, and Dad. They were a class act. They started in vaudeville when the boys were little, but Dad eventually got tired. Anyway, they decided to change it to Hines, Hines, and Channing, which was a dream come true for me. So I learned all I know of tap through Gregory Hines and no less than Honi Coles, and that's not bad.

With Hines and Hines, I had huge bows on my shoes like Minnie Mouse, great big black ones, and Cuban heeled tap shoes. We thought we had the greatest dialogue material since Anton Chekhov or Neil Simon. We took our entire show with our band and chorus of dancers all the way across the country and around.

I saw Dad Hines backstage at *Jelly's Last Jam*, my favorite Broadway musical to attend. He still looked young to me and solidly healthy enough to tour. His sons are busy now. Maybe *he'd* like to tour with me. Please? Dad? I know the routines.

Laurence Olivier

*L*aurence Olivier once announced he was presenting *Guys and Dolls* with himself playing Nathan Detroit. He said to the press that he was looking for a Carol Channing type to play Miss Adelaide. I read this in the Edinburgh, Scotland, newspapers, jumped on the next plane, swung into his backstage dressing room, and announced, "But, Lord Larry, I'm here! Why do you want a type? I want to be your very own Miss Adelaide." He laughed and hugged me and kissed me and sat me down on the sofa with him, where we cuddled like Jerry Herman and I used to. Can you imagine? Being hugged by the great Laurence Olivier like that? I was in euphoria.

But I didn't get the job! Why did he never call me? He got somebody else in the part? No! I just looked it up on the Internet. He never did the production. I should have looked it up long ago instead of being hurt all these years. Even though you left us all in the eighties, please do forgive me, dear Lord Laurence, for my hurt feelings, I never really stopped adoring you, just like the rest of the world.

I *have* a friend who lives up the hill near my current home in Rancho Mirage, California. She said, "Carol, you've got to put that in your book."

Me: Put what?

Cynthia: About you having cancer during the first two runs of *Hello, Dolly!*

Me: Why?

Cynthia: It'll help other people.

Me: But will it give it power? With eight shows a week and sometimes sixteen in concerts, I never had time to let it stop me.

Cynthia: That's what I mean. That's what helped me.

My friend Cynthia does fabulous oil paintings. I told her it gave me strength over size C (the extremest) cancer of the uterus to create and re-create as constantly and as long as I was privileged to play Dolly and never stop in between. (Cynthia is on strong chemotherapy now for her lung cancer. She promises she'll keep painting every day no matter how tired the chemo makes her.)

I've only talked about my cancer with people who are on their way to the hospital for their operations. That was the only frightening time for me, because I wasn't working. But something told me clearly, "You are going to find, Tootsie, that you're exactly the same girl you were before this operation. Nothing will change you, basically, not even the extreme pain." Are our lives all preordained? Many people have told me what's going to happen to me and it does. George Burns told me I'd be just like him, performing till I die. I asked him, "How do you know, George?" Again he said, "Don't ask me that. I just know it, that's all. I know it as sure as I'm standing here telling you." Well, now that I've told you, I'll have to do it. I can't let George be proven wrong.

Let me preface this. Long after my hysterectomy, I read Bill

Moyers's book *Healing and the Mind.* It covers methods of healing all over the world. Part of the American method spoke of cancer patients who were given one week to live. Many of them were sent to a place in Big Bear, California—or was it Big Sur?—where they were told to create something, anything, every day—a poem, a song, a painting, a story, even a sand castle would do. They lived and lived. Then I saw in the paper that Mayor Richard Riordan of L.A. had blocked off a street on Sundays to exhibit paintings by people with AIDS so they could support themselves. They also lived and lived, and this was years before any of these medications that are sustaining AIDS patients now.

By the time *Dolly* got to something like Louisville, Kentucky—it seemed like years later—I was bleeding. I went to a gynecologist, and he said I should have this checked the moment we got to our next city, which was Washington, D.C., and he made an appointment for me there with a caring Dr. Thompson. He stopped his own work and that of a specialist in his building, who examined me right up until show time. Most doctors are dedicated, aren't they? They phoned my Dr. Bill in New York, and he took over from there.

Because I never missed a performance of *Dolly*, not even for a vacation, which Equity arranges we can take, I've always told Dr. Bill he should take a bow with me at the end of each show. I did miss in Kalamazoo with violent food poisoning. I'm a Christian Scientist right up until 6:30 P.M., and then, if I have no voice or whatever, I get frightened and rush to Dr. Bill. Mrs. Eddy writes about it sometimes taking time for one to see clearly the real nothingness of one's problem, so sometimes one cannot receive healing immediately. Well, my shows began promptly at 8:00 P.M. I had to do something one way or another by 6:30. Bill fixed me.

He insisted I'm still a Christian Scientist. He says nobody could drag into his office all the trashy bacteria I pick up, or the broken bones or occupational hazards, without some other healing process to hang on to (with me it's creative work). My father used to say to me, "Never forget, God loves you the most when you're active. God seems to flow through you stronger and faster." I heard one bone specialist whisper to Dr. Bill, "How can she go onstage tonight with these broken ribs?" Bill whispered back, "Well, it's a combination of willpower and Mary Baker Eddy. What I do is the least of it, I'm sure."

Dr. Bill was wrong. He parentally cherished every one of his patients, including me. That's partly what heals them, I'm convinced. Betty Comden, of Comden and Green (who wrote *Billion Dollar Baby*, *Hallelujah, Baby! The Will Rogers Follies*, and lots more), had cancer of the tongue. Dr. Bill did such a careful job of cutting it out that the operation left her with only a slight lisp. It gives her a baby vulnerability she never had before. She was always a lovely, highly intelligent woman, but now she's adorable. That has to stem from affection from Dr. Bill. He did it right and in such a way that it suits Betty's nature. Wasn't I fortunate he was the uterine cancer specialist of Memorial Sloan-Kettering Hospital anyway? I mean, after years of his piecing me together from falling into the pit, I finally came in with something in his territory.

We were on tour, so I had to return to New York every second weekend for cobalt and chemo treatments. Charles and I left Reno, Nevada, first, then other cities, after the Sunday shows, slept in the Dallas airport on a bench until our plane connected with a New York–bound plane, slept on that, arrived at Memorial Sloan-Kettering for treatments, with Dr. Bill explaining to the specialists that my name was Rifka Schwartsbarg. No one ever found out.

I don't remember how many months this went on, but I came out fine. Dr. Bill wouldn't trust any hospitals on our tour to give me precisely the treatments he was controlling at his own hospital. I understand cobalt and chemo drain one's energy almost completely, but I get stage fright before most every show anyway, and I found there's nothing like sheer panic to create adrenaline. Adrenaline pierces through everything in your body and charges you on. But at the time nobody told me chemo drains you. Dr. Bill was so wise not to tell me. The tightrope one walks while onstage requires the concentration of an athlete before a game or a bullfighter prior to entering an arena. I heard an interview with Manolete, the greatest of Spain's bullfighters. They asked him, "Aren't you afraid of death, which is possible every time you face the bull?" The translator said Manolete just said, "Never! I'm only afraid of losing the audience." How true! Death is dignified. Losing the audience is embarrassing, even if it happens only once. And you have to live the rest of your life with the memory of it.

After *Hello, Dolly!* Jerry Herman wrote *Mame* for me. Gower convinced Charles to turn it down, saying it was too much like *Dolly*. It was the exact opposite of *Dolly*. They never discussed it with me, ever.

In order to get my mind off the pain of the cancer operation, I studied *Mame* carefully.

By this time it had already been done on Broadway during the newspaper strike. But it healed me much more quickly to work diligently on something well written. Bea Arthur, as Mame's friend Vera, was, I hear, at her best. I always wanted to work with her. I am Angela Lansbury's fan in anything Angela thinks is wrong for her, like Jessica Fletcher in everyone's favorite *Murder, She Wrote*. I am Bea Arthur's ferocious fan in anything Bea does. I wanted to play Mame as much as I wanted to play Dolly. But I got to play her only in a sketch for our tour of *Jerry's Girls*. *Jerry's Girls* was a revue-type show of Jerry Herman's music and lyrics.

Mame is an outrageously comic character. I would have adored to play Mame. What a mistake! Jerry wanted me, too, I'm proud to say. We could have asked Mrs. Miller to sing the high notes. You don't know Mrs. Miller? She used to rent Carnegie Hall for her once-a-year recitals and sold out to theatre people. She could certainly sing the high notes, but she was completely tone-deaf, unbeknownst, of course, to herself. We wouldn't think of missing her. We'll end this chapter right here so I can get some carbohydrates in me to try to stop this hypoglycemic sink.

It turns out it is not a hypoglycemic sink. You are sickened, Carol, by facing the true facts concerning your own weaknesses in demanding what you know to be right for you.

As I've said, Barbara Walters is the most remarkable friend of all to me. I turned to her when I had no one else to turn to. She called off all her most important appointments. I asked her if we could not meet in a public restaurant, because the subject I wanted to discuss with her was too private. We met in her apartment. I dumped the entire problem of my warped nature on her. She really helped me. She said, "Look back over your life, Carol. Your big mistake is that you hand yourself over—body, work, and soul—to people who haven't proven themselves." I, Carol, have watched my life ever since and been stronger on my own because of it. What I mean is, if we have to, we can force our bodies, works, and souls to add up to something that is needed by our fellow man all by ourselves, with no help from anyone.

Then Barbara phoned a man in Canada who has booked her on lecture tours that Canadian audiences pack theatres to see and hear. She asked him to book me. He did. I'm sure he did it because he might have lost Barbara if he didn't. That's Barbara when she's helping a friend in need. She reconstructed my life right then, and I've been following her advice ever since. Then she put me on her TV show *The View* and interviewed me herself. I discovered the next day, flying back to my son in Florida, that almost the entire airport watches *The View*, especially when Barbara is interviewing, and aren't those women all great? But then, you knew that. However, they're even greater off camera. They want their guests to come off well, so they automatically befriend and love every one of them. They give you invaluable tips on how Barbara likes to be teased.

Loretta Young

My most understanding friend who lives near me here in the desert is, I'm proud to say, Loretta Young. She's eighty-seven and looks like most everyone's imagination of Mary, Queen of Heaven. Loretta looks just like Loretta Young, only her beauty has taken on even more magnificent proportions inside and out.

When I was growing up, she was always my most favorite movie star. In the third grade, when I was seven years old, she was my very own personal fairy godmother, just from seeing her on screen. Much later I used to see her every Christmas at the Marvin Davises' Christmas party. Like Merman, she must have sensed my adoring respect. I never told either one of them of it. They just seemed to know. The surprise is she really was a fairy godmother, even to a strong Cinderella like me.

When her two sons were at our house and everyone was talking, she'd unnoticeably drift over to me and say, "How are you doing? When you start to slide down under again, call me please." I did.

Whoops! This is what happens every single time I come to a firm conclusion about anything. One night at my cousin's house Loretta had to lie down on my bed during dinner. The next day she was in St. John's Hospital in Santa Monica in the intensive care unit. She was operated on, and when she was opened up they found the cancer was everywhere. Just as I thought I had something that might help other people, I learned that it was too late. Our beautiful, gentle Loretta had the endurance of a mule . . . all stars do, John Gielgud told me.

And now that the pain has subsided a great deal, she wants to overcome it! Can you imagine the happiness that has descended on her friends and me? Okay! Now she's got to create something. She watched her loving husband, the great designer Jean Louis, so she could design a huge, all-enveloping apron for me, and we left it in our favorite restaurant because she couldn't figure out how I got food on the back of me. The front she understood. I ate very carefully, so as not to spill, with Loretta watching me like a hawk, but the moment I stood up there would always be a lettuce leaf or bits of food on the back of me and all over, and no one, including Loretta, saw how it got there. As soon as she's back, we all get new aprons, so that she's creating something. That's final.

This is now Saturday, August 12, 2000. Loretta died this morning at 3:30. I've been following all her guidance. I've purchased a little house that is perfect for me now. Dickie is giving me a golf cart so I can see him often. He says he wants my house close by so he can keep an eye on me.

And I finally got back the apron that Loretta made me. The restaurant we kept it in saved it for me. It doesn't look at all like a professional seamstress made it. It looks like Loretta made it.

I do hope this doesn't violate the privacy of a friendship—but I do not know any other words with which to tell you about my feelings for Lady Bird Johnson. I mailed this letter yesterday to her. It is good news that she's out of intensive care and has her own room and is able to say four new words each day.

My Dear Lady Bird,

You have been such a power for good in just my life alone, that I am knowing no harm can come to you. No stroke, nothing can keep you from being the positive force you are.

One of the great things you did for me around two years ago was when you asked for me to be one of the speakers at the Johnson clan reunion along with so many writers and brilliant orators. It was my first meeting in Austin of the Johnson clan. It was thrilling!

Naturally, I was on no par with them, so I told, as accurately as I could, the happy, sad, funny, and affectionate experiences I personally had with you and President Lyndon.

As soon as I got home to Rancho Mirage, California, you phoned me. You said, "You are brand-new, Carol, I never saw you so clearly before. You are truly you now, up on that platform." You repeated, "You are brand-new." You told me I was on the right track, which, at that moment, nobody I knew thought but you.

How did you know how direly I needed to hear that said by someone whose opinion means as much to me as yours? You made it possible for me to ignore everyone else's opinion at that time but yours, and now I have finished my book with no criticism particularly in it; my publisher, Michael Korda, likes it; and I am coming through just fine.

You are still my role model, always will be, and those qualities you possess cannot be harmed or weakened. I am holding to your words: "You are on the right track."

Along with so many, I am praying for you in my own way. I want it so to help you, and at least it can't hurt, I'm sure.

With my very dearest love,

Carol

ME

10/02